The Three Graces of Raymond Street

The Three Graces of Raymond Street

*Murder, Madness, Sex, and Politics
in 1870s Brooklyn*

ROBERT E. MURPHY

excelsior editions

State University of New York Press
Albany, New York

Published by State University of New York Press, Albany

Printed in the United States of America

Excelsior Editions is an imprint of State University of New York Press

For information, contact State University of New York Press, Albany, NY
www.sunypress.edu

Production, Diane Ganeles
Marketing, Kate R. Seburyamo

Library of Congress Cataloging-in-Publication Data

Murphy, Robert E. (Robert Emmet).
   The Three Graces of Raymond Street : murder, madness, sex, and politics in 1870s Brooklyn / Robert E. Murphy.
       pages cm. — (Excelsior editions)
   Includes bibliographical references and index.
   ISBN 978-1-4384-5562-4 (paperback : alkaline paper)
   ISBN 978-1-4384-5563-1 (ebook)
   1. Murder—New York (State)—New York—History—19th century.   2. Women murderers—New York (State)—New York—Biography.   3. Female offenders—New York (State)—New York—Biography.   4. Brooklyn (New York, N.Y.)—Biography.   5. New York (N.Y.)—Biography.   6. Insanity defense—New York (State)—New York—History—19th century.   7. Sex role—New York (State)—New York—History—19th century.   8. Women—Legal status, laws, etc.—New York—History—19th century.   9. Brooklyn (New York, N.Y.)—Social conditions—19th century.   10. New York (N.Y.)—Social conditions—19th century.   I. Title.

   HV6534.N5M87 2015
   364.152'3092—dc23   2014015550

10 9 8 7 6 5 4 3 2 1

I dedicate this book to my sisters and brother
and the people they married.

Of all the great cities in the world, one stands pre-eminent in the preservation of public order and in the purity of public morals. That city is Brooklyn.

—William E. S. Fales, *Brooklyn's Guardians* (p. III), 1887

Contents

Acknowledgments

A warm thank you to three old companions from Manhattan College who wisely advised me during the writing and rewriting of this book: Peter Quinn, Tom Quinn, and Lou Antonietti. Peter actually read two full drafts of it, which is more than a writer of his magnitude, with many demands for his attention, should be asked to do. But I will probably do it again. I also thank his wife, Kathy Quinn, for some special and important advice.

It will be immediately apparent to any reader that the composition of *The Three Graces of Raymond Street* depended heavily on newspaper archives. So I salute and thank the New York Public Library for its wonderful microfilm resources and its helpful (mostly quite young) staff, and I am especially grateful to the Brooklyn Public Library for bringing the nineteenth-century *Brooklyn Daily Eagle* into my workspace. I also send an appreciative shout up to Fulton, New York, where diligent and generous Tom Tryniski has put scores of other New York State newspapers online.

Readers who become interested in the characters and scenes described here will likely be curious to see what those persons and the places where events took place looked like. To present images of a quality suitable for publication, I have been helped immeasurably by my friend and Park Slope, Brooklyn neighbor Tony Spengler, a professional photo-enhancer who enthusiastically donated his time and skill and whom I now designate Illustrations Editor of this book. I am grateful also to another neighbor and graphics professional, Oliver Yourke, for his valuable advice.

Introduction

Unlike the great majority of books, this one began with a title, and I owe the title to the Brooklyn Public Library and its admirable initiative to produce an online archive of all the nineteenth-century pages of the *Brooklyn Eagle* newspaper. The discovery of the phrase "The Three Graces of Raymond Street" was serendipitous. I was searching that archive for information about the connection between James Jourdan, Brooklyn politician, city official and gas-company executive, and the Standard Oil trustees H. H. Rogers and Charles Pratt, who were partners in a Brooklyn refinery in the 1870s. I found nothing about it, but the computerized pursuit of "Pratt" brought up, in addition to Charles (best known today as the founder of Pratt Institute), Justice Calvin E. Pratt of the Kings County court, who presided over the trial of one of the "three delicate and feeble women" housed at Raymond Street Jail and dubbed "The Three Graces of Raymond Street" by a Brooklyn editor who mischievously compared them to the graces of Greek mythology. Each had been arrested for murder and was "in peril of judicial strangulation."

Well, what Brooklyn writer with an interest in local history would not want to know everything that could be known about these young woman and what they might have done to land in such vexing circumstances? Not I. So I searched and searched in the *Eagle* and other Brooklyn and New York newspapers, and wherever else their names could be found. Their alleged crimes, I learned, were local sensations, and at least two drew widespread interest. Their trials or other court hearings were in each case judicially historic—and for that reason I have recounted them at some length.

1

My searching also became time-travel: into post-Civil-War New York and its very different yet very large and significant bordering city of Brooklyn; into a period of increasing social mobility that contributed to rapid and vast urban growth and concomitant turmoil, danger, violence, sexual license, and predation—in effect, the development of the modern American city. I had entered a pulsating age in which the role and nature of woman was in flux and in dispute, in which members of the professions of law and medicine were laboring to understand better the motivations, complexities, and pathologies of the human mind.

The searching was also an especially fascinating path to what once was Brooklyn, the unique city and borough that in the following centuries would be my lifelong home. Unlike in those later years, 1870s Brooklyn didn't bow before New York, but it well understood its relation to that greater city while it proudly attended to its own business, struggled to manage its own speedy expansion, and carefully considered and eloquently commented on its identity and problems. It nurtured and attracted an impressive roster of outstanding citizens who operated its courts with distinction, enforced its laws with prudence, led its churches with panache, but also entangled each other in vicious, overlapping political, moral, religious, and ethnic controversies.

This book is not a history, but it is, I hope, historical—a narrative that describes a certain place at a certain time, appealing to the nostalgia that most people in some degree share for the past, even the past that long preceded our own lives. At the center of this picture that I've tried to paint are the three female murder suspects who became acquainted with each other at the county jail. And surrounding them, connected to them, directly or peripherally, are the policemen, prosecutors, defenders, journalists, politicians, clergymen, physicians, activists, bigots, and adulterers who formed a small portion of the big city that they lived in. My purpose, then, has been to focus on those killings and their aftermaths as interesting in themselves, while also presenting those events in the rich context of Brooklyn and New York City of the early 1870s, when persons who touched or participated in or commented on those events were living out interesting stories of their own, some of those stories of related nature to those of the imprisoned "Graces," and likewise reflecting a vital, formative period in American urban history. So I have included passages and full chapters that flesh out the "lost" nineteenth-century city of Brooklyn.

Much of this story, or these stories, depends on the rushed and not always conscientious accounts in those many daily and weekly newspapers of New York and Brooklyn. But I have purposely recounted some events through the eyes and words of the newsmen and very few newswomen of the period. Those words bear the time's color and flavor, and in many places I have put them in quotes because I cannot improve the phrases and sentences in which those writers described events, such as the reaction of a defendant in a capital trial when the jury foreman announced its conclusion, or the manner in which a police chief whose competence was questioned confronted a commissioner. Those feisty, faulty, sonorous papers are an important strain of the narrative. Because they survive, some bits of the dear and so valuable past have not altogether died.

1

Living Dangerously

City Air Breathes Free

To chance their ambitions and desires, men and women came to New York from everywhere in the second half of the nineteenth century. And to Brooklyn, long since a lost American city.

Some hankered for property and wealth. Others sought only work and freedom of movement, including the freedom to find each other. But some also found danger.

In 1872 and 1873, in the sprouting, hyperactive city of Brooklyn, three persons of property found sudden death, and three young women with very different origins, owners of nothing, were accused of murdering them. Two of the dead and two of the suspects were settlers in the big cities; a third presumed murderess was the daughter of immigrants.

What happened to the second of the victims would not be immediately clear; how the third died would never be. But there was no question about who had killed George W. Watson.

Mild midwinter weather had turned frigid during the fourth week of January 1872. On Thursday, the 25th, the skating-ball had risen at the Lullwater in Brooklyn's sparkling-new Prospect Park,[1] and on Friday, as Henry Hyde dressed for work in his and his wife Fanny's apartment on Wythe Avenue in the Williamsburg section, the first light of day revealed a frozen blue sky above the East River.

Both were within easy walking-distance of their workplaces, which were in opposite directions from their home. Henry would head for the massive Appleton book-bindery, several blocks south on

5

Kent Avenue, which bordered the river; Fanny, for George Watson's hair-net factory in the Merrill Building a few blocks north.

Fanny dressed at her bureau. Atop her petticoat she put on a plain, slate-colored poplin dress, buttoned the sides of her ankle-high shoes, and, gazing into the bedroom mirror, pulled low on her dirty-blonde head a gray jockey cap with embroidered red flowers and a brown ribbon that secured a black feather.[2] She wrapped herself a in a thick winter cloak, grabbed her satchel, and left for work. But this day she carried, in the bosom of her dress,[3] a possession she had never brought there before.

Watson's business in Williamsburg was winding down. He had sold machinery about ten days earlier and taken the materials that were not yet finished into the third-floor shop of Fanny's uncle, where Watson had use of one table and worked side by side with Fanny, now his only employee.[4] This morning, after hanging up her coat, jacket, and hat, she stepped over to the table with reluctance, for the previous day she had quarreled with him before she left the shop.[5]

Again this day they were seen talking heatedly, but were not clearly heard over the machinery's hum.[6] She could no longer sit still beside him. At about eleven o'clock, she put down her work, dashed to the back of the shop and dropped herself into a soft chair beside the pot-bellied stove that vented through the back wall. She sat there for several minutes, staring across the room, until her Aunt Mary walked over to her.

Family members sensed something was amiss with Fanny when she seemed unconcerned about her appearance. "What an old dress you have on," her aunt remarked.

"It's good enough for me," Fanny responded. She had partially covered it with a shawl.

Mary asked how she was.

"I wish I was dead," she said.

"What for?"

"A good many things."

Mary Dexter was the first of several persons to observe a painful, distraught look in Fanny's face—"wild," she would call it, and "pale."[7]

There was a problem with third-floor toilet,[8] so Fanny left the shop, went downstairs and knocked on the door of the velvet-weaving shop. Henry Potts, one of the weavers, opened the door, and Fanny, without speaking, stepped briskly past him and headed to the "water-closet." There was something "singular" in her expression that he could "hardly describe"—"Her eyes were red and swollen." He waited for her, so that he could let her out of the shop, and when she didn't come out as soon as he expected, he went back to work.[9]

Fanny's stepmother, Sarah Windley, was working on that floor that morning, and Fanny stopped to talk to her. The girl at the same table noted that Fanny, uncharacteristically, ignored her, and that she looked "wild and very much excited."[10]

When she returned upstairs, Watson accused her of making love to Henry Potts, charged that she was "nothing but a prostitute and a whore," and pressed her to "go with him."

At about 11:45 Fanny again found the toilet unavailable, and once more went downstairs and knocked at the door of the velvet-shop. But she was not heard in the workplace din, and headed back upstairs, intending to try once more at noon, when the lunch whistle would halt all work. At the top of the stairs, on the third-floor landing, she saw George Watson.[11]

It was Watson's habit to leave for lunch about five minutes before the whistle, but this day he left earlier, about three minutes after Fanny had stepped out.[12] He was wearing a light overcoat. No one witnessed their encounter in the hallway, but between Watson's leaving and the next time anyone saw Fanny, there would have been enough time—seven or eight minutes—for the scene that Fanny would remember to have occurred:

"I saw him there before I went up the stairs. I asked him if he was going downstairs. He said no; he had to go back for something. I thought he had gone in; when I got to the top of the stairs, he seized hold of me . . . in a very indecent manner."

She did not remember exactly what he said, only that he repeat-ed what he had demanded in the shop: "He wanted me to go to a room outside somewhere."

She tried, she said, to break loose from him—"we had quite a struggle. I got free from him, and he seized me the second time."

She claimed to remember nothing else, except one detail that seems unlikely—that she had already taken a pistol from between her breasts before he had grabbed her the second time.[13] In fact she must have been downstairs from him when she released what she said was the only bullet in the gun,[14] for it struck him from several feet away through his coat collar and into the neck below his right ear, and traveled upward across his brain. Watson dropped and tumbled past her down the 15 iron steps until his torso and the back of his head, with its spurting, fatal wound, settled on the second-floor landing—his splayed legs tilting upward onto the bottom stairs.[15]

A native of the little sheep-raising town of Plainfield in Massachusetts's Berkshire Hills, George W. Watson had arrived in Brooklyn in 1850, when he was 23. He had come, most likely, to work for Ager Pixley, a widower and manufacturer of hosiery who lived with his 20-year-old daughter, Eliza, on Hicks Street on Brooklyn Heights.[16] In that brick-and-brownstone neighborhood above the East River, which would be known as New York's first suburb, Watson rented a room, and in September 1853 he married Eliza Pixley.[17]

It was the month Fanny Windley was born.

The Windleys were from Nottingham, a fast-growing industrial city in the middle of England, where they all labored in its signature lace and silk trades.[18] Hattie Windley died when her children, Samuel, Fanny, and Alice, were five, four, and two, and John, their father, unable to earn enough to support them, sent them to work as soon as they were able.[19]

They came to New York during the American Civil War on three-masted, iron-hulled British ships that were hybrids of steam and sail.[20] John Windley, just turning 30, landed on the *Edinburgh* in February 1864, and the next October his second wife, Sarah, 26, brought her stepchildren on the *Louisiana*. Their steerage tickets from Liverpool cost about $30.

On the Port of New York manifest, 11-year-old Fanny, christened Frances, who had been a factory-girl at eight, was entered as a "boy" named "Francis."[21] That was an ironic error, for the clamor that would surround her American story would be all about her being female.

Something troubled Eliza Watson's health in the early years of her marriage to George, and a Brooklyn doctor took the odd notion that she should move away from the sea. Her husband brought her back to the bucolic Berkshires and sold produce. But manufacturing had become George Watson's vocation and path to a substantial income, and in the 1860s he picked up that trade again in Hartford, Connecticut.[22]

The Windleys of Nottingham had New York connections that had been formed in England, and Samuel and Fanny were hired right away—she by the velvet-manufacturer A. P. Bachman of Franklin Street in lower Manhattan. She later worked for more than two years for a lacemaker who had been the Windleys' neighbor back home. John Marr remembered her as having been, at age 12 and 13, the brightest and most competent girl whom he and his wife employed. "A good girl in the work-room, and her conduct, too, was very good," said Sarah Marr, who supervised her. She was "as good a girl as I would wish to have." Fanny often visited the Marrs' home to play with their children, and between factory jobs she sometimes made money caring for kids. When not at work, Fanny was a dutiful student at night school and Sunday school.[23]

As she reached her teens she no longer looked like a boy. She grew to five-feet-two, slender but well-figured. She had alluring blue eyes and a healthy flush in her face, and was considered pretty.[24]

By the end of the 1860s, while Eliza Watson raised five children in Hartford, her husband stayed mostly in Brooklyn. He had returned south to become a supervisor for and perhaps a partner of A. P. Bachman, Fanny's former boss, who now owned operations in the Charles Merrill and Sons Building in the northern Brooklyn industrial hive of Williamsburg. There, on the corner of First Street and South 11th Street, across from a riverside gas-works, Watson opened the shop that produced silk hair-nets.[25]

Ager Pixley, now in his late 60s, also worked in the Merrill Building, and would remark that his son-in-law was a "dutiful husband" who returned every other week to Hartford, where the youngest of his and Eliza's children was a toddler, and the eldest was about the age of the teenage girls that her father employed.[26]

A few years after landing in New York, the Windleys too moved to Brooklyn, settling amid the factories and docks of Williamsburg,[27] where all the family went to work in the Merrill Building. Fanny transferred to the Bridge Street Primitive Methodist School in downtown

Brooklyn, which she attended regularly for two years. Officials there also described her comportment as "good" or "excellent," and invited her to speak at one of their evening presentations.[28]

John Windley conceded that he was more strict with his children than he "would have been if their own mother had been alive," and Fanny would say that both her father and stepmother had been strict with her.[29] But a girl who begins working for wages as a child, and in a strange city before puberty, feels other influences and grows up quickly.

She was 15 when, in February 1869, she reported to George Watson's third-floor hair-net shop.[30] At 42, he was trim and hand-some, five-feet-nine, with a full black beard tinged with gray; with wavy, receding black hair, high, prominent cheekbones and deep-set eyes.[31] Watson was sportive and indulgent with the girls who worked for him, and to some other men in the shop he seemed inappropri-ately familiar with them. These men noticed him frequently joking with the girls, leaning over them and talking to them as they worked, or tapping their shoulders and laughing when they turned to him. He ordered treats brought into the shop for them—oyster stews and sweets. At least two co-workers chided him about these things.

His obvious favorite was Fanny. He appointed her a forewoman, and by the fall of that year he seemed to be constantly near her, working beside her at a table and talking to her, or, if she left the shop, following her. "Hundreds of times" he was seen going after her into the corridor or into another shop. He also followed her to Sunday school, and on the evening of her presentation he tossed a bouquet onto the stage, an act that a staff member at the school "never saw anything of the kind" in 10 years there. In the middle of one November afternoon, one of the men at the factory opened a door to the corridor and found Watson with an arm around Fanny's back and kissing her. She was not resisting him.[32] The same man and other workers were aware of several times when Watson asked Fanny to stay and work with him alone after everyone else had left.[33]

By that time George Watson and Fanny Windley, who turned 16 in September 1869, had been sexually intimate for months.

He Told Her Not to Do It

Fanny Windley's own recollection would be that she and George Watson became involved during the first summer she worked for him. One afternoon he gave her a job to take home and told her to come back at nine the following morning for elastics to attach to the nets. She didn't describe how it happened, but said that there, that morning, he seduced her. He had access to at least one third-floor room that could be locked, and there was a bedroom on the second floor. Perhaps it had been a Sunday, when the shop was closed, but Watson was hardly discreet about his ardor. He also began to visit Fanny at her family's apartment.[34]

During these months, and into early 1870, her parents noticed changes in her appearance and manner. She grew pale and thin. She seemed careless about her dress, and her father found her to be less obliging, inattentive to his requests, and increasingly irritable.[35] Apart from any emotional conflict that she might have been feeling, Fanny suffered from painful menstruation—"dysmenorrhea." It bothered her on the day of that first experience with Watson, and she thought that it was aggravated by their relations. Her periods were also irregular, and Watson, fearing that she was pregnant, gave her abortifacient pills and asked her to move to New York and to see a physician there. She refused to do either,[36] and it is unclear that she ever did become pregnant by him.

During that first part of 1870, John Windley heard a rumor about Fanny's relations with Watson, but believed this was malicious talk that had been put in motion by a man who held a grudge against him. He did mention the rumor to Fanny, quietly, if for no other reason than to determine whether or not she was aware it. She reacted sharply, and told him that she was old enough to take care of herself. He never mentioned it again.[37] And shortly afterward, in March, she left his home and moved into a place she called "the homestead"—a boarding-house.

There she met Henry Hyde, a thin, boyish-looking 21-year-old who, in addition to his job as a bookbinder at the Appleton plant on Kent Avenue, also began to work in Watson's shop.[38] On May 6th, 1870, without telling her family, she married him.[39] John Windley did not know about it until two months later. Fanny told him one day when they were both at work, but she didn't explain why she had married so quickly and secretly. Nor did he ask, because he "thought if she had married and made her bed, she had better lie in it."[40]

Fanny did inform Watson of her coming marriage, and he promised that if she did marry, he would "leave her alone." She made him swear to this on a bible. But a few days after the wedding he began to follow her again, and he attempted to rent a room across the street from the Hydes on Wythe Avenue, a block from the river. Although Fanny may have had the option of quitting and taking a job with her father or uncle, she continued to work for Watson because the money—$10 a week—was better. Within two months they had sex again.[41]

The geography changed for a while in the spring of 1871. Fanny traveled to Washington in April to stay with her mother-in-law and visit a Dr. Elliott, president of that city's medical board, about her condition. She told Margaret Hyde while she was there, "I feel that there is a curse hanging over me."[42]

Fanny had a chance to make this trip because Watson, having dissolved his arrangement with Bachman, had gone north to operate a factory in New Britain, Connecticut,[43] and there was little or no work for her in Brooklyn. Henry had moved to New Britain, and he sent Fanny in Washington a letter asking her to join him.[44] She traveled up about the first of May, and she and Henry remained there until sometime in July, when they went back to Brooklyn.

In the fall, Watson also returned, and, in Fanny's telling, he did not leave her alone. He threatened to expose her, and he applied sexual blackmail. Their intimacy resumed, and his lust had become entwined with nagging jealousy. "He was always accusing me of going with other men," said Fanny.

He would call at her home on Wythe Avenue, where she worked during the last months of 1871, while Henry resumed his job at the Appleton Bindery. It was a time, Fanny would remember, when she was "always thinking about" the liaison with Watson and "cried about it continually."[45]

Yet it went on for months, despite some stormy moments between them. A friend of Henry Hyde remembered occasions during those months on which he heard Henry ordering Watson to leave the house, and Fanny telling him that he was no longer welcome.[46] But she admitted that, after doing that in January 1872, she had sex with him again the next week.[47]

Her feelings, though, had turned poisonous. One day around the middle of that month, after she had returned to Watson's shop in the Merrill Building, she and her brother Sam walked into the gun-and-locksmith shop of Nelson J. Stowell at 86 Broadway in

Williamsburg and asked to see some pistols. Stowell handed Sam a Sharps four-barrel revolver; Sam held it toward Fanny and asked if it "would suit" her. She said it would. Fanny would claim that she bought it for her husband as a delayed New Year's gift, but Stowell would remember that Sam had paid for it. When they got it to her apartment, neither Henry nor Sam could figure out how to operate it, so "two or three days" later, according to Stowell, Sam returned for a lesson; then, on Wednesday, the 24th of January, or Thursday, the 25th, he purchased cartridges for it.[48]

Ellen Curley, who worked for Fanny's uncle, John Dexter, had left the shop in the Merrill Building at 11:50 that Friday morning and gone to a grocery on nearby Division Avenue to pick up the makings of her lunch, which she would bring back to the factory. She returned a few minutes before noon, entered through the door on the South 11th Street side, and, climbing the first flight of iron stairs, was startled by the sight of Fanny Hyde kicking at the door of the second-floor "plush" or velvet room, wringing her hands and making a sound that Ellen first thought to be singing, but soon realized was moaning. She would report that, before anyone answered the knock, Fanny turned to her and told her that she had killed George Watson, and that he was lying at the foot of the second flight of stairs. Ellen didn't see a gun, and no one in the buzzing building had heard the shot.

Go tell the men in the plush room, Fanny shouted, that Watson is dead and lying in the hall. Ellen, in a frenzy, banged on the door.

It was opened at last by Ager Pixley. The only words that Ellen could get out were "Watson! Hall!"—then she bolted past him to tell the others.[49] Pixley, then Henry Potts and Charles Merrill, rushed to attend to Watson. Pixley heard Fanny say something about Watson's having fallen down the steps, and, before picking up his son-in-law's head, he tried in vain to stop the blood that flowed "as thick as a pipe stem" from the wound below his ear. He still had a pulse, so Potts ran off to find a Doctor Brady, but when he returned another doctor had arrived and was just pronouncing Watson dead.[50]

The noon whistle had sounded, and Ellen had run up to tell the news on the third floor. It was getting crowded around Watson and the pool of blood spreading on the second-floor landing. John and Mary Dexter and John and Sam Windley came down. Mary at first assumed that Watson had fallen down the steps, then, seeing her niece crying, asked what was wrong.

"Watson has been the ruination of me," said Fanny, "and I shot him."[51]

Sam grabbed the stair-post with one hand, and turned to his sister, who stood with a hand on her forehead, staring into Watson's face. Ager Pixley would be clear about what he then heard and saw.

"Fanny," Sam called to her, raising, then sweeping down his free arm, "I told you not to do it!" Then he swung himself over the victim and rushed up the stairs.[52]

A Terrible Thing to Tell

Pixley took charge of the body, and helped to move it onto a table in the plush room. Then Coroner Lawrence A. Whitehill allowed Pixley to take the remains to his home on Hudson Avenue,[53] on the other side of the Brooklyn Navy Yard, where police surgeon Joseph Creamer conducted an autopsy. He removed the dead man's scalp and found the bullet—he called it a "ball"—lodged in his brain. Traveling obliquely, it had crossed the top of his spinal cord. There were abrasions above Watson's left eye and down his face, and a wound atop his head that Creamer attributed to his fall, not to a struggle with his killer.[54]

Between one and two o'clock, Fanny's husband, father and brother walked with her to the Fifth Precinct station-house, more than half a mile north at the corner of North First Street and Fourth Street, which would soon become Bedford Avenue. Henry Hyde spoke first and handed the pistol to Captain Cornelius Woglom, a square-faced, 56-year-old former alderman who was called "the Chief of Williamsburg."

"I have a terrible thing to tell you," Henry said to him.

Fanny said that it had been her idea to "give herself up,"[55] and she was not reticent when she got there. She told her story and admitted the shooting to Woglom, to the desk sergeant, to the detective who brought her by streetcar to downtown headquarters the following day, and then to Chief Patrick Campbell.[56] She also spoke briefly to reporters at the precinct-house.

A man from The *Brooklyn Eagle* arrived there the same afternoon, and had to push through "a great crowd" on the corner to be admitted. He was allowed to visit the prisoner in the captain's office, but she "very snappishly" declined to talk to him. Her husband, though, had a few things to say—that she had shot Watson because he had insulted her, and that he "had committed a rape on her" before their marriage.

The *Brooklyn Union's* reporter got more out of her that evening, although she had seen a lawyer by then and would not discuss the shooting. When he asked if Watson had ever "wronged" her, "the blood mantled to the cheek of the woman, her eyes even flashed with fire, and drawing nearer to the bars of her cell, and pressing her arms even more closely around her, she said, 'Yes, sir; he wronged me, cruelly wronged me, both before and after marriage.'" She "thereupon retreated to a distant part of the cell," and he understood that the interview was over.

To the *New York Herald's* representative she would only speak, tearfully, of her early childhood in Nottingham and her coming to America. And when she found time to relax in the following days, she passed part of it reading a novel, *Put Yourself in His Place*, by a popular English adventure-writer, Charles Reade.

The newsmen each appraised her appearance differently through engaged masculine eyes. Her figure, wrote the *Eagle's* man, was "only medium in size and attractiveness." But the *Union* found her "delicately formed," with "calm, quiet, intelligent features, and a dark, lustrous blue eye." Her hair seemed to him light-brown and somewhat short, but to the *Eagle* it was "long" and "yellow." To the *Herald's* observer, she was "an interesting and *petite* woman of mild and pleasing aspect, and her large blue eyes have a kindly gleam in them very different from what would be expected in those of a malicious and ferocious murderer."[57] Such differences in observation are symptomatic variations of nineteenth-century reporting. Yet even the two available drawings of her seem to depict different women, although in each she is wearing the same dress and boa and her head is poised in an identical attitude. In one portrait, a drawing that may have been rendered from a photograph, her hair is light and neatly combed, her eyes limpid. It shows a more feminine, more traditionally pretty, face than the full-front-page engraving in the *National Police Gazette*, where her hair is as dark as a headline and straight, parted in the middle, above an oval face with deep eyes and a long, straight nose. Despite the variation, the latter, according to one professional opinion, may have been copied from the first. It could have been that the *Gazette*'s artist had seen Fanny after her arrest, and incorporated his impression of an agitated, somewhat disheveled young woman.

No one had yet remarked on her voice, and whether it retained any traces of middle England. But it is likely that such features had all but disappeared in a girl who had emigrated so young.

The coroner's inquest began on the evening of the murder, as close as possible to where it happened—in the plush room of the Merrill Building, to reach which the participants had to step around the wide smear of George Watson's blood that had been blanketed with ashes. The room was a large loft, heated by a central stove and lit by four kerosene lamps. At a small marble table sat Coroner Lawrence A. Whitehill and Fanny's attorney, Patrick Keady, who was Brooklyn fire marshal and had also served as a Democratic assemblyman. At another, larger table sat representatives of many Brooklyn and New York newspapers. Ellen Curley was the first of several witnesses of the shooting's aftermath to be examined before a jury of eight men who sat around them.

Fanny was not able to change clothes in her jail-cell, but she had a chance to freshen up and add a few articles that had been delivered to her. Still wearing the plain gray dress that her Aunt Mary had demeaned that morning, she had fitted over it a bright-blue velvet "sacque," or bodice, and about her neck the boa of gray fur with matching muff. She sat serenely in an armchair before the stove, those limpid eyes moving around to all the faces in the room. Near her still were her husband, father and brother, joined now by her 16-year-old sister, Alice, whose face was puffed from crying. After Henry Potts had testified, Fanny took the stand, but, at Keady's direction, offered only her age, address, marital and employment status. Whitehill then granted him an adjournment, and Fanny was escorted back to the station, where she dropped onto the mattress in her cell and, moaning, hid her face in her hands. Henry was allowed to sit all night with her, relieved in the morning by Sam.[58]

The next night, Saturday, the venue switched to the courthouse at Fifth and South First Streets. By ten minutes to eight, when she was let out of her cell, the precinct-house was filled with friends, the sight of whom brought her to tears, and she dabbed her eyes with a sheer veil that she was carrying. An unidentified woman of about 40 embraced her and cried, "Oh, Fanny, Fanny, I'm sorry for you, my child!" The group then followed her on her route of a few blocks, "like people," wrote one reporter, "going to the funeral of a dearly loved friend." They were joined by many others along the way, and he estimated that five hundred persons had gathered at the court, only half of whom were admitted, jamming the room beyond capacity while the others pressed at the doors.[59] Fanny was wearing her veil when she arrived, and when, after several minutes, she removed it, her "calm, cold features" drew every eye in the courtroom.[60]

Keady was now joined by Samuel D. Morris, the just-replaced Kings County district attorney, who would lead Fanny's defense. She was recalled, and again gave no material information. Neither did her husband, who followed. Mary Dexter stated that Fanny had admitted to the shooting, and John, her husband, brought laughter to the room when he mentioned that he never had heard the killer and victim talk to each other "because they would stop as soon as I came up." Ager Pixley recalled Sam's remonstration that he had told his sister not to do it[61]—and from that point Sam was no longer seen in public.

The curious masses thronged to the courthouse again for the inquest's conclusion the following Tuesday night, and those who weren't admitted hooted and shouted in objection. Fanny was upset and slumped at her table. It was 8:30, a half-hour late, when testimony, which included the responses of Stowell the gunsmith, Dr. Creamer, and Captain Woglom, began. At evening's end, six of the eight jurors agreed on a verdict:

"We find that George W. Watson came to his death by a pistol shot fired from a pistol in the hands of Frances Hyde, with malice aforethought."

The *Eagle* described this verdict as one of "the most sensible of modern times," but had "small apprehension that in the present temper of Brooklyn the trial of Mrs. Hyde will not be as fair and unsentimental as the trial of a man murderer would be."[62]

She was transferred the next day to the County Jail at Raymond Street, where she was given a cell in an unoccupied tier, the entire corridor of which she was free to walk in.[63]

Determined to disparage her, the *Eagle* raised two hostile theories about her motive. One was that Watson "was perfectly innocent of any criminal relations to her," but had objected vehemently to her carrying on with someone else at the factory. Another was that he had paid her for sex, and that she had shot him when he decided to end the deal.[64]

And it forcefully rejected all favorable assessments of her appearance and character:

> She is a small, thin undersized girl of eighteen, with a pinched face, all the thinner for her worry. Her eyes are small, but bright, and her cheekbones protrude far enough to spoil any beauty she might otherwise possess. Her hair is colorless and thin, and her figure scrawny and fleshless. She speaks in a little piping querulous voice, betraying an evident lack of resolution. There is nothing of the heroine about her. She looks like a small souled, uneducated, factory girl, whose head has been overturned by flash literature and whose mind is almost overturned by the daily growing realization of her condition. She looks evidently what she is, a wretched little creature, who committed a crime whose magnitude she is only just beginning to comprehend, and from whose effects she would, if she could, shrink into the very dust.

It hardly seemed possible that George Watson could have "follow[ed] to the death such an uninteresting young woman." Indeed, such a folly would have been "a sufficient reason for his death."[65]

Many newspaper-editors in New York and Brooklyn complained about judicial delay and growing sentiment for killers who had been motivated by jealousy or related passions. Such murderers, wrote the *Herald* the same week, "always find their apologists among decent people, who never saw the gashed, riddled or jellied corpse of the victim."[66] And the apologies were most predictable when the avengers were women. An outcome often maligned was the ballyhooed prosecution of Laura Fair of San Francisco, who had shot her lover in front of his wife and children in November 1870, then pled temporary insanity, associated with menstrual problems similar to Fanny Hyde's. She had been convicted and sentenced to hang, but the California Supreme Court had overturned the verdict on technical grounds, and she was acquitted on the insanity plea the second time around.[67]

The twin cities had become preoccupied by murder. They had been shocked the previous spring by the unprovoked slaughter of a passenger on a midtown Manhattan streetcar by a drunk wielding the driver's "car hook." Another clubbing-murder, of the financier-philanthropist Benjamin Nathan in his 23d-Street bedroom in 1870, remained vivid in the public mind because it had not been solved. And most vivid of all was the shooting to death on January 7th, 1872, of the railroad tycoon and bounder Jim Fisk by his romantic rival Ned Stokes in a downtown New York hotel. On the day of the Watson killing, before it was reported, the *Eagle* had ruminated about murder and punishment in New York. There had, it stated, been 146 murders counted in Manhattan during the previous year, while in the state of New Jersey, with "about an equal population," there had been fewer than "one every two months." But "that Commonwealth has a habit of hanging murderers. . . . Oh, for one year of Jersey justice in New York!"[68]

So the undoing of George Watson also was announced as "Another Murder"[69] to a City of Brooklyn that felt itself to be under a siege of violence. Indeed, the people's anxiety had been whetted during the week by a deadly attack near the Brooklyn Navy Yard against a quiet, slightly built, gentlemanly piano-instructor heading home from a lesson.

John B. Panormo, a 42-year-old native Londoner, was well-known as both a teacher and performer, and had been featured with his pupils in a recital at the Brooklyn Institute on the evening of Monday, January 22nd. The next night he resumed his rounds of private tutoring, and sometime before ten o'clock he left a house on Cumberland Street and turned toward Myrtle Avenue to catch a horsecar. The district, known as "the Hill," was largely residential but the vast navy yard brooded dourly over it on a winter night, and it had become one of the most dangerous areas in the city, known to be haunted by a nocturnal gang intending to rob houses or pedestrians. On that evening two men attacked "Professor" Panormo and swiped his watch, and he was found lying on a sidewalk battered and profusely bleeding. Some Samaritans took him to a druggist who exhorted them to find a doctor, suggested that the victim would be better off remaining in the "fresh air," and shut down his shop after they left. When they returned Panormo was gone.

He had found his way to Myrtle and hailed the car, which was headed west to downtown and Brooklyn Heights, where he lived in a boarding-house at the corner of Fulton and Pineapple Streets. The people's outrage was exacerbated by reports that neither a physician nor a policeman on the car had raised a hand to help the grievously wounded little teacher, who insisted that he simply wanted to be let off at Pineapple. At home he was treated at last by a doctor, but there, in Mrs. Snow's parlor, he died the next morning.[70]

The papers wailed in unison about the inefficiency of the police departments, particularly after it became known that on the night of Panormo's killing 24 officers of the Fourth Precinct had been assigned to a primary-election polling-place where their captain's brother was winning a race for a committee-seat.[71] And, by week's end, both the *Brooklyn Eagle* and the *New York Herald* were exclaiming "Murder Mania"—outraged by more street attacks, by a ferocious beating of a man who'd been dragged from his home by an inner-Brooklyn gang, and by the shooting of a young New York man by his father,[72] as well as the Panormo and Watson murders. Then on Sunday morning 25-year-old Alfred East shot himself in his room at Mrs. Snow's boarding-house.[73] One account stated that he had shared that room with the professor, and that they "seemed to be on terms of the utmost intimacy."[74]

The *National Police Gazette* printed a full-page illustration of four of these alarming events around a central scene in which George Watson leaned and whispered over Fanny Hyde's shoulder.[75] And it was noted as "a singular coincidence" that Watson, in his early years in Brooklyn, had lived in the same accursed residence on Pineapple Street where Panormo and East had died.[76]

~

Lost City

Up with the flag; be far the day
When Brooklyn's ever-honored name
From glory's role is wiped away
And buried in the book of shame.

—song opposing consolidation of Brooklyn and New York

Where the city of Brooklyn bulged into the East River at Fulton Ferry, less than half a mile separated it from downtown New York. Between their two city halls was a mile-and-a-half. Twin cities, yes and no. New York was firmly established as the leading commercial, financial, industrial and, with a nod to Boston, literary and cultural city in America. Brooklyn lived in its long shadow, but lived generally well, as "the City of Homes and Churches." It did not lead the country in much except in baseball and Protestant oratory and the manufacture of certain goods like rope, sugar, and whisky,[77] but it was a major city, no doubt, a very big port city that, since its late-occurring incorporation in 1834, was growing faster than any comparably sized place in America. In 1860, spreading south and east in block upon block of brick, brownstone, and wooden-frame homes, and having annexed the northward city of Williamsburgh (and dropped the "h"), it became the nation's third-largest city, and would remain so until 1890. Its 1870 population was just a tick under 400,000,[78] and, as New York's neared a million, its leaders and editors realized that Brooklyn was far too substantial an entity to ignore.

Big it was and, like New York, lively, tumultuous, contentious, and abundantly interesting. And in Brooklyn, as in New York, the newspapers, in an age of expanding, passionate, eloquent journalism, embraced with relish the growing complexity of urban life, the pains and challenges of growth itself, of the development of the modern American city. They reported vividly, if, in the rush to press, often inaccurately, and they savored particularly the competition to describe crimes like the murders of George Watson, the trials of criminals, and the battlefields of politics. In fact, they were themselves batteries on those battlefields, and nowhere was the action hotter than between two Brooklyn dailies edited by fiercely partisan political operators.

In the winter of 1872 one of these partisans, Thomas Kinsella, had left his editor's desk at the *Brooklyn Daily Eagle* to take one of Brooklyn's two Democratic seats in Congress, where he was involved in clearing the many illicit whisky distilleries out of the Fifth Ward and in arguing for the construction of a federal building in his bulging city. He had just turned 39, and had traveled an admirable distance since arriving in New York, supposedly as an orphan boy or adolescent, from Ireland's County Wexford. Kinsella, who most likely accented his name on the first syllable, was described by Dr. Henry

R. Stiles in his 1884 Brooklyn history as "an ideal self-made man," who, "while the basis of his character was Irish, its development and embellishment were wholly American." The newspaper he ran was the oldest, most popular and influential of the city's three dailies, all published in the afternoon, and indeed it had become the most widely read afternoon paper in the country. He had started there as a typesetter and become its very young editor in 1861, when his predecessor, Henry McCloskey, also an Irish-born Catholic, resigned after his pro-secession policy had prompted the postmaster-general to bar the paper from the mail, and federal authorities had threatened to suspend its publication. Kinsella's *Eagle* supported the government and the war against the South, although it remained Democratic and critical of President Lincoln, and his editorials were no less forceful and stylish than McCloskey's.

Combining journalism with civic service, he became one of Brooklyn's most prominent public men. He was a member of the Board of Education, where he advocated equal pay for women, and sat on the water-and-sewer board. He was a very active trustee of the East River Bridge, which began to be built in 1870. And in Congress, allied with the Liberal Republican movement, he was, a rival paper would write, "chiefly responsible" for *New York Herald* publisher Horace Greeley's presidential run on the Democratic ticket in 1872. Yet his time in Washington was a detour in his career. He would serve just one term, and return to the *Eagle* full-time at the start of '73.[79]

The *Eagle*'s alignment with the national cause was not thorough enough for the city's radical Republicans, who one night at the start of the war had marched to the paper's Fulton Street offices and demanded that a man who appeared at a window "hang out your flag," which he promptly did.[80] Then, in September 1863, some party leaders established a paper with a title that made their allegiance explicit—the *Daily Union*. It was linked in spirit to the less forthrightly named *Independent*, a weekly organ of the Brooklyn and New York Congregational Church, which Brooklyn's celebrity pastor Henry Ward Beecher regularly contributed to and later edited. Both papers were eventually owned by Henry C. Bowen, a Connecticut native who had come to New York and made a fortune in dry goods, settled in the grandest, most lavishly appointed home on elegant Brooklyn Heights, and prevailed upon Beecher to establish himself at Plymouth Church. It was Bowen too who invited candidate Lincoln to visit

Beecher's church and deliver his groundbreaking campaign-speech at Cooper Union in New York. The *Independent* prospered in the 1860s under Beecher as editor and the talented young managing editor, and Beecher companion, Theodore Tilton, whom Bowen would also appoint editor of the *Union* in 1870.[81] In these years Beecher, Bowen and Tilton were joined in the public mind as "The Trinity of Plymouth Church."[82] But in the 1870s the bonds that linked them would strain and break under public pressure, and in history they are linked as the three central male figures in the thunderous Henry Ward Beecher adultery scandal. In the same period the animosity between Kinsella and Bowen burst into flame.

Beecher was much more than the city's best-known citizen—a recent biographer has called him "The Most Famous Man in America." The son of a fiery, sometimes controversial New England clergyman, he had set out to surpass his father, as well as several ministerial brothers, in theological demagoguery, and sensationally succeeded. He first drew wide attention in Indianapolis, from where, in 1847, at age 34, he shifted to Brooklyn and oversaw the construction of a massive but bland Brooklyn Heights church, on the platform of which he would perfect the theatrics that included voice-modulation, weeping, foot-stamping, fist-thumping, and a variety of solo acts such as a drunk appealing to a judge or a fisherman landing a trout. His celebrity grew during the turbulent pre-war years when he became the most eloquent abolitionist voice in the country and sealed his position by conducting mock slave-auctions on his stage. His histrionics yielded hysterics. So desirable was one of the 2,100 upholstered seats, or a supplementary chair, or even a space to stand in the auditorium of Plymouth Congregational Church on Orange Street that policemen were employed to regulate admission. Many applicants crossed from New York on Sunday ferries that were known as "Beecher Boats." According to different accounts, by 1870 the great man they came to see and hear earned or had humbly turned down a salary of $20,000 a year, and made nearly that much in speaking-fees and from publications that included a collection of his sermons and a novel.[83]

Many well-known Brooklynites were citizens of two cities, with homes in Brooklyn and offices in New York. The 11 intercity ferries[84] in the 1870s were thronged in the mornings and early evenings in only one direction, yet it was hardly the case that New York sucked away all of Brooklyn's talent. While it remained a city—until 1898— Brooklyn proudly represented itself and proclaimed its own identity. It did not want to be New York, but was glad enough to have New York stirring beside it. It wished to be better-governed than its neighbor, to have cleaner, more-verdant, less-congested streets, and fewer crimes, especially murders and political malfeasances. It wanted and had its own institutions: dozens of theaters through the decades, the Brooklyn Institute, which would become the reputable Brooklyn Museum, the Leopold Eidlitz-designed Academy of Music, the first two enclosed baseball grounds in America, and, completed in 1873, a great Vaux and Olmsted park painfully planned and financed to match, or surpass, the one they had built in the middle of Manhattan Island in the previous decades.

At the same time it was plagued by the thousand miseries of runaway growth, with symptoms not so different from those of wicked New York. It was enormously hard, and not growing easier, to manage its expansion—to pave its streets, fill its water-pipes, instruct its children. And of course there was corruption; of course there was squalor and poverty and violent crime. Its exalted Protestant clergy and Republican politicians may have conceived of Brooklyn as an Anglo-Saxon New Englandite city, but in fact about half of its people were foreign-born, most of those Irish and Germans[85] who had transported and probably aggravated their cultural tendency to drink hard, most notoriously on Sundays. And the papers were filled with tales of drunkenness inclining to mayhem, often involving husbands and wives. One of the city's most newsworthy crimes was the operation of those tax-dodging distilleries in the Irish Fifth Ward, an industry that became so vigorous that from 1869 to the mid-1870s U.S. revenue officials enlisted federal forces, including Marines, in a series of invasions that became known as Brooklyn's "Whisky War," for they were stoutly resisted by the moonshiners and brick-and-stone-flinging residents of the district. One raid, in 1870, deployed 1500 troops.[86]

Brooklyn's distinguished Americans included an impressive contingent of Civil War generals, such as James Jourdan, president of the Board of Police and Excise, Congressman Henry Slocum, Judge Calvin Pratt and a pair of legal bigwigs, the brothers-in-law Benjamin F. Tracy and Isaac Catlin, who would each defend a suspected Brooklyn murderess in the 1870s. Another alleged female assassin would be represented by a former governor of Maryland, Enoch Lowe, who joined Brooklyn's estimable legal community after the war.

Jourdan and Tracy were two of the three Republican operatives, along with the banker Silas B. Dutcher, whom a journalistic wag had dubbed "The Three Graces" of that party, because they controlled all federal patronage in the city.[87] Tracy would end his term as U.S. attorney in 1873, return to private practice, and become a defender of Henry Ward Beecher.[88]

Beecher was not the only admired and influential preacher in a city of 200 churches. Farther south on the Heights his fellow Congregationalist Richard S. Storrs was known as "the Chrysostom of Brooklyn"[89]—though one wonders, given his anti-immigrant prejudice, if he quite appreciated the comparison to a Roman Catholic saint. DeWitt Talmage's so-called "sensationalist" oratory might attract bigger crowds than even Plymouth could handle to the Presbyterian Free Tabernacle on Schermerhorn Street.[90] And Theodore L. Cuyler's Lafayette Presbyterian had the most congregants of any Reformed church in America. All were prolific writers of articles and books, as was Abram N. Littlejohn, Brooklyn-based Episcopal bishop of Long Island.[91]

The Roman Catholic Diocese of Brooklyn, also including Long Island, had been carved out of the Archdiocese of New York in 1853. It was led by Irish-born Bishop John Loughlin, who had little interest in writing books and much in building churches and schools and caring for the poor. How such care should be managed was one of the most contentious issues between the Christian branches, and Brooklyn was sharply divided religiously, socially, and politically between an old Yankee establishment and European immigrants and their offspring. Loughlin had hardly settled into his episcopal seat when nativist mobs rallied and marched against his church, attacked Irish Catholics, threatened church property and provoked riots that required the deployment of the state militia.[92] No more blood was shed in the following decades, but events in the 1870s would demonstrate how the city remained a Protestant-Catholic battleground.

Brooklyn did not yet extend, as it would at the end of the century, across Long Island from the East River to the Atlantic Ocean, to cover all of Kings County—not by a long distance. It ended at the borders of Flatbush and Bay Ridge to the south, beyond which there were scores of mainly Dutch farms. Indeed there was still farmland within the city limits. But the city managers foresaw its expansive destiny, and when they determined that they wanted an extensive bucolic park like New York's, they placed it at the edge of the city, with its southern end jutting substantially into the town of Flatbush. Construction began in 1866, but its heavy cost became a lingering controversy, and it was not completed until 1873, the year that Calvert Vaux and the partner he had mentored in the field of landscape-architecture, Frederick Law Olmsted, parted ways.

The park they left behind is generally considered their greatest achievement. "It is admitted by strangers," the *Eagle* would write the following year, "that Brooklyn has in Prospect Park, taken for all in all, the handsomest place of public outdoor resort of any city in the world."[93] This was only slightly hyperbolic. Olmsted would walk through it in 1886, as the thousands of trees and shrubs he and Vaux had planted there were growing full, and remark, "I am prouder of it than of anything I have had to do with."[94]

And in the same years that it was being completed, the greatest technological and architectural accomplishment in America was rising in the harbor. The towers of John and Washington Roebling's long-envisioned East River Bridge emerged painstakingly above the swirling waters, block by granite block, through the first half of the decade. When crowned, on the Brooklyn side in 1875, on the New York side the next year, they would reach 276 feet above water, higher than every steeple in the two cities except that of Trinity Church at Wall Street. The span that joined them would be the longest in the world.[95] And few things ever built would better express the view of the Roman poet that "he wins every point who combines the useful with the beautiful."

Government was messy, sharply contentious, and too generally ineffectual and corrupt—hardly unique characteristics among American cities. Yet there were more than a few men of probity and intelligence who hoped to make it more honest and efficient. Venality and dullness were, wrote Harold C. Syrett in his excellent political history of Brooklyn City, the particular properties of the municipal aldermen—it was said that the council chamber of either New York or Brooklyn could be emptied by a boy who yelled, "Hey, mister, your saloon's on fire!"[96]

Voting fraud was rife, and in the mayoral-election year of 1869 too obvious to ignore. But when Democratic District Attorney Samuel Morris, who would defend Fanny Hyde, diligently pursued the wrong-doers, he butted against party boss Hugh L. McLaughlin,[97] and the confrontation would eventually cost him his position. The 1871 election was no purer, and again Morris delivered indictments.[98] When he left office the following January, this work was apparently done. But there would be much, much more heard about it after another Democrat, Winchester Britton, succeeded to the job. About the same time the Republican comptroller, Frederick Schroeder, was demonstrating a refreshing determination to examine the books of the City of Brooklyn, an initiative that apparently no official had shown for some time. He found that his predecessor had left a gap of $100,000, and the man eventually would be charged with stealing nearly twice as much. Then, one July morning in 1873, the president of the Brooklyn Trust Company, E. S. Mills, drowned in the ocean at Coney Island, and was mourned in verse by the *Eagle* as a man of virtue before it was discovered that he had scooped up $150,000 in bank funds to cover personal losses. Schroeder dug up the further news that the bank secretary, who was also the City's deputy treasurer, had conspired with his boss, Cortland A. Sprague, and Mills to relieve Brooklyn of another $200,000.[99] Schroeder, in recognition of his integrity and diligence, would be elected mayor in 1875,[100] presumably by an accurate count of the votes cast. Reform was in the air, and would be achieved more thoroughly by Mayor Seth Low in the following decade.

It was no surprise that Hugh McLaughlin, who would become known as "the sage of Willoughby Street," where he dispensed favors and enforced discipline from a perch in Kerrigan's Auction House, sniped at Schroeder. McLaughlin had become entrenched as the Irish Catholic Democratic boss that nearly all big cities—with the temporary exception of William Marcy Tweed in New York—seemed to require. He would remain in place until 1903, picking candidates, influencing the courts, swaying votes to the gubernatorial nominees he favored. He may not have chanced his arm by sticking it directly in the City's cash-register as others had, but he got rich through what George Washington Plunkitt of Tammany Hall would describe as "honest graft"—investing in real-estate, for example, in areas of his city that he knew to be bound for improvement, such as the proposed entrance-route to Prospect Park.[101]

In his own party, Boss McLaughlin's greatest nemesis would turn out to be Thomas Kinsella, a sometime ally who decided at long last to engage a strong and eloquent campaign against one-man rule in 1879. It shook the Sage more noticeably than any other force directed against him during his long reign, and it largely caused the election of Low.[102] A few years earlier, Kinsella had also been influential from a distance in bringing down the mighty Tweed.

Brooklyn, city and lost city, would grow and grow until its population far surpassed that of the borough and world cynosure of Manhattan. But it would be viewed as the vaguest, least definable of very big places, its flag lowered, its name, as the anti-consolidationists had feared, all but "buried in the book of shame." No other place of such size and distinctiveness has lost so much of its history and individuality, and most of its own residents today are hardly aware that it was once such a very different, and fascinating, place.

Jailhouse and Courthouse

Fanny of Raymond Street

"Fanny, my child!"

"Father!" she responded, and kissed him through the bars of her cell.

This meeting was observed one day in March of 1872 by a man who had supervised factory-girls for 25 years.

"I have generally found in every factory two or three wayward girls," he wrote in a New York paper, "over whom I had complete control—could have been either guardian or monster." No death, he added, "would have been too inglorious for such a wretch" as had violated this trust.[1]

Yet there continued to be much public disdain as well as sympathy for Fanny Hyde.

She was arraigned on March 6th at the Court of Oyer and Terminer, the quaintly named nineteenth-century venue for felony trials in New York State. Court buffs were frustrated when she appeared concealed behind a nearly opaque veil at the County Court House, where Messrs. Morris and Keady entered her plea of not guilty and agreed with District Attorney Britton to begin the trial on the 19th of the month.[2] The *Eagle* looked forward to "a notable legal tourney,"[3] but the following week the court granted Morris a postponement,[4] so Fanny waited at Raymond Street as the spring of 1872 brightened the busy city outside the prison walls.

The Kings County Jail, faced in brownstone, graced with Gothic windows, and said to be "modeled after a West Point fortress," was known as "Brooklyn's Bastille" for its thick, massive walls, crenellated roofline, and corner turrets. Located northeast of downtown, across Flatbush Avenue at Raymond Street—later, Ashland Place—and Willoughby Street, it was built in 1836 and '37, when Brooklyn had just become a city, and it was described 36 years later as "a relic of the age so fondly remembered." Its cornerstone was laid on the 60th anniversary of the Battle of Long Island, and the grounds abutted the site of Fort Greene, one of the Revolutionary army's defenses on that day. After Olmsted and Vaux reconfigured that site into Washington Park, its opposite boundary became one of the city's most prestigious residential streets, home to Police Commissioner Jourdan and other civic leaders.

That "Raymond Street Jail," as it was always called, was antiquated had been one of the milder complaints about it. Rev. DeWitt Talmage once compared its atmosphere to "that of the Black Hole of Calcutta," and added, "When I swept through the wicket it almost knocked me down." Vermin thrived, and supervision was so lax that prisoners got drunk in their cells. Talmage believed that, as a corrective institution, it was counterproductive: "Yale College is not so well calculated to make scholars, nor Harvard so well calculated to make scientists, nor Princeton so well calculated to make theologians as Raymond Street Jail is calculated to make criminals." In the 1870s Sheriff Aras G. Williams ran it humanely and was credited for making many improvements, but described it nonetheless as a "mean" and "badly laid-out prison." The original, or men's, wing had been built to house about 50 inmates on its three floors, but now held up to 200, with three or as many as six packed in nine-by-six-foot cells. Noise was constant, as the men entertained themselves with thrusts of irony and steady rounds of banter and song. Williams saw that halls were kept clean, the floors scrubbed, and the cells disinfected and their walls whitewashed as often as twice a week. But there was no bathing facility, nor running water for commodes. Inscribed in plain black letters above an archway inside the main entrance was an admonition from the Book of Proverbs: "The way of the transgressor is hard."

The women's wing, built a few years later, was described by a commentator in 1872 as not at all noxious, but "in admirable condition" and "exceedingly clean." It was constructed of red brick and contained three tiers of double rows of cells, 80 in all, accommodating in these years about 100 residents. A later visitor interviewed two women being held for trial on felonious charges. "I am treated kindly here," said one. "I have good food." The other found the surroundings to be "just like home." When Fanny Hyde was encountered at Raymond Street, she was found to be "polite and cheerful, as usual."

But by the middle of the decade a general call arose in the county for the replacement or expansion and renovation of its jail, and a new wing was completed by the summer of 1880. Its exterior granite was acquired from the same firm that supplied blocks for the East River Bridge. After some argument about cost, each of the 448 new cells was equipped with a water-closet.[5]

The end of Samuel D. Morris's nine-year span as Kings County district attorney in January 1872 had been involuntary,[6] so his confrontation with Winchester Britton in a popularly fascinating murder trial was laden with some prickly recent history.

Morris, 48, handsome, blue-eyed, dark-haired, side-whiskered, had come to Brooklyn from New Jersey in 1851, and his early political affiliation was with the "American Party," or "Know Nothings," a vigorous and very influential national nativist movement of the 1840s and '50s. Drifting to the Democrats, by his early 30s he had served as a state assemblyman, city corporation counsel, and County Court judge. He was district attorney at 38.[7] In politics and in prosecution he was viewed as pugnacious, fearless, effective, and adept at making enemies. He admitted to a relish for "taking the scalp" of an opponent, and pursued criminals even after his life had been threatened.[8] Once, during a cholera epidemic, he exceeded his authority but won plaudits for ordering the release of Raymond Street inmates—the most serious offenders were housed in tents. As a political speaker, he was said to have "few equals in this state," and to have once been complimented for his skill by Henry Clay.[9] Certainly he was smart, shrewd, and partisan, and nine years was a wide period in which to accumulate power. But in his third term as district attorney he had been overtaken by a more powerful Brooklyn Democrat.

In May 1870, Boss Hugh McLaughlin, offended by Morris's indictment of poll-meddlers and his accusing Democratic judges of obstruction of justice,[10] moved to undo him, charging that he had played with bail money and put more than $1,000 in his pocket. Morris coolly conceded that he had done so, because the county had owed him the money. The matter made its way to the Democratic governor, the Tammany-Hall- and Boss-Tweed-endorsed John T. Hoffman, and was resolved when Morris agreed to nullify the remaining indictments. But, as the pressure had mounted, Morris had angrily scored "the Ring" for "trumping up the frivolous charges against me . . . but this was to be expected after exposing their frauds."[11]

The upshot was that, in the fall of '71, Morris yielded the Democratic nomination for district attorney to Winchester Britton. And, though the retiring D.A. played the good soldier and "heartily" endorsed the party's ticket, the issue of who had done what about those odd-smelling election results lived on. Morris had stated in a letter to Britton that there were no more convictions to be had, but the former D.A. would claim that these letters had been written (and pre-dated) as a favor to Britton, who was anxious about being viewed as ineffectual. Britton, he insisted, knew that there were actionable cases against persons who "had 'cleared out' and could not be arrested during my term," but had since returned; and Britton responded that he did look further into the lingering indictments, tried one man, who was acquitted, then decided that it was not worthwhile to pursue any others.[12] He was clearly being cast, however, as the Democratic Ring's prosecutor, by whom McLaughlin's minions at the polls did not feel threatened.

These events, whatever version of them was true, were taking place just as the men were also preparing for the much anticipated trial of Fanny Hyde, and Morris's animus against his adversary would fester as the year 1872 wore on.

Winchester Britton, about two years younger than Morris, had also migrated to Brooklyn—out of western Massachusetts, the New York State city of Troy, and San Francisco. The "Bench and Bar" contributor to Stiles's *History of Kings County* commented on "his remarkably brilliant black eyes," and the accompanying portrait indeed depicts a stern, penetrating stare coming out of a strong, square, full-bearded face. A reporter once fixated on the prosecutor's coiffure:

> It is silvery white, but full of electricity, when the District
> Attorney gets excited or nervous—and whoever saw him
> cool? It does stand up and bristle, like quills upon the
> fretful porcupine. All the rubbing down, all the running
> through of the fingers that Mr. Britton can do, does not

affect it. It is like *Poor Pillicoddy* in the play, perpetually "turning up again." Various intimate friends of the District Attorney have recommended to him numerous compounds *pour fixer les cheveux*, but his hair perpetually refuses to be fixed. Pomatum, apparently, it scorns; hair oil it scorns; cosmetic is its abomination. And the result is that Mr. Britton looks, at whatever time or place one may meet him with his hat off, like a venerable mop that has experienced a very bad scare.

The writer added that "he is full of nervous fire, and in any case where his best abilities or his sympathies are engaged, his fine eyes flash with the fire of combat."

Britton had gone west during the Gold Rush years, and reportedly made his fortune, then lost it somehow in one of the big San Francisco fires. He ran for the California assembly and failed, but served as a city alderman and county supervisor. In 1853 he sailed back to New York to get married and settled in Brooklyn. When his young wife died, he married her sister, who bore 11 children. He too had temporarily strayed to the Know Nothings, then practiced privately in New York for nearly two decades before he returned to politics in 1871. But when he died suddenly at his home on Carroll Street in 1886, Judge Calvin E. Pratt complimented him for having been "too bold, frank and outspoken" to be politically successful. Others praised his honesty, loyalty to friends, and exceedingly fine knowledge of the law.[13]

A pedestrian or horsecar-passenger coming along Fulton Street from the direction of the ferry-house would face two Greek Revival buildings designed by Gamaliel King: marble-clad Brooklyn City Hall, completed in 1849 at the junction of Court Street, and just behind it, flanking it on the left, the County Court House, topped by a massive global cupola and inscribed on its pediment with the Roman numeral for 1861, the year that its construction had begun. Modeled on classical temples, they were about equal in height,[14] but the courthouse was much deeper, extending in three sections from Joralemon to Livingston Street. Very handsome buildings they were, yet there was a raffish flavor to this "Civic Center" area, for it was supplied, according to Harold Syrett, with "an inordinate number of liquor establishments," as well as "oyster bars, restaurants, chop houses, merchant emporiums, centers of the policy game, lawyers' offices, and, in fact, almost anything at which money . . . [could] be made."[15]

The courtroom was thick with prominent Brooklyn jurists when Fanny Hyde's trial began on Monday, April 15th, 1872. Three judges presided: Justice Abraham B. Tappen and Associate Justices Stephen I. Voorhees and Barnett Johnson. County Judge H. A. Moore was also on the bench. Beside Britton was Assistant District Attorney Edgar M. Cullen, whose name survives to this day at the downtown Brooklyn law firm of Cullen and Dykman. Morris's assistants, in addition to Patrick Keady, were General Isaac S. Catlin and Thomas E. Pearsall, and Morris would tell the jury in his summation that they were all, himself included, working for nothing. Every square foot of the seating area and the gallery above was occupied by spectators sitting and standing, and the room became so stifling on the second day that Tappen ordered all the windows to be opened. A more than usual number of women were present, "young and old, . . . with flashy costumes, and at times lively if not brilliant conversation."

"No trial which has been before the courts in a great while," wrote the *Brooklyn Union*, "has attracted the attention this one is receiving, and both at home and abroad the result will be looked forward to with painful anxiety."

The crowd hushed when Fanny entered. She again wore a veil, which was brown, and sat with her father and husband, to whom she spoke steadily and with apparent lightheartedness. Her "neat but plain" attire included "an overskirt of slate colored alpaca," a black cloak, embroidered with silk, "a black hat which was jauntily set on her head," and black kid gloves. Henry Hyde was described as "quite a fancy looking individual," with "slightly curled" brown hair parted in the middle, clothing "not new" but "well brushed," and wearing a seal ring, a watch-chain and diamond-like jewel on his shirt-front. John Windley, blue-eyed and gray-haired, with a slight mustache and a pointed "imperial" beard, wore a black suit.[16]

Although Morris felt that the district attorney's juror-challenges were excessive, twelve men were selected by two o'clock,[17] and later that afternoon Winchester Britton opened for the prosecution.

"It would seem," he declared, "that the facts, as I have stated them to you, would constitute a plain case. Well, add to what

I have already stated, that the brother came out from [the room below] . . . stepped across the dead body of this man, the defendant being still there, and, showing some emotion, said to her, 'Fanny, I told you not to do this,' to which she made no reply."[18]

He then defined and explained the statute on first-degree murder, which required a premeditated design, and discussed the meaning of justifiable homicide.[19] And added:

> [I]t will be your duty to rebuke this mawkish sensibility which seems to be pervading in our society, and which in many instances even leads our citizens to sympathize with crime. . . . And if there should be developed any mitigating circumstances which the law recognizes and which those principles that I have suggested to you recognize, leave it where it belongs, where, in our administration of the Government we have entirely placed the pardoning power—in the Governor of our State.

"I trust," he concluded, "that you will not, by your verdict, say that vengeance for any supposed personal wrong shall be taken into the hands of private persons."[20]

As testimony began, Morris conceded that Fanny had shot Watson with a pistol that she and her brother had bought at Stowell's shop.[21] Then Britton brought forth witnesses who had been at the Merrill Building on January 26th, none of whom had seen the shooting. Morris and Britton began to disagree about admissible evidence during the cross-examination of the first witness, Ellen Curley.[22] There would be several more clashes.

After noontime recess, many of the factory-women gathered around Fanny and chatted briskly with her.[23]

The following morning, Fanny again wore hat and veil, and carried a grey squirrel muff, in which she steadily kept her hands as she looked about the courtroom or bowed her head on her breast. She was joined now by her stepmother, described as tall and thin, wearing a striped brown-and-gold poplin dress, trimmed in velvet, a dark straw hat, and a black veil. Henry, looking pale and anxious, leaned constantly on his wife's chair, while a contingent of "stalwart policemen" struggled to limit the overflowing crowd. In the afternoon, the prisoner was joined by Alice, her sister, who was just turning 17. She was said to closely resemble Fanny and wore a dress of green-and-black plaid. George Watson's similarly bearded but taller and heavier brother sat beside Britton, and other family-members sat among the spectators. Mrs. Eliza Watson remained in Britton's office, out of hearing of testimony that would be painful to her. She wept nonetheless.[24] After the examination of Dr. Creamer, the police surgeon, who estimated that Watson had died about eight or ten minutes after being stricken, and the recall of Watson's father-in law, Ager Pixley, who identified a light-weight overcoat with a bullet-hole in the collar as having been worn by his son-in-law on his final day, the prosecution rested,[25] and Morris dropped a surprise. He motioned that he need not mount a defense:

"I submit to the Court that there is no proof of the first element of the crime of murder. I submit that they have not, to begin with, proved that Watson was killed by the defendant."

This was particularly odd because Morris had conceded that she had shot him, so he was making the legal point that, even so, it was the prosecution's burden to prove she had. Britton remonstrated that he had indeed so proved, and that the defense had no right to have the jury charged with such a claim until the case was closed. But the district attorney seemed a bit flummoxed, and Morris seemed to be flaunting his superior knowledge of the law. He launched a monologue of several minutes, in which he insisted further that, even if the prosecution had proven the act, it had not established an intent or motive necessary to convict the defendant of first-degree homicide.

Judge Tappen denied the motion and announced a one-hour recess, after which General Catlin opened for the defense.[26]

A powerfully built man of 36, Catlin, a famously brave officer, had lost a leg at Petersburg[27] and moved about with a cane. He declared that the defense would now present the case "in full." Gathering all his reserves of bluster, he insisted that he had never considered the defendant guilty, but "believed, and still believe" that her act derived from "the convulsion of a mind upon which great wrong, outrage and provocation had been heaped," that it was "the result of some sudden, irresistible, overpowering impulse, some convulsion of the human mind as irresistible and uncontrollable as the decree of fate."[28] Here was the defense of temporary insanity. It too had dropped this day as a surprise upon the prosecution, and the trial of Fanny Hyde would be a significant chapter in the history of its development.

The insanity defense he was introducing had become a trend in mid- to late-nineteenth-century America, and his use of "irresistible" twice in a sentence was not a rhetorical lapse. It tapped the terminology that American jurisprudence had developed to refine the definition of legal insanity established in the international-landmark Daniel McNaughtan case in 1843 England. Beginning in the year 1800, with the trial of James Hadfield for aiming a pistol at, but not shooting, King George III, British courts had been enlightening their view of the mental conditions that justified finding defendants not guilty—advancing from an eighteenth-century judge's instruction that this verdict could only apply to one who "doth not know what he is doing, no more than . . . a wild beast." Hadfield was shown to be brain-damaged and delusional, and was acquitted because judge and jury concluded, with the aid of expert medical testimony, that, although he had often seemed sane, he had committed his crime in a delusory state in which he could not distinguish right from wrong.[29]

The McNaughtan (or "M'Naghten") case was a watershed not because it substantially changed the definition of insanity, as related to the unawareness of right and wrong, but because of how it solidified the definition. The defendant was a Scottish woodworker who had shot and killed the secretary of British Prime Minister Robert Peel, believing that he was assailing Peel himself. He was found "not guilty by reason of insanity," but this verdict was broadly unpopular and, specifically, displeasing to young Queen Victoria. Her complaint led the House of Lords to present five questions to the justices of the court about what exactly constituted a state of mind that absolved a person from responsibility for a criminal act. Among their carefully considered answers was a formulation that guided judgments in English-speaking countries for a century or longer: that "at the time of the committing of the act, the party accused was laboring under such a defect of reason, from disease of the mind, as not to know the nature or quality of the act he was doing, or, if he did know it, that he did not know that he was doing what was wrong."[30] Thus the factors of knowing right from wrong and of the state of mind at the time of the act were stated more precisely than before, but at about the same time the Scotsman James Prichard was refining the understanding of insanity to distinguish between the "cognitive" insanity defined in the "McNaughtan Rule" and "moral" or "emotional" insanity, in which "the will is occasionally under the influence of an impulse" that "is in some instances irresistible."[31]

As early as 1844, American courts began to supplement the McNaughtan Rule with this "volitional" element, by which they could attribute insanity even to someone capable of knowing that his or her criminal act was wrong.[32] Although New York was not one of the states that had adopted the "irresistible impulse" test by 1872,[33] Isaac Catlin was clearly appealing to this precedent.

It was not a long step from here to the concept of "temporary insanity," or *transitoria mania*, and the first trial in which an acquittal was delivered on this basis was that of New York City attorney, Congressman, soon-to-be Civil War general and outsized character, Daniel Sickles. In 1859, in Washington's Lafayette Park, Sickles shot and killed the son of Francis Scott Key, Philip Barton Key, the city's district attorney, whom Sickles accused of adultery with his young wife. A sympathetic jury in the sensational trial agreed that the Congressman had been driven temporarily mad by jealousy.[34] That trial's focus on passion stirred by sexual intimacy and betrayal underlined its relevance to the case of a humble Brooklyn factory-girl. And many more precedents would be offered.

Catlin may also have been thinking of the McNaughtan trial transcript when he peeled the onion of Fanny's lamentable past. The Scotsman's counsel had told the jury of the death of his client's mother when he was a boy, and of his being raised by a stepmother who did not offer the "kindness which is usually shown to legitimate offspring."[35] Likewise with Fanny: " 'Motherless!' . . . In that one word is Fanny Hyde's fate. If that sainted mother, that kind-hearted mother had lived, Fanny Hyde would not be on trial for her life to-day. She would have been educated to avoid the adulterer; her tender heart and mind would have been disciplined to have saved her from the wiles and treachery of the seducer."[36]

And so on. He believed, he said, that God was "on Fanny's side." And a good thing, too, because "the poison and mildew of licentiousness are corrupting our society."[37]

Not only that, but this case also poised the poor and weak against the wealthy and powerful—labor against management. The defense had learned that the Watson family had spent thousands to add a New York lawyer to the prosecution's force and to hire detectives, "under the guise of charity [toward Fanny], to get some confession out of this defendant."[38]

The oration lasted two hours, during which many women in the courtroom sobbed.[39]

Then Britton and Morris went back at each other. Hardly had the defense testimony begun when the district attorney objected to an inquiry about the evening that George Watson had tossed a bouquet to Fanny at the Bridge Street Church presentation, an objection that opened a long argument about the relevance of this to the defense's claim of temporary insanity. This allowed Morris to ruminate about this evolving issue. Noting that Fanny's "intercourse" with Watson was involuntary and had begun when she was a "child," he asked what "are the causes of insanity? What are the causes that operate on the mind and produce this? Who can tell them?" He suggested that the district attorney had not advanced his knowledge beyond the "wild beast" analogy: "According to the idea of the counsel, there could never be such a defense as insanity set up with any success unless you could prove that the person was a raving maniac, and had been all her life."[40]

But he followed this appeal for a more advanced understanding of human behavior with a rather regressive contention that the dysmenorrhea from which Fanny suffered was "one of the fruitful sources of temporary insanity." And he added: "There is not a married man but that knows the effect of this disease upon the mind and intellect of the female sex. Why, there are girls here in this city to-day laboring under this disease who are crazy at home and would be perfectly irresponsible for any act they might commit while that was upon them."[41]

Britton responded that it was clear that some things did and some things did not produce insanity, and he begged the court to distinguish between them. This business of claiming that madness "comes on in a moment and passes away in a moment," that a killer can be sane immediately before and after his act, but not during it, was unconvincing to the prosecution.[42]

One newspaper of the period described those who experienced such phenomena as being "cured of their disease by their crime."

Judge Tappen allowed Morris to continue his questioning of the witness.

At the end of the day, the prisoner was thronged as she was escorted to her carriage through the courthouse corridors and across the sidewalk on Joralemon Street.[43]

On the third day Morris asked those who had seen Fanny before the shooting to describe the distracted look in her face. "Very wild and very much excited," said her co-worker Mary Gleason, ". . . she did not look natural." The defender homed in: "what impression was made upon your mind as to whether she was in her right mind or not?"

Britton objected, but Tappen admitted the question.

"I don't know," answered Mary Gleason, "I think she was not in her right mind."

But Britton came back hard at her.

"What do you mean by saying her right mind?"

"She seemed to be excited, and not natural."

"Was it an impression on your mind that she had not her faculties?"

"I do not know as it was."

"That she hadn't her senses?"

"She didn't act as if she had."

"Was that the impression that your mind had at the time?"

"I cannot say for certain."[44]

Still, the defense had another tack to move along. Mary Dexter, Fanny's aunt, succeeded Gleason, and was asked, suddenly, "Did you know her grandfather?" She responded, "Yes. I lived in the same house with him."

"How did he come to his death?"

"Drowned."

Objection. This was "totally immaterial and irrelevant" to what the defense was trying to establish, because it was not competent proof of the ancestor's insanity. "It is impossible," Britton complained, "for us in any way to meet such testimony as this."

Tappen, stating, "Tradition is testimony," admitted the inquiry, and Dexter submitted further responses that turned tradition against the prosecution. The grandfather had attempted to poison himself with laudanum, and to hang himself in his room, and he had slept with a butcher-knife under his pillow. And John Marr remembered that the old man had offered to "bite an inch out of the chair back" if someone would lend him a sixpence, and that he was tended to by his younger brother "because he was said to be out of his mind."[45]

After a brief examination of Sarah Windley about Fanny's worsening health and loss of weight, John Windley took the stand and recounted his life with his older daughter, and their falling-out. And yes, he said, it was understood that his father "was not entirely in his right senses."[46]

The courtroom became silent for perhaps four minutes, as Samuel Morris stood talking in a low voice to his client. Then he turned to Justice Tappen, paused briefly and "slowly and distinctly called out 'Fanny Hyde.'"

"A suppressed buzz or stir ran through the bar, the seats outside and the gallery as the pale-faced Fanny rose from her seat and went forward to the witness stand. Amid breathless silence she was sworn, her hand trembling as it lay upon the book she was about to kiss. She took her seat."

Again Morris paused a moment, then asked:

"When was it that you went to work for Mr. Watson?"

"The latter part of February, three years ago."

"About how old were you then?"

"Just turning fifteen."

"You were a virtuous girl at that time?"

"Yes, sir."

"Have you ever had any improper intimacy except with Mr. Watson?"

(Firmly) "No, sir, I have not."[47]

The issue of Fanny Hyde's character was now in play.

You Have Had Me

It had been journalistic hearsay of a kind likely to be printed at the time—an account in the *Brooklyn Union* a few days after Watson's shooting that implicated the 13-year-old Fanny in a blackmail scheme against a "prominent citizen" of Williamsburg who had been amorous with a friend of hers.[48] But it had suggested a version of the defendant that would linger beside Isaac Catlin's portrait of the tender girl who had been prey to "the wiles and treachery of the seducer."

Now his associate Sam Morris had anticipated that the prosecution would attempt to demonstrate that she had not been "a virtuous girl at that time."

As he neared the end of his questioning, he asked if she had cried much about her situation with Watson.[49] When she didn't immediately answer, wrote the *Union*, "the crowd surged forward, and in the gallery, men perched on the shoulders of others to gain a view." She "cried about it continually," she said, and she wanted Watson to leave her alone. Then she bent her head and, swaying in her chair, cried into her handkerchief.[50]

On cross-examination, Britton went where Morris expected, to New Britain, Connecticut, during the summer of 1871.

The Hydes had boarded there at the home of a Mr. Woodhouse, and George Watson had returned to his family in Hartford. But the peculiarly close association that that they had formed in Brooklyn continued.

On two occasions Fanny and Henry stayed with the Watson family, and on one of those visits Fanny spent at least two nights there without her husband, sleeping one of those nights with the youngest daughter, who was two, and the other with the oldest, who was 16—exactly one year younger than Fanny. On a Sunday in July, Fanny went to church with Mrs. Eliza Watson.

At some point, also, while the Hydes were staying at Woodhouse's, Watson took a room there. This arrangement may have spared him the nine-mile trip back and forth from Hartford, but for George Watson there was never an innocent motive for being close to Fanny. She would state at her trial that in New Britain she had told Henry, with Watson present, that he had seduced her, and that Henry had become very angry and threatened legal action. Watson, she said, had begged him not to do so, "for the sake of his wife and children," and had promised again "to leave her alone." After this scene, the Hydes went back to Brooklyn.

Britton had other information:

"Don't you know it to be a fact that your husband asked Mr. Woodhouse to have Watson come there?"

"No, sir."

"How long was it [after] you went there that Watson came there?"

"Two or three weeks, or a week."

"While you were at Mr. Woodhouse's place, did you all the time occupy the same room?"

"Yes, sir."

. . .

"How many rooms were there then?

"Three."

. . .

"Who occupied the other two?"

"Mr. Watson occupied one, and Mr. Woodhouse's son and another gentleman the other."

"Did the other gentleman and Mr. Woodhouse's son occupy it all the time?"

"Yes, sir."

"Sure about that?"

"I won't be certain."

"What was the other gentleman's name?"

"Stephen Roberts."

"Was he a single or a married man?"

"A single man, for anything that I know; he passed for one."

"Was he there all the time you were?"

"Yes, sir."

"You have said that you stated to Mr. Watson, or stated in the presence of your husband, that Watson had improper associations with you; on that occasion, was there any talk about having a couple of men come from New York and work up there?"

"Not that I know of."

"Didn't you ask Mr. Watson to bring up a couple of men from New York to have them work up there in the factory?"

"No, sir."

"Isn't this the language you used, when [he] made these, what you have designated 'accusations,' 'you have nothing to say about it, for you have had me?' "

"No, sir."

. . .

"What was the last occasion before Watson's death that you were intimate with him?"

"Monday night."

"What day was he killed?"

"Friday."

"You don't mean to say that you did not have intercourse with your husband?"

"Of course I don't."

"Did you have any intercourse while you were in New Britain?"

"No, sir."

"Did you have improper intimacy with Roberts while you were in New Britain?"

"No, sir, I did not."

"Did you go to his room while you were there, in the night, from your own?"

"No, sir."[51]

The "accusations" that Britton referred to were Watson's, regarding her being with other men—charges that she had described as having become constant and obsessive before the shooting. Now the jury would have to wonder if there was any basis for them, and if Fanny Hyde's behavior had become so depraved that her husband had served as her pimp. They might also have wondered where was the man, Stephen Roberts, who might have clarified the matter.

In re-direct examination, Morris led his client through the shooting of Watson—or through the moments leading to the shooting, for she claimed to have no recall of the act itself or the minutes immediately following it.[52] The district attorney pursued this reportage, asking the obvious question, "How did you happen to have the pistol with you on that day?"

"He had abused me the day before, and I took it intending to frighten him."

She believed it had been loaded with just one bullet, and denied knowing that Henry had later fired off additional ones. She did not think it was cocked when she slipped it between her breasts, and did not remember how she had cocked it. She did not remember removing it on the stairs and aiming it. But she knew that she had not intended to shoot him.

"I don't recollect when I shot it or how I shot it. . . . I have no recollection how it went off. I have no recollection of it at all."

She had never practiced with the pistol. She did not know how Henry had got hold of it so that he could hand it to Captain Woglom of the Fifth Precinct.

Had she told Woglom why she had shot her employer, that she "could not stand it any longer," that she "shot him for satisfaction"?

"I don't recollect saying that."

Fanny held up very well. The only possible lapse in her amnesia was her answer to how many shots she had fired: "Only once, to my knowledge."

Near the end of her testimony, Britton asked if she knew where was her brother, who had been indicted as "an accessory before the act." She did not, nor whether or not he was still in the city.

Morris spoke up: "He will be on hand any time you desire him."

"I have desired him for the last two months," responded Britton. ". . . I would like to try him now. It has cost me a good deal of money to try to find him."[53]

Sam Morris arrived at court on Thursday morning followed by a clerk carrying "a small library of law books, books of reference, pamphlets, etc.," which he spread out on the defense table. Fanny entered before ten with her parents and sister. On one side of the spectator area sat more women than on any previous day, counted at "some forty." And in anticipation of the legal significance of this day's testimony, several "prominent New York lawyers" also attended.[54]

It was the day for medical testimony, a procedure all but dictated by recent jurisprudence. Dr. John Byrne, a solidly built, grey-haired clinical professor of uterine diseases at Long Island Medical College and staff physician at St. Mary's Women's Hospital, both in Brooklyn, stated that dysmenorrhea "is oftentimes disturbing to the mind, and in nervous temperaments will intensely increase nervous irritability."

Morris then summarized Fanny's family- and health-background and her long experience with Watson, up to the moment of his allegedly seizing her in the hallway, and asked what effect this might have on her mind.

"I think," Byrne answered, "its effect would be to temporarily destroy her reason entirely."

Morris followed with a very long and further detailed description of the prisoner's suffering—her dysmenorrhea, her presumed pregnancy and medication-induced abortion, her weight-loss, Watson's obsession. And, again referring to the moment of his "attack" on the stairs, asked "what, in your opinion, was the effect upon her mind?"

"Premising, sir, that before this last act of shooting, from the statement made that her mind was in a state of incipient menstrual mania, as described by authorities, I say, premising such, I would say that at the time of the act she was not in her right mind, she was insane to all intents and purposes."

"Can you state whether producing an abortion upon a young girl sixteen years of age, by drugs and medicines, would have a tendency to affect the mind of a person of nervous organization?"

"It would, as any other debilitating circumstances would, by depressing her physical powers and working upon her nervous system."

"In your general practice, is it unusual for you to find young girls, during certain periods, when they are affected with menstrual difficulties, to be affected mentally during that period?"

"They are affected mentally to the extent of hysterical paroxysms."[55]

Up then came Dr. Charles Corey, a specialist in "the mind and its diseases" at the Bloomingdale Asylum on Morningside Heights in upper Manhattan, who had sat among the spectators on previous days. Morris now referred to some of the research materials he'd had brought into the court, and asked if it was "well recognized" that "delusion, or transitoria mania," was "a form of insanity [that] may be suddenly caused and suddenly disappear."

"I think it is," replied Corey, a tall, thin man with gray hair and mustacheless beard, who wore gold-rimmed glasses.

"It is brief in its duration?"

"It is in its more marked symptoms."

"Is it not a fact that the more sudden the attack the shorter its duration?"

"Generally so."

"Is insanity in the family considered a predisposing cause?"

"It is."

"And is it not a recognized fact that it may escape generations and appear again?

"That is so."

The remarkably thorough Sam Morris read from the writings of an international array of 11 medical authorities and one French jurist on the subject of temporary or transitory insanity, while Corey nodded in agreement to all of them. One of the medical men had written: "the sympathetic connection existing between the brain and the uterus is plainly seen by the most casual observer. Many women are completely prostrated while menstruating, and suffer intensely in the head . . . more girls between the ages of twelve and eighteen are insane than boys; then we should expect to find every girl at this time in peculiarly susceptible nervous irritation." Corey agreed.

Another authority had found "certain evidences of mental disturbances immediately following the criminal act," and Morris asked Corey, "Would one of those evidences be an imperfect recollection of the occurrence?"

"Yes, sir."

"Making no effort to conceal the act?"

"That is one of the most marked."

"Delivering themselves up to the authorities?"

"They frequently do so."

A third doctor had written of "the subject [being] urged in a moment to automatic acts which could not have been foreseen," and Corey agreed that this conformed to his own "experiences or knowledge." It seemed to be forgotten at this point, however, that Fanny Hyde had carried a pistol to work on the morning of January 26th, which made the phrase "could not have been foreseen" a clumsy fit with her case. Nonetheless, Corey echoed it in his final, definitive responses on the stand.

"I have no doubt that she was insane. . . . I believe the act was from the result of a sudden impulse, the occurrence of which she did not foresee and which she was not able to restrain; I believe she had no knowledge of what she was doing at the time the shot occurred."

District Attorney Britton, who was also familiar with some of these sources, did not believe that their descriptions and definitions applied to the defendant, and he cross-examined the witness with a skillful precision that soon eroded his certainty. He got Corey to concede, first of all, that the symptoms that Fanny had displayed before the killing might have indicated "great nervous disturbance" that was not necessarily a predisposition to insanity. Yet the witness restated his conviction that "her agitation, her willingness to surrender herself, her making no effort to escape, are all facts we usually expect to find" in cases of *transitoria mania*. That was not, though, the same as proof. Moreover, Britton sensed a contradiction in the doctor's opinion that "imperfect recollection of the occurrence" was also indicative of the condition.

"If she did not recollect she had [killed him], and no one told her, be kind enough to suggest what would induce her to go the station house?"

"She would certainly know she had killed the man."

"That's the point I want to get at. She would not have gone to the station house unless she knew she had killed the man?"

"No, sir."

Britton yielded another concession out of Dr. Corey—that sane killers frequently made no attempt to escape. Then he pressed hard again on the distinction between violence derived from passion and from temporary insanity:

"What is the difference in the condition of the brain or of the mind between a person insane killing a man, and a person sane killing a man?"

"There must be some disturbances in the condition of the brain, probably a degree of cerebral congestion, an unnatural fullness, in the insane state."

. . .

"Would there not be congestion in a very high state of passion when the person was not insane?"

"There would be, but it would be of a different kind."

"Well, what is the difference?"

"I do not know that I am able to define the difference."[56]

Insane?

Detective Langan, who had brought Fanny by streetcar to headquarters the morning after the shooting: "she said she did not mean to kill him," that "she could not help it. She was sorry for it."[57]

Or just impassioned?

Captain Woglom, brought back to the stand by the prosecution to give a fuller account of what she had told him at the Fifth Precinct station-house, remembered a phrase that she could not recall having used: "she was worked up so in her mind that she shot him for satisfaction."[58]

Ellen Curley, also recalled to reinforce the prosecution's view that Fanny had recollected what she had done, stated that she had.[59] Evidence was swinging both ways.

The session ended with the judge's indication that he expected the case to go to the jury the next day.[60]

Look at Her Now

As Fanny Hyde traveled from her Raymond Street cell to the Kings County Court House on the last day of testimony at her trial, two advocates for women's rights, Sophronia Kilbourn and Helen Walton, issued a sharply worded statement of several hundred words complaining that, since all jurors were men, "Mrs. Hyde" was not being fairly tried: "Men are not the peers of women. They are her masters, self constituted. . . . A jury of women are better fitted and entirely able to judge and weigh such evidence as comes before them, and to decide according to that evidence in the case of another woman, than man can possibly be. They have a clearer perception of the right, a finer inception of truth, are less corruptible than man, and are therefore the natural judges in all cases of woman. . . ."[61]

The crowd that Friday, which began to form outside the courthouse an hour before it opened, was the largest yet, and hundreds of curious citizens were left outdoors. Fanny, said to be looking "haggard," yet "calm and placid," arrived wearing "a close-fitting black grenadine dress," trimmed with a silk fringe and a fancy white-lace collar. Around her neck was a pendant brooch that matched her earrings. All of her family except her still-missing brother were with her, and her cadre of female supporters vocally greeted her.[62]

After one more spat, about admitting a final witness, Morris opened his summation.

He went right after the district attorney, whose technical quibbling about procedure, he felt, was unjust to a defendant whose life was in the balance. He pointed at Fanny Hyde and told the jury: "Upon your verdict depends the question of whether this unfortunate girl shall live or die . . . sent to an awful or ignominious death upon the scaffold. . . ."[63] She and her stepmother wept for minutes.

"This is not a case of blood-hunting," Morris went on. "This is not a fox chase, this is a court of justice; here is where we are supposed to elicit the facts and the evidence."

During the oration, Winchester Britton now and then smiled derisively.[64]

Even if there were doubt about the reality of temporary insanity, Morris insisted, the benefit of it must be given to the prisoner in a capital case: "[O]h what can be said when a person is executed, suffers an ignominious death—when it afterwards turns out, as it has in many of these cases, that the persons at the time they committed the acts for which they suffered were irresponsible. . . . Better that ninety-nine guilty go free."[65]

On and on then he went with citations from medical texts, some already quoted, and with examples of earlier trials. He spoke of the advance of science, the developed understanding that the knowledge of right and wrong was no longer the test of responsibility for an act. He spoke of intellectual and moral insanity, of how "no man can conceive of the misery that exists in the world today, following on the track of the libertine,"[66] such as George Watson.

"Look at her now," he lamented, "a wreck, a wreck produced by the persecutions that have been heaped upon her . . . reduced to a skeleton."[67]

He addressed some points of law. The prosecution had proposed murder in the first degree, and he agreed that the charge was that "or nothing."[68] But it had not been proven because no one had corroborated Watson's father-in-law's testimony that Samuel Windley had remarked, "Fanny, I told you not to do it!"[69] And Britton's insinuation, without testimony, that Fanny had prostituted herself in New Britain was "a gross outrage upon all propriety."[70] Detective Langan was "a miserable sneak, worse than a spy, "who was "a disgrace to the force and ought to be turned off." Morris thought he could see in Langan's late revelations the glitter of some of the gold that had been paid to Charley Spencer,"[71] the New York lawyer engaged by the Watsons.

And at long last he gusted to an end:

"Oh, gentlemen, I beg of you, as you love your families, as you love your children, by your hope of salvation hereafter, by your expectation of mercy, I ask you to let this prisoner go free, let her return to her home. Oh, lift the great load that now oppresses her; say to her, you are innocent, God bless you, God bless you, Fanny Hyde!"[72]

Many in the crowd applauded, and Judge Tappen hushed them. It was ten minutes past five. Sam Morris had spoken, before and after a recess, for 5 hours and 20 minutes.[73]

They began at an early hour on the bright spring morning of Saturday, April 20th. When Fanny entered with her father, mother, and jailer, Sam Morris, seeming emotional, walked up and silently shook hands with her.

Winchester Britton began his summary at ten past nine. His "nervousness," wrote the *Eagle*, "extends to his fingers' ends. He trembles with excitement from head to foot and his voice partakes of the same characteristics."[74] No doubt his white hair was constantly popping out of control.

A riposte to his adversary's thrust against him seemed in order. The defense counsel's charge of excessive emotion in the prosecution "must have caused a smile upon the countenances of some of the gentlemen in this courtroom, who remember his action during his nine years of official career."[75]

Britton had two main arguments to deliver, and would deliver them cogently: Fanny Windley Hyde was no innocent child, and the defense of temporary insanity in this case was specious nonsense.

The story was simple enough in his telling. "Here is a woman who, early in life, voluntarily entered into cohabitation with a man much her senior in years . . . she exerted her wiles through her feminine influence . . . continuing this intercourse she gets married, and yet still continues to beguile him from his duty by greater charms than those of his home. . . ." The affair ended, as adulterous relations "always do." Fanny grew tired of the older man. He, spurned, grew jealous and obsessive, called her names, accused her of being a proverbial rag in every bush. "She then prepares herself with a pistol and shoots him."[76]

"Some women would have quailed at this contemplation. But history shows that some of the worst crimes are committed by women."[77]

As at the trial's opening, he bid the jury to not to be deceived by sympathy, although he understood that there was "a growing feeling in the community against capital punishment" and "a particular reluctance to inflicting this penalty upon women," for "there is more deference to women among the educated American people than any other on the face of the earth."[78] But sympathy for a murderous act was "petty, contemptible," and more: "this defense is conducted upon an hypothesis which, if successful, would strike at the foundation of human society, and overturn the results of the experience of ages."[79]

He mocked Morris's elaborate efforts to prove that insanity could be manifested suddenly after having been latent. No one was denying that this was true, but "the question here is; is this such a case? That is all."[80]

Now about experts, whose testimony was "a mode of proof that has crept into jurisprudence": The problem with bringing experts into an insanity trial was that these were the only forums in which they departed from their proper function of providing general technical information and pronounced particular judgments on defendants' mental health. This was "a grave error"—"it is left to the jury alone and exclusively to apply those general principles and opinionate the facts of the case."[81]

Then came a telling point from a prosecutor who had knocked a peg or two from under the position held by the defense's principal medical witness: "Men in pursuit of a single idea, men in pursuit of a single principle all their lives, become enthusiasts on that question. They are always radical; they always carry it farther than the common sense of the community will justify. They are unsafe judges of such questions when you come to apply them to specific acts."[82]

Moreover—and here he had to regret that he had not managed to put up his own countering witnesses—it was possible to present "a score of witnesses on each side"[83] testifying to and against a person's sanity.

"Did it occur to you," asked the district attorney, "before these physicians were placed on the stand that there was any evidence in this case, outside of the testimony of the prisoner, which tended to show that she was insane? . . . Did that even suggest itself to your minds?"

No? Then follow your own judgment, for, "Gentleman, that defense, so far as this testimony is concerned, is as sham and a farce."[84]

Morris had slammed the prosecution for insinuating, without proof, that Fanny had played the strumpet in New Britain, and Britton excused himself for this because he had felt at the time that he did have testimony, but later determined that it was not clear and convincing enough to properly introduce.[85] Yet in regard to Fanny's enduring relations with Watson, "there is no getting away from the conclusion that her husband connived in this matter; . . . that he gave his assent to this relation."[86]

Morris had claimed the she had shot Watson at close range—during a struggle, in a moment of madness. Now the D.A. argued convincingly that she had fired from "some ways below," at least three feet,[87] for the ball had entered behind the ear and vectored toward the top of the head. He could have been no threat to her at that moment. Her clear, quiet purpose would have been to kill him.

She was guilty of first-degree murder, but if the jurymen concluded that she she shot the man in passion without intending to kill him, then they were free to convict her of third-degree manslaughter.[88]

After 3 hours and 40 minutes[89] of reasonable argument before the jury-box, he slipped a little at the end, whipping up commiseration for Eliza Watson and her four children, and, after all his warning against misplaced emotion, concluding that "if sympathy is to determine the case, I ask you, gentlemen, that your sympathy shall go out not to the wicked and vicious alone."[90]

Applause was again stifled by the bench, and the court recessed.[91]

The trial, wrote the *Brooklyn Eagle* in a long and mannered commentary, had been "a contest between the two men." And "on the side of the defense were necessarily enlisted all the sophistical, morbid and sympathetic elements which now-a-days dominate in trials for life." The writer did not share the spectators' concern for "the demure defendant who so potentially pistolled her path to prominence, and attracted attention to her career by putting a period to her paramour."

"The outside impression," he added, "was that Mr. Morris examined witnesses much more effectively. . . . But when the argument day came, it was apparent that Mr. Britton had been husbanding as many resources. . . . Mr. Britton surpasses Mr. Morris in subtlety."[92]

In the afternoon Justice Tappen charged the jury, narrowing the details of a trial that "present[ed] issues not ordinarily found even in cases of great celebrity." He repeated Britton's warning that the gentlemen not be swayed by sympathy or passion. He defined first-degree murder and manslaughter, and explained that they could acquit the defendant if they believed either that the prosecution had not proven the crime, or that her act was justified, or that she was insane at the time. He reviewed the meaning of insanity, which, he stated, must be established beyond reasonable doubt.[93]

The jurors began deliberating about a quarter to two, as the room remained crowded with expectant, speculating and contending spectators.[94] At about six the jury sent a note to Tappen asking for specific instructions on the charges of first-degree murder, third-degree manslaughter, and justifiable homicide. He read the statutes, and they took the printed matter back to their room.[95] All evening Fanny, now doubly veiled, and her family sat in their places.

About 10:30 p.m. the jury returned, and Tappen asked if they had agreed. Fanny "perceptibly trembled" as her parents' eyes surveyed the jurymen. The foreman was Hugh Allen, a New York shipping-merchant, who stood and stated calmly, "We have not, your honor." The remaining crowd murmured, and Fanny's head fell to her breast. The judge said some words about the significance of the case, the interest it had raised, and the effort that had been dedicated to trying it. He had to ask them to go back and deliberate further,[96] and Juror Rowan remarked, "Your honor, it will be impossible for us to agree if we stay together until next January." But back they went, several of them smiling wryly.[97]

Much of the crowd, including about twenty women who had watched the whole trial, remained, and those spectators who left were replaced by others. When Fanny, her mother and mother-in-law, attended by a court officer, left the courthouse sometime after eleven, an overeager gang rushed after them into the street, and found that they were headed to a local restaurant.[98] The diners had hardly returned when the jurors came in again at 12:30 a.m.

Allen declared that "We stand now just as we stood when we first went out, and there is no possibility of our changing our minds." But Tappen would still not let them go, nor sleep. He appointed to meet them again at 7 a.m. Then he cleared the courtroom.[99]

The Hydes and Windleys retired to a private room, while the four justices divided their forces between another judge's nearby home and their chambers, where pranksters removed the boots of both Voorhees and Johnson while they slept.[100]

The twelve weary men took their seats again at exactly seven, as the Sunday-morning sun splintered through half-closed blinds into their faces. Every head in the room bent toward and every eye focused anxiously on the foreman as Tappen spoke.[101]

"Gentlemen of the jury, have you agreed upon your verdict?
"Your Honor, we have not!"

Fanny Hyde, sitting with her parents and three of her lawyers, again "trembled," this time, wrote the *Eagle*'s man, "like an aspen in the summer wind." She groaned and sobbed, and her stepmother cried once more.[102]

Judge Tappen remarked that if it were any day but Sunday, he would send the jury back again. Then he thanked and discharged them. Eleven of them shook Fanny's hand as they left, while the twelfth exited quickly at a side door. Everyone soon knew that their immutable vote had been ten for acquittal and two for manslaughter in the third degree.[103]

The *Eagle* got the attention of several jurors and asked who had held out for conviction. Hugh Allen was one, and the other was his fellow shipping-executive James Tapscott. Both had departed, and their adversaries stayed behind to malign them. Tapscott, said one, had looked into Allen's eyes "as a spaniel does into the eyes of his master. Allen was immovable, and Tapscott was the same because Allen was."

Further comment charged that Allen, being rich, had no sympathy for "the poor and friendless," that, though he was "a pillar in some church," he was unchristian.

"May every man who loves his wife and daughter," prayed one, "and would see their virtue kept pure and unspotted, point the finger of scorn at Hugh Allen, as he passes along the streets." And still there was "other and much more vehement language" used, which the paper shrank from revealing.

So much for the district attorney's admonition against misplaced sympathy for the defendant.

"May God forgive him!" exclaimed another juror. "We asked Hugh Allen had Fanny Hyde been his own daughter, what then? He replied: 'I would convict her! She is a [whore], always has been a [whore].'"[104]

A reporter found the dissenters at their lower Manhattan offices on Monday. Allen, at No. 15 Old Slip, politely stated that he had left the case in the jury-box and had nothing to say about it. Tapscott, at 86 South Street, graciously sat for an interview. He dismissed as "ridiculous" the impression that Allen had "led him by the nose," and explained that he was sure that the defendant was guilty, but not of first-degree murder. Then, when the judge defined the manslaughter charge, it seemed to him "to be just her case exactly." He also revealed that nine of the ten voters for acquittal accepted the insanity defense, and the tenth felt her act to have been justifiable homicide.

"For my part," he added, "I think her husband has acted the most like an insane person all through the case, from the time he married her until the close of the trial. If ever a man had a vacant look, he has it."[105]

The *Times* of New York and the *Times* of Brooklyn, as well as the *Eagle*, stood firmly with the minority, and they editorialized on the verdict at length. It became known that the majority of jurymen had attempted to cajole the holdouts by proposing conviction on fourth-degree manslaughter, which would have freed Fanny upon payment of a thousand-dollar fine—and that they then offered to produce the money themselves. The *New York Times* thrust at the ten with a satirical sword: had they been "anxious to be whipped for her sweet sake, the public would have been entirely willing to permit them to gratify themselves."[106]

The "growing disinclination to hanging people," especially women, suggested to the *Eagle* that capital punishment be discontinued or prescribed only for men. The revealed behavior of the prurient triad of Windley, Watson, and Hyde, it felt, was "as revolting as anything in the records of our courts."[107]

On the other side, as ever when the *Eagle* had spoken, was the *Brooklyn Union*. And it fired directly at the "Ring-Organ," as it always called the *Eagle*, and its Irish-born editor, for printing the vituperations of the majority jurors against their rivals. That a jury's privacy was sacrosanct was obvious to "every native-born citizen and every other person, come from what badly organized and governed country he may, who has been here long enough to really understand our institutions."[108]

On the morning of Tuesday, April 24th, two bondsmen posted $2,500 bail for Fanny Hyde, and Samuel Morris wrote a check for the full amount to indemnify them. The prisoner, informed, was "almost entirely overcome with emotion," and was taken by her father to his home on Rodney Street in Williamsburg. The *Eagle* expostulated further and predicted that she would never be tried again.[109]

Yet the district attorney's office intended that she would be, and on Friday, the 27th, it replaced Fanny in Raymond Street Jail with her brother, "defiant-looking" Samuel Windley, who had been captured the previous night in Philadelphia.[110] If she were to be retried, he seemed likely to be seated beside her. But no case was built against him. He would be bailed out in August and hardly heard of again.

Britton moved to retry her in October, but Morris, stating that both he and his client were in poor health, won a postponement.[111] When the case came to court again on January 21st, 1873, Fanny did not appear, and the prominent lawyers re-engaged their battle. Morris insisted that he and the D.A. had agreed that she wouldn't be tried again. Not so, responded Britton, who demanded payment on the bond.[112]

Detectives searched for her, and, on March 23rd, when Brooklyn and New York were gripped by another killing of which a woman was suspected, Fanny was arrested on Washington's Capitol Hill, where she had been living with her husband and mother-in-law. Morris had agreed to the trip because of her bad health, and it seemed to have benefited her. Sent back to Raymond Street wearing a flounced purple dress in a carriage beside Morris, she "shook hands warmly" with Keeper Conrady and was escorted to her cell. There a newsman found her relaxed and, to a degree, communicative. She laughed "merrily" when asked if she'd been enjoying herself, and replied, "Oh, yes. I used to walk on the avenue every afternoon, and improved so much in my health that I weigh twenty pounds more than I did when I went away." She had no fears, she said. She "only wish[ed] that it was all over."[113]

During these same months Samuel Morris led a campaign to impeach Winchester Britton. He and others submitted an elaborate list of 11 charges to Governor John Adams Dix, accusing the D.A. of failing to prosecute against election fraud, of not pursuing an abortionist called Madame Van Buskirk, of bribery to gain a salary-raise, of protecting friends, political allies and the City's finagling tax-collector from indictment, and of using "foul and insulting language," such as "Go to hell!"[114]

Morris was particularly rankled about Van Buskirk, who had been an accomplice in the brutal maltreatment in August 1871 of a sadly seduced and deceived New Jersey woman, who eventually died at Brooklyn City Hospital.[115] He railed that Britton's discharge of her case, freeing her to resume her trade, was "a monstrous outrage against society."[116]

Then another murder-trial squared them off. In April of 1873 Morris defended Dr. Lucius Irish against the charge of dosing his lover's husband, the City's assistant tax-assessor, with arsenic. This trial also ended with a hung jury, but Morris was incensed by the district attorney's failure to produce a witness whom he wanted to cross-examine,[117] and he blasted off a long, condescending letter to the prosecutor:

> . . . permit me to volunteer a little advice. Review carefully the first year of your official life. Set down in one column that which you have done properly, and in another column that which you have done improperly, as well as those things which you have left undone. Add up the columns, strike a balance, and see how the account stands between you and the public.

Britton's extraordinary public reaction to this was that he did not hold his correspondent "accountable" for what he had written, because "there was evidence of suffering on his part from aberration of intellect."[118]

~

Adulterous, Militant Brooklyn

> I presume there is no city in the world equal to Brooklyn for gossip and scandal.
>
> —a letter to the *Brooklyn Eagle*, January 21st, 1873

These were the City of Churches' most turbulent years. Sexual fever infected all classes, and religious and political contention combusted into war. Courtrooms and meeting-rooms and even schoolrooms shook with controversy. This was the context in which Brooklyn pursued and tried its concupiscent female murderers.

In the fall of 1872, notorious Victoria Woodhull, the woman who ran for president nearly 50 years before American women won the right to vote, the advocate of free love and socialism, the spiritualist and apparent crackpot, ignited the flames of Rev. Henry Ward Beecher's public purgatory when she released the secret of his shocking liaison with the wife of his protégé Theodore Tilton. She had been told of the affair by the suffragist leader Elizabeth Cady Stanton, who, with her ally Susan B. Anthony, was a regular visitor to the Tilton home on Livingston Street.[119]

Blurting the revelation to Woodhull, Stanton would admit, was "an awful blunder," for which she deserved to have her "ears pulled." It wrought such sentences as this, in the publication that Victoria edited with her sister: "I conceive that Mrs. Tilton's love for Mr. Beecher was her true marriage . . . and that her marriage to Mr. Tilton is prostitution."[120] It was a sizzling discourse that deposited the sisters in New York's Ludlow Street Jail for a month on the charge of circulating obscene literature.[121]

Some papers tried to avoid the sudden sensation, but a prurient scandal involving the leading clergyman in America could not long be stifled, and the *Eagle* had particular reasons for focusing on a particular villain in the story. As a correspondent had written to the paper in January, "almost every man in Brooklyn has an ax to grind,"[122] and Thomas Kinsella and his *Eagle* were ready to swing at Henry C. Bowen, Tilton's employer at the *Independent* and the *Union*.

The "Trinity of Plymouth Church," comprising the persons of Beecher, Tilton, and Bowen, appeared to be quite unholy. It had become something like a game to estimate how many mistresses the pastor preached before on Sunday.[123] In addition to "Libby" Tilton, two likely candidates were the poet Edna Dean Proctor and Chloe Beach, who was married to the publisher of the New York *Sun*, and with whom Beecher is believed to have fathered a daughter.[124] And Tilton, tall, curly-haired and in his mid-30s, also had a roving eye. He was reported to have dallied amorously during lecturing journeys and to have propositioned a young woman who lived in his house as an unofficial daughter.[125] Bowen was accused of different sins, such as vindictiveness and unscrupulous business practices,[126] but it was rumored that, eight years earlier, his wife and the mother of ten, Lucy Maria, had revealed on her deathbed her own intimacy with the minister whom Woodhull approvingly described as "amative."[127] If that did happen, it would have contributed to the growing estrangement of the two men in the late '60s and early '70s. They disputed over money and disagreed about the management of the church, the content of the *Independent* and Beecher's participation in it; and repeatedly Bowen hinted or declared to friends and colleagues that he knew enough about Henry's infidelities to shake the Christian world.[128]

Bowen was having problems, too, with Tilton's evolving liberal views and the moral charges circulating about him. So when Tilton ineptly revealed his own wife's confession, Bowen had weapons that could injure both men, which he would manipulate sharply to keep them squirming. He betrayed Tilton by not backing him, as he had indicated he would, in confronting Beecher, then fired Tilton from both newspaper positions and kissed (literally) and made up with the great clergyman.[129]

In her dissertation on the scandal, Altina Laura Waller has keenly explained how the entire drama was inextricable from the lethally charged political rivalries of 1870s Brooklyn. One of the most vicious of these faced Bowen against the come-lately Benjamin F. Tracy, the great lawyer who was overtaking him as a Republican power-broker. And it further nettled Bowen that the very shrewd Tracy had also joined Beecher's congregation and cuddled with the pastor, for Plymouth was the church that Bowen had largely built.[130]

"Machiavellian,"[131] one author has described Bowen. Apparently so, and he was also an anti-Catholic bigot. One of his chief campaigns when he took over the *Union* editorship from Tilton in 1872 was to prevent the election of the presumably disloyal papist Francis Kernan as governor.[132]

This was a lingering breath of the nativism that had infected Brooklyn around mid-century, and that ignited street brawls in 1844 and 1854. In the latter year, preachers appeared on city streets to attack the Catholic Church and the first papal nuncio to the United States, Cardinal Gaetano Bedini. When crowds of angry Irishmen, many of them refugees from the recent potato famine, began vocally and physically to object to these presentations, mobs of Know-Nothings invaded from New York and perhaps as far as Philadelphia, ready to take them on. In June of that year one such oration ignited a promiscuous battle, conducted and witnessed, by one report, by 20,000 people.[133]

Nativism was activated by the mid-century deluge of destitute, crudely mannered, hard-drinking immigrants, and fueled by paranoia. Its devotees believed that Catholics answered to the pope and not the institutions of American democracy. They feared that Catholics would outvote them and take their jobs, and that superstitious papist beliefs and practices would undermine public education. In the 1870s these remained concerns of Henry Bowen and the *Brooklyn Union*, and he had hordes of allies.

His darkest *bête noir* was the Catholic-bred Thomas Kinsella, who may have been generally loyal and principled, but was also tough, bellicose, and vindictive. Even a newspaper of which he was a principal founder, the *Brooklyn Sunday Sun*, spoke of his "hauteur," conceded that he was "rarely amiable," not to be described as a "good fellow," and had "contrived to make for himself more enemies than any other man in Brooklyn." Yet this journalist—it might have been Kinsella himself—felt that "if we wanted a friend to swear by we would choose Kinsella."[134] That is, he was the opposite of Henry Bowen.

In April 1873, Thomas Kinsella had been a member of the Board of Education for five years, and was chairman of the committee for the local school, No. 13, on Degraw Street. When Kinsella concluded that its principal, William Reid, a fierce Protestant partisan, refused to send students from crowded No. 13 to a new, half-empty school because he didn't want to expose them to Catholic influence, Kinsella got him fired.[135] The *Union* objected, fueling its ire with information that the rival editor had paid a scandalous visit to No. 13 during which he had failed to remove his hat or the cigar from his mouth, complained in front of students that it was "hot as hell," and asked a teacher to fix him a brandy-and-water.[136] The paper thenceforth would rarely print his name without adding, in apposition, that he was a "half-drunken, profane loafer" or "a man of low, even brutal instincts." But then no better was to be expected from "an Irish importation of questioned naturalization."[137] It demanded his eviction from the Board, and then, in common cause with Reid, the replacement of that entire body by Christian citizens like themselves.

When Kinsella struck back, he had the then-breaking accusations against Beecher to work with. What else would these rumors be but the crowning blow of a man whose career was dedicated to scandal? It was "well known," the *Eagle* wrote, "that, in order to blast the reputation of the pastor, whose ministrations he still ostentatiously professes to profit by, Henry C. Bowen was prepared to subject to the world's pity, or scorn, a member of his own household."[138]

Alas for the cause of Catholic virtue, Tom Kinsella was another unholy Brooklynite. And the *Union* knew his biggest secret sin, which, with what seems to have been extraordinary good luck, it was able to dramatize just in time for a big nativist rally at the Academy of Music.

That spring a corps of 100 laborers began to shape the last piece of the Prospect Park landscape, along its western boundary at Ninth Avenue. By summer, then, this splendid enclosure, a source of enormous civic pride, would be essentially complete,[139] and in the fall, after the Panic of 1873 had struck, Calvert Vaux and Frederick Olmsted would amicably end their historic partnership.[140] The park was still surrounded by a wooden fence, later to be replaced, in part, by squat stone walls. To the west of where the workmen dug and raked, farmers still harvested fruits and vegetables, but sidewalks were being paved with bluestone flags, and some frame row-houses were being constructed, though not yet the grand Park Slope brownstones.

Among Prospect Park's major features was the carriage-drive that wound like a lariat around its elegant Long Meadow and artificial lake. If, in the late afternoon of Tuesday, April 15th, Thomas Kinsella was heading toward the park drive from his five-story brownstone at 430 Clinton Street, he would have ridden his buggy up Union Street to the main entrance at the plaza that would later be dedicated to the Civil War dead. If he had come from his *Eagle* office on Fulton Street, he would have approached the plaza along Flatbush Avenue. In either case, his wife Elizabeth knew where he was going, for she had lately received anonymous letters about his indiscreet meetings with Mrs. Emeline Field, and the most recent of these had informed her that they would meet again at a certain time that afternoon at the tavern in Olmstead's Hotel.[141] Although this resort was not named for the great park's co-designer, it stood directly across from its Park Circle entrance, on the Coney Island Road in the town of Flatbush.

Emeline was the wife of Thomas W. Field, a poet, historian, and former city assessor whose recent appointment as superintendent of the Board of Education had been influenced by Thomas Kinsella. The couples had once been friendly, but not since Kinsella and Mrs. Field had grown intimate. It was said that Field had discovered an affectionate letter from Kinsella to Emeline and barred the editor from their home.[142] Emeline, aged 23 or 24, was a relative child in this group. Her husband was 52 or 53, and she had married him—his third wife—at 16. They had a daughter who was about five. Kinsella was 40, and Elizabeth around the same age.[143]

Newspaper accounts varied,[144] but it seems likely that the triangle of lovers arrived at Olmstead's in three vehicles within several minutes of each other, and the episode the journalists described was dynamic and concentrated. Elizabeth had had time to dress very well for her part, and had engaged a coachman, who raced through the freshly verdant park so closely behind her husband's buggy that it seemed she were following him. What route Emeline Field was taking is not known, but she was carrying an unlikely passenger to such a tryst—her young Ada. Kinsella arrived first at the hotel described by Bowen's *Union* as "a neat, frame dwelling of the better class of country inns," operated and hosted by a genial gentleman with a weathered face earned in his earlier career as the captain of a coffee-trading clipper. Kinsella sat for a short while chatting with some acquaintances on a balcony at the front of the barroom before Emeline and her child arrived. They met him there, then moved off with him to a parlor area on the left with rooms for seating ladies. They took a room in the back.

A few minutes later Elizabeth's carriage arrived at a fast gallop.

"There is hell to pay," a "well-known city official" remarked to a group of companions gathered outside. "Here comes Mrs. Kinsella." A boy of about 17 who worked at the hotel also saw her, then walked into the parlor, knocked on the open back-room door and announced to the editor of the *Eagle* that his wife was arriving at the premises. Just as the young fellow was leaving, she rushed into the tavern, stepped up to a mirror in the front room and "arranged her bonnet." Her husband came out to meet her, and she turned to address him.

"So you are here!"

"Yes, I thought I would take a ride. Mrs. Field is in the next room. You must come and see her. We met by chance."

"Yes, you accidentally met her, you scoundrel!" She shook her fist and declared, "I've got you now!"

He drew her into the back room and shut the door. Patrons on the other side of it heard voices shouting, but could make out no words. A woman worker came out of the barroom, and warning, "we are going to have some trouble here," urged them to leave the area.

When Elizabeth came out of the parlor, the *Union* stated, she turned to a woman who was watching her, and commented, "That was Thomas Kinsella, father of ten children, of which I am the mother." But that was inaccurate. The couple in fact had four daughters, no sons. The paper had her adding, "I was young once, but now I am older."

She left the tavern, and directed the porter at the door to bring around Mrs. Field's carriage. To its passenger, she ordered, "There, you strumpet, leave this house."

In "a low moan," Emeline responded, "Do not call me that." But Elizabeth, far from being pacified, reached out and slapped her rival below her left ear. Kinsella and Captain Olmstead rushed over to separate them. As they then assisted Emeline into her carriage, she, "casting a withering glance at Mrs. Kinsella," parried the blow with a nonviolent stroke of her own, asking the editor if he would "call on her this evening."

He told her he wouldn't be able to.

"No," his wife added, "He won't, but I will. I mean to see this thing out."[145]

Emeline drove off, soon followed by Kinsella in his buggy and his wife in her chauffeured carriage.

The *Union* gleefully recorded it all, and remarked that "the scene furnished another of those peculiar evidences of the gentlemanly nature so often exhibited by the moral member of the Board of Education, Mr. Thomas Kinsella." It also gleaned reactions from prominent downtown citizens.

"Oh, this thing was bound to come out sooner or later," one remarked. "We have heard queer scandals whispered about Kinsella long ago."

Another, a lawyer, felt that "this thing wouldn't be talked much about if a private citizen was involved but, Kinsella being the chief editor of a newspaper which pretends to teach you and me morality and then being a member of the Board of Education, I tell you his position is terrible."[146]

The morality that the chief editor pretended to teach at this time focused on a recently slain Brooklyn man's "coarse and commonplace lust."[147] Yet the philandering that the paper had condemned had not been adulterous, as allegedly had been those of Henry Ward Beecher, Lucy Maria Bowen, Elizabeth Tilton, and now Emeline Field and Thomas Kinsella, for whom Henry Bowen's newest epithet was the "——— master" who managed "the Ring Organ."[148]

The educational meeting at the Academy of Music[149] drew a brimming crowd of about 3,000. Tickets, the *Eagle* had learned, had been distributed liberally at the lodges of the Order of the United American Mechanics, a leading nativist association, and its members were especially cheered by the Rev. Dr. Ingersoll's resolve to "defy any system that may be controlled by hierarchical church power." Although the Reid/School-13 affair was not supposed to have been on the agenda, the defrocked principal spoke for several minutes, and the organizers resolved to recognize him as "an educated and highly cultured Christian gentleman."

In May and June, Reid got his hearing before the Teachers' Committee of the Board of Education, at which he and Kinsella contended face to face, and the editor charged that Reid and others present and "acting here as jurors" were "members of a secret political, religious organization." The ex-principal denied it.

"Is that so?" Kinsella came back. "I think I can show that he is."[150]

Indeed, at a Republican Association meeting the next week meeting in South Brooklyn, a former Assembly candidate, himself "no Catholic," spoke out vehemently against religious bigotry in his party and identified Reid as a past "presiding officer" of one of its engines, the Order of the American Union, in the city's sixth ward.[151]

Later that month the Teachers' Committee delivered its finding that Reid had "promulgated" the order to transfer students, but had not enforced it, and was therefore guilty of insubordination. The only blame that they could pin on Kinsella was that, at least on some visits to School No. 13, he hadn't doused his cigar or doffed his hat.[34] He had admitted as much about the cigar—that he had kept it lit during short visits, but had not left it in his mouth.[153]

3

Her Poor Betsey

Come in Here and See Him

Before Brooklyn ever heard of Charles Goodrich, it had heard much of his younger brother, the Honorable William W.

They had been born in 1831 and 1833 in the Finger Lakes region of western New York State, then taken as young boys to Albany, where the more studious William became a practicing attorney at 21. At about the same age as George Watson, he headed for New York City to make his living, and he would become there a widely recognized authority in maritime law. Eventually he settled his growing family in a grand brownstone on the border of Brooklyn's Washington Park. Then he ran for public office. He served twice as a Republican state assemblyman, but he was defeated in elections for the State Senate and U.S. Congress. Full-bearded and less than five-and-a-half feet tall, he would be dubbed "The Fighting Gamecock of Kings County." In law and politics, he was always "W. W. Goodrich." To family and friends he was "Billy."[1]

And Charles was "Charlie." He was about five-eight, slender, with a dark mustache, clipped side-whiskers and a hairline that retreated as he approached middle age. In Albany he followed his father into the lumber business, but all the Goodriches eventually migrated south—the parents first, then Charles, who arrived in New York in June 1868 and opened a lumberyard on E. 18th Street. Nearing 35, he had been a widower for six years,[2] and it was a solace to him to rejoin his remaining family, with whom he was close.

Close, yet distanced from them, too, by his well-developed secrets—for in the loose-jointed cities of New York and Brooklyn, where he too would eventually reside, Charles Goodrich began to live dangerously.

After Charles moved into 731 Degraw Street, Brooklyn, in March 1873, his brother often stopped to see him in the morning[3] as he was being driven in his carriage to the ferry that took him to his law office at 59 Wall Street. This course took William out of his way, and may have indicated concern for a brother whose intemperate habits had begun to be found out. Charles also seemed anxious. There was one newspaper report that he would sleep with a loaded revolver under his pillow.[4]

On Thursday, March 20th, William carried a pail containing a half-loaf of bread to the basement door. He would say that this gesture was a joke conceived by his wife—perhaps a comment on the scantiness of the single man's household. William noticed that the shutters were drawn, a sign to him that Charles was not home or had not yet risen, and he reacted with agitation. He "rang the bell steadily half a dozen times," kicked the door and threw a stone against the window of the room where Charlie slept. Drawing no response, he left the pail at the entrance and went to work.[5]

Charles was seen in Brooklyn several times that day and night. A messenger named Bunker Hill would remember the exact spot on Fulton Street where he had noticed him talking to another man that afternoon,[6] and three persons would state that he had been on the Fifth Avenue car traveling from Fulton Ferry between 9 and 10 p.m. on that rainy last night of winter: the driver, the conductor, and Alderman William Richardson, who exchanged bows with him.[7]

W. W. Goodrich stopped again at Degraw Street the next morning, Friday, March 21st. Again, as he would put it, "no sign of life was visible," and he was alarmed to find the pail with the risible half-loaf of bread exactly where he had left it. Once more receiving no answer to his ringing and knocking, he hurried to the house of a real-estate agent, and got from him a key to one of the adjoining houses. He climbed the stairs and opened the roof-hatch above the top-floor hall closet, crossed over to the roof of 731, found that hatch unlocked and dropped down into the closet, broke open its door, and entered the house, which was sparsely furnished and partly carpeted, and contained two beds on the third floor. Descending from floor to floor, he found all quiet and in what he'd call "absolutely painful" good order. On the ground floor were the kitchen in back and the dining-room in front, to which there was a hallway door that he found locked.

"I forced it open," he would report, "and immediately found my brother lying on the floor. My first impression was that he was sick, as his eyes were partly open. I thought I saw an expression on his face as if he was glad somebody had come."[8]

He opened the shutters, and, looking back, got a different impression. Charles Goodrich lay two feet from the mantelpiece, in which was installed a space-heater. His feet pointed toward the front windows, his face to the ceiling, and below his head was a pool of blood that was later found to be leaking in slow drops into the cellar. He was fully and handsomely dressed in a brown "business coat" and vest, dark-blue check "pantaloons, dress-shirt, collar and tie." In his coat pocket was a perfumed handkerchief. His arms were stretched at either side, his left toward the door where William had entered, his right toward the mantel, and an inch or two from his right hand was a dark-handled pistol. William noticed some blood on the hearthstone and on the edge of the mantel shelf. He felt his brother's face, which was cold and shaved close. The face and the slicked-back hair atop his head were free of blood and seemed to have been wiped clean. Then he noticed something even odder. The head lay on the dead man's boots as if they had been placed beneath it as a pillow. And, as if to compensate for their displacement, his feet were shod with slippers, which had had been pulled over his toes but not secured behind his heels.

William ran to the front door, completing his reverse circuit through the house, and found it secured by a stick propped between it and the wall. Pulling it away, he stepped outside and approached his "colored coachman."[9]

"Oh, Joseph," he called. "My brother is dead! Come in here and see him."

"He was crying when he told me this," Joseph would remember.[10]

In a front-page newspaper list published in July 1871, William W. Goodrich had been placed among the wealthiest persons in

Brooklyn—although his stated worth of $312,000 fell well below that of the city's eight millionaires. His total had mounted not only from his law practice, but also from a bundle of real-estate investments he had begun to transact the previous year. One of these, in March 1871, was the acquisition of four contiguous lots on the north side of Degraw Street, between Fifth and Sixth Avenues,[11] in an area called South Brooklyn. The spot was described by the *Eagle* as "bleak and desolate," and "dotted over with little shanties."[12] But it was ripe for improvement, being within a half-mile of Prospect Park, which was just being completed, and in the development of which Goodrich had long been politically involved.

William related to his brother as if he, not Charles, were older. He indulged him and took interest in his financial and personal welfare. At the end of 1871, as if presenting a substantial Christmas gift, he turned over the Degraw Street property to Charles for one dollar, in an agreement under which Charles would manage the construction of six brownstone houses there. Some he was authorized to sell, but he was also free to "peaceably and quietly have, hold, occupy, possess and enjoy the above-granted premises."[13] Or so it was hoped.

They went up fast. In April 1872, on the day that every afternoon paper transcribed the trial testimony of Fanny Hyde, Charles posted an ad in the *Eagle*:

> FOR SALE—HOUSES—SIX 3 STORY, basement and subcellar, brown stone houses; three blocks from Prospect Park, finished handsomely, and with all the modern improvements; will be completed on or before the first of May, price $10,000 each, of which $7,500 can remain on bond or mortgage; would exchange for well located lots in Brooklyn. Inquire on the premises, in Degraw st., north side, between Fifth and Sixth avs. C. GOODRICH[14]

But they did not sell fast. The price may have been too high for that still chancy location, for they remained empty nearly a year later. During that period Charles stayed in one or the other of the houses, but kept his rooms in New York until he moved into the house nearest Sixth Avenue in that late winter of '73. He got a second house ready for tenants to occupy in April, and intended to move his parents into another.

A local stove-dealer who did business with Charles found him to be "amiable." To others he was "temperate and quiet."[15]

Among the shanties on or near Degraw Street were some more substantial houses, both brick and frame. One resident of Charles Goodrich's block, in fact, was rather famous: Ferdinand T. L. Boyle, an artist and professor at the Brooklyn Institute. Charles's brownstones were numbered 721 through 731; Boyle and his family lived at 757, toward Sixth Avenue. In back of his house was the carpentry shop of C. V. Snedeker, who had done some work for Goodrich; and Snedeker and his son, who was his assistant, lived with their families in separate houses across the street. These and other neighbors had become slightly acquainted with Charles. They assumed he was wealthy and wondered about his personal arrangements, for all of them had seen a woman either in his company or coming or going from a house where he was staying.

Boyle, walking frequently to and from the horsecar stop on Fifth Avenue, had begun to notice Charles around the middle of 1872. That summer, returning from his downtown studio around twilight, he saw him several times sitting on a stoop with a woman whom he described as "very handsome, fine, noble-looking," and, to his artist's eye, "Diana-like." These sightings continued well into the winter, including an occasion late on a "cold, unpleasant" night in February, when he "thought what an uncomfortable spot it was for a trysting place."

Around the same time, both the younger Mrs. Snedeker and her father-in-law saw a woman leaving one of the houses in the early morning. The elder Mrs. Snedeker's live-in servant, Rosalie Logan, once met a woman on Degraw Street who asked her where Mr. Goodrich lived; then Rosalie watched her go into the house that she had indicated.

There had been another February night on Degraw Street when a female companion of Charlie Goodrich was not seen but heard, and the sound disturbed the person who heard her, a Sunday School teacher and friend of the Boyles named Emma Leland. At about seven o'clock, she was passing the third of the Goodrich houses, attended by "a little lame girl" who was one of her "scholars," when "a strange noise, as if someone's head had struck the door," came from the downstairs entrance. She stopped, and heard it again, then a woman's voice shouting, " 'Help, help, don't, you will knock my brains out!' " Ms. Leland sent her young charge up the street, then boldly stepped into the areaway to examine the doorway. As she approached, Charles Goodrich emerged alone from the house, and their eyes met. She backed away onto the sidewalk as he came forward and shut the gate; then he looked up and down the street and returned inside. By then Miss Leland had spent all her courage. Turning, she ran up the street to the Boyles's "as fast as ever [she] could."

The artist was no coward either. He answered his doorbell, listened to Emma's story, took up his walking-stick, put on his hat, and rushed down to number 725. The night outside was "as still as death, and as dark as Egypt." He tried the outer basement door and found it locked.

"Halloa, there," he called two or three times, but "not the slightest sound of any kind" came back. He left, but with misgiving—"all the time feeling that I ought to have burst in the door and found out just how the matter stood."

The story quickly passed along the block. But when one resident asked Goodrich the next day about "that scuffle," he muttered, "What scuffle?"[16] seeming quite annoyed. It was the only time the woman had found him out of humor. Otherwise she had known him to be a gentleman.[17] His brother would describe him as "exceedingly abstemious"—he had never seen him drunk. Nearly every Sunday Charlie was Billy's and his wife's guest for dinner at the house on Washington Park.

"From the time we were children," said William Goodrich, "I don't think I had a word of disagreement with him."

But that winter brought a change, if not a disagreement. William realized that his brother was hiding a part of his life from him. One evening, while visiting Degraw Street, he too glimpsed a woman, very briefly, and heard the rustle of her dress in an adjoining room.[18] And in mid-February both he and his father received copies of a plaintive letter from an unknown woman who had been Charles Goodrich's lover.[19]

My God, It Is Plain!

The eastern end of Degraw Street, South Brooklyn, where Charles Goodrich lay in his peculiar death scene, was in the Tenth Police Precinct, stationed about a half-dozen blocks away at Sixth Avenue and Bergen Street. But W. W. Goodrich, important public figure that he was, directed Joseph to drive quickly to police headquarters at the northwest corner of Court and Livingston Streets. There they found the detective chief Harry Van Wagner, who sent two "smart" men back with them—Charles H. Videto and William H. "Billy" Folk, 35-year-old son of the former Superintendent John S. Folk.[20]

At just this hour, William Foster, the "car-hook murderer," was hanged at New York's original Tombs prison. "Thousands feel," wrote the *Daily Graphic*, that capital punishment "is a coarse, harsh, barbarous way of dealing with the gravest of problems." Nor was it an effective "preventive of crime." But in his study not far from the mid-Manhattan Street where the killing had occurred, George Templeton Strong had proclaimed in his diary, "All honor to the Governor's firmness" for not commuting the sentence.[21]

Back at Degraw Street there was immediate confusion and disagreement about how W. W. Goodrich's older brother had reached his bloody end. And the uncertainty, peppered at times by rancor between contending parties, would linger for weeks.

The pistol immediately suggested suicide, but William was sure that his brother had been murdered. The way that the slippers were not fully fitted on his feet indicated to him "that they were put on after the deed was committed." He also had searched Charles's body and found that his watch, pocketbook, and seal ring were missing.[22]

Folk and Videto did not agree with him. The way that the slippers were worn did not seem strange to Videto. The dead man, he surmised, had dressed himself. That the boots and a piece of carpet lay beneath his hemorrhaging head seemed accidental. That there was just a spot of blood on Charles's freshly clean collar did not seem significant. Charles Goodrich, he concluded, had killed himself with the gun that lay beside him. Folk noted that there was no sign of a struggle in the room, and could discern only one bullet-wound. The shooting was a case of "suicide, certainly." Detective Van Wagner, who arrived at the scene about 20 minutes behind his men, saw nothing to contradict them.

But when Coroner Whitehill arrived about 11 o'clock, he quickly noticed that a bullet had entered the left side of Charles's head, but the pistol lay near his right hand.

There was another possible clue in the kitchen to support William's burglary theory. A small pane of glass in the window leading to the backyard had been broken, and the latch had scraped the sash when it had been unfastened. The yard was bounded by a wooden fence, beyond which there was open ground stretching ahead to St. John's Place and left to Fifth Avenue. An observer looked that way and noticed "dirty children playing in the mud, pigs and cows grazing on what is left of intramural pasture." Indeed, a truckman who lived back there sold pints of milk to his neighbors, including Goodrich. Van Wagner searched the soggy yard, but found no footprints, and the next day the younger Mr. Snedeker told reporters that the window had been broken for some time.[23] So the intruder theory receded.

Coroner Whitehill, who was not a physician, began his own examination of the body, which had been placed on a long, wide board brought in from the yard, propped on chairs and carried to the front windows. The dead man's eyes were still open, "with a dull, leaden stare." When Whitehill lifted Charles's head, William Goodrich pointed to the back of it and cried out, "There, see! My God, it is plain! That has been washed off this morning." In the kitchen they found a wet, blood-stained towel hanging above the sink, a piece of reddened soap, and, below the sink, a copy of the previous evening's *Eagle*, also bloody. Whitehill went back to the corpse, and judged that the cause of death was so obvious that there was no need to strip it. He concluded that there had been one pistol shot, and that three other wounds, behind the right ear, at the left temple, and on the forehead, had been caused by a blunt instrument.[24] He was entirely wrong.

In the evening, with Charles still lying in the same spot on the same makeshift examining-table, a proper post-mortem was conducted by Drs. A. Warner Shepard and Robert F. Speir, watched by a group of Goodrich relatives and friends. They found three bullets in Charles's skull, which were said—by whom it is not certain—to match the gun at the scene, identified as a "seven-chambered 'Ethan Allen' revolver." The bullets that had entered at the left temple and behind the right ear had crossed paths and penetrated well into the brain. The one that had struck behind the left ear had hit bone, split, and flattened. Dr. Speir hypothesized that the forehead wound had been caused by a fourth, grazing bullet. Indeed, four chambers of the gun were empty—but where was the last bullet? Shepard thought, correctly, that the falling man's head had struck the mantel, accounting for the bit of blood that was found there.

Shepard also observed that the hair had not been burned behind the right ear, but had been singed around the other openings. So one shot had been fired from a distance, perhaps not more than a couple of feet, while the others came from a pistol held very close to or against the skull.

"The wounds," he stated, "could not have been inflicted with his own hands unless he was more than mortal."

But if he'd been more than mortal, "he couldn't have committed suicide,"[25] quipped the same Alderman Richardson who had bowed to Charles Goodrich on the last night of his life.

Still the Brooklyn police, despite the multiple bullet-wounds and the bloody kitchen towel, kept the suicide theory alive. Billy Folk conjectured that W. W. Goodrich had wiped his brother's skin and hair. So what if William denied this—he would have been so excited that he had forgotten he had done so.[26] Van Wagner, in fact, suggested that the face-wiping had been calculated:

"If you had a brother that committed suicide, wouldn't you a great deal rather have it appear that he was murdered?"[27]

So this perplexing case had spawned both the theory that a murderer had attempted to create an impression of suicide, and the theory that a mourner had tried to make a suicide look like murder. As late as five days after the event, Chief of Police Patrick Campbell insisted that murder and suicide were both possibilities, and protested that "people who deny that he has committed suicide are not acquainted with as many cases as the police are—peculiar cases, I mean."[28]

The theory was nonetheless pilloried in the press. The *Eagle's* reporter made fun of "the old veteran" Van Wagner in the way that Holmes and Watson would toy with dull-witted Inspector Lestrade. And on its editorial page it labeled the notion of suicide "exquisitely ridiculous."[29] To the *New York Times* it was "absurd to everybody but some detectives who still profess to believe that a man, having sent one bullet through his brain, could have sent another from the opposite side of the head." Moreover, the burglar theory had "hardly a single fact to rest upon." What burglar would have taken the time to wipe his victim's face and head, while neglecting to snatch his golden shirt-stud and cufflinks or other valuable items upstairs?[30]

The *Eagle*'s man stopped snickering when he realized that the Brooklyn dicks might only be pretending to be mad. "The chimerical idea of suicide raised by some," he concluded, was "solely and mainly, the writer thinks, for the purpose of concealing the true trail upon which some of the detectives have departed."[31] Their purpose may have been to lull the murderer into thinking that he or she was not being pursued and need not flee from town. His editors agreed with him, partly. "We no more believe," they would write, "that the detectives believe Goodrich committed suicide, than we believe that the detectives murdered him themselves." But, being in the habit of lambasting the police force, they were not ready to credit these men with the cleverness to form a policy of deliberate deception: "They appear to have lighted on the absurd idea in order to excuse themselves from all labor or care in working up the case."[32]

These papers were among a dozen or more dailies in Brooklyn and New York that covered the "Brooklyn Mystery" on their front pages and in editorial columns—for the case "occasioned more excitement in the city [of Brooklyn] than any thing of the kind reported in many years."[33] And in the days following the discovery of the body, especially on Sunday, a stream of curious citizens visited the scene and stood around in groups discussing their notions of what had happened there. On Monday the *Daily Graphic*, which claimed to be the world's only illustrated daily paper, offered a half-page of sketches depicting the house and the hubbub outside, the interior scene of Goodrich's body stretched on the dining-room floor, and a head-and-shoulders portrait of the good-looking, mustachioed man who lay there.[34]

The *Eagle* was one of several journals that took credit for outsleuthing the sleuths. Its immediate canvass of the neighborhood had pointed out the likely involvement of a woman in the case. And it amazed its readers with its discovery of a female who had been intimate with Charlie Goodrich.

It was noon on Saturday, March 22nd, and the reporter, "who was on the watch" at 731 Degraw Street, saw a carriage drive up, and from it emerge "a lady attired in deep mourning." She rang the bell, was admitted, and he followed her into the second-floor back parlor, where the woman removed the heavy black veil from her face and revealed herself to be "a handsome blonde." She asked if William Goodrich was in the house, and was told that he was not. The reporter must at that point have identified himself, for she seemed to speak for many puzzled readers when she remarked, "Which of these accounts is correct? I have read the *Sun*, the *Herald* and the *Times*, and they are all different."

"Did you know Charles Goodrich?" he asked.

"Oh, yes. I knew him quite well."

"Do you think he committed suicide?

"Oh, no; don't you believe it. He was murdered for his money. I'm quite sure of it."[35]

She may, like his neighbors, have believed that Charles was well-off, but it would soon be revealed that he had died intestate, leaving no more than $3,000. Meanwhile, his well-heeled brother, who would later state that Charles had owed him $15,000, had offered $2,500 for the capture and conviction of his killer.[36]

Having revived a theory that one of the papers she had read had dismissed, the handsome blonde began to sob, and "fell back on the lounge as if she were going to faint." Her interviewer asked her name, but she wouldn't provide it. She told him that she had last seen the peripatetic Charlie Goodrich on Wednesday night, two nights before his death, at her home in New York, and, repeating her certainty about the burglary theory, explained that he carried a lot of money, and that his watch and ring were very valuable. Turning away then, she walked across the room, sat on a chair and stared out the window. At that point W. W. Goodrich came in with Detective Videto, who "scowled at the reporter, who laughed in return."[37] But it was time for him to go. The lady, a dressmaker who lived on E. 59th Street, was labeled in the following day's headline: "A Mysterious Woman in Black."

Other papers also learned about her and described her in angelic terms. She was, wrote the *Sun*, "of considerable beauty." Her blonde head, said the *Times*, was "profusely curled," and "her relations with the deceased" were "honorable."[38] She could hardly then be the imperiled woman who had shouted through the door of the third house on Degraw Street, or the one who had been noticed leaving that house early on more than one morning, or seen stoop-sitting at midnight with her paramour. No, she represented another side of Charles's complicated life.

"It is believed by those in a position to know," wrote the *Times*, "that she was engaged to be married to Mr. Goodrich."[39]

Her name was Adeline Palm.[40]

Charles Goodrich's closely examined and well-chilled body lay in the kitchen icebox[41] at 731 Degraw Street until it was removed on Saturday, the 22nd, and laid out in an open rosewood coffin in the home of W. W. Goodrich that the *New York Herald* considered a "mansion." The wound on his forehead was evident, and the "general contour of his features," it was said, was such as "might indicate the deceased to be a man of fretful and even misanthropic disposition." The wake on Sunday drew a crowd that extended onto the sidewalk, and was "so densely packed" within that "it was impossible to view the coffin." At 3 o'clock, Rev. Theodore Cuyler of Lafayette Avenue Presbyterian Church, one of the best-known clergyman in this city nationally identified with its clergymen, began a funeral service and intoned a long oration in which he referred to the lonely life that the deceased had led after losing not only his wife but also his only child. He bemoaned the conditions of current urban living in which no one could walk the streets with a sense of security, and prayed that the government and the law would deliver justice to the people. He remembered that he had seen Charles Goodrich among his congregation and recalled that he had been converted to Christian faith by an Albany clergyman, after which Charles gave most satisfactory assurances of having entered upon a Christian life: "His daily walk was that of a quiet, unostentatious Christian, loved by those who knew him best." Then, after the dead man's mother and father had kissed his face, and the casket-lid had been screwed in place, eight pallbearers carried it to the hearse that took it to the Grand Central Depot and a train to Albany, where it would be laid in the family vault.[42]

On Monday, the 24th, the *Eagle*'s reporter, lurking around police headquarters, observed another "mysterious" New Yorker, this one a man, six-feet tall, sandy-whiskered and wearing "a Kossuth hat and a blue chinchilla overcoat," entering the offices of both Chief Campbell and Coroner Whitehill, to be interviewed at length. But the paper was sure that he was not a suspect, for it now had information from "one who had thoroughly examined the premises, and made himself acquainted with all the circumstances," that Charles Goodrich "was killed as the result of a quarrel with a woman, who was either jealous of him, or whom he had refused to marry."[43]

She was a "bold and scheming adventuress" who had been living with Charlie "in adultery"—although, unless she were married, that word would not have been accurate—and she had borne his child. But he wanted to be rid of her, and had become involved with the lady in ringlets whom the *Eagle* was so proud to have interviewed before the police had. Now it presented a bad-woman-good-woman scenario. Miss Ringlets had "no stain whatever" on her reputation. The other, whose character was "bad in every sense," had seen her enter one of the houses with Charlie, and this had convulsed her into rage. Besides the battle in the doorway, there had been another fracas, in which she struck him and threw things at him "with the utmost venom, vindictiveness and fury." On the night of March 20th they had wrangled again in the third-floor sleeping-quarters of house number six—where, it was now revealed, a panel of his bedroom door had been split, and it was assumed that she had damaged it after he had locked her out.

Police officials, among them Board President James Jourdan, who searched the upstairs rooms on Saturday found in Charles's closet evidence of one of these engagements—a blood-stained shirt with its collar torn and buttons pulled off. They also observed what William Goodrich had not when he found the house in "painful" good order on Friday morning—that both beds on that floor had been lain in.

The writer somehow knew that Charles had given into his volatile mate that Thursday night, and so she had slept with him. Then in the morning she had followed him downstairs. "No doubt with the stealthy movement of the paw of a tiger, she had possessed herself of his seven shooter." When he'd turned away from her toward the fireplace—presumably to light the space-heater—she had shot him "in the side of the head." After he'd fallen, striking his forehead on the mantel shelf and spilling his blood on the marble slab below, she had drilled him once behind each ear, then moved him and laid his riddled head upon his boots. Not very shrewdly, she'd placed the gun beside his right hand to present the appearance of suicide. Then the reporter or his imaginative source supposed she had become suddenly remorseful for what she had done to "the father of her child," and respectfully washed his head and "laid him out."[44]

There was no speculation about where the child might be, but the *Eagle*'s man was pleased to announce that this version of events had received "an emphatic indorsement" from "one of the highest officials in the county."[45]

It was becoming apparent that the political and operational sides of the police department were at cross purposes. While its chief was still working the suicide theory, Commissioner Jourdan was kicking it out of sight. "I have never, from the first," he said, "entertained the least shadow of belief that it was other than a murder."[46] It was also suggested that the paper's source may have been a detective whose lips had been loosened in a downtown tavern. But whatever the derivation, some members of the force reacted against the scoop by appealing to the residents of Degraw Street, in the interest of justice, to stop talking to reporters. The *Eagle* scoffed at this attempt to muzzle it or its sources,[47] but was willing to meet its adversaries half-way:

"The name of the woman who in all probability shot Charles Goodrich has been discovered," it reported on the 26th, "but at the request of the police, who fear its publication might render her more difficult to capture, the *Eagle* withholds it from the public for the present. Suffice it to say that the history of her relation with the deceased, and the manner in which she committed the deed, given in last night's *Eagle*, is recognized as true by the authorities today."[48]

Within a week, after events around police headquarters had clouded the case with further confusion, every paper in the two cities had printed her name as "Kate Stoddard."

The Same Type of Woman

Why couldn't the Brooklyn police find Kate Stoddard? All the editorialists in the two cities seemed to agree that these men were fit for only routine tasks, and that this case had them overmatched. The *Eagle* expounded on police mediocrity:

> The system is the creature of politics. The Democrats succeed and Father Briggs has everything under his immediate eye. The Republicans succeed and General Jourdan ceases to be an experienced assessor and becomes an empirical policeman. Neither the Commissioners, the Chief nor the patrolman feel that they are in for life. They owe their

places to political patrons, and while with one eye they are watching disorder with the other they are watching the chances of continuance. The fruits are not better than the tree which bears them. The detectives are commonplace, faithful enough, but entirely ordinary men, who never by any possibility can die of brain fever.[49]

Father Briggs and General Jourdan—Daniel D. Briggs and James Jourdan, with the accent on the second syllable—were two of the three Brooklyn police commissioners, Jourdan having succeeded Briggs as president the previous year when the state administration had turned Republican. The department he oversaw was actually just three years old, for in the 13 years before 1870, New York and Brooklyn police had been united by the state legislature in an unlamented experiment called the Board of Metropolitan Police. Patrick Campbell, who had been Kings County sheriff, was in that year named Brooklyn chief of police.

The paper's snipe about Jourdan's sudden transformation into a policeman was a reference to his being the local assessor of internal revenue, a position he owed to his leading role in the Republican party—one of its "Three Graces." Jourdan, in fact, may have worn more hats in his time than any other citizen of the short-lived City of Brooklyn. Born in Ireland, with French Protestant roots, in 1832, he had been brought to Brooklyn as a boy, and as a young man made some money in real estate. In 1861 he headed to the Battle of Bull Run as a major in the Brooklyn regiment that would win praise as "The Fighting Fourteenth"; later he led a brigade in North Carolina, and he came out of the Civil War as a major-general. At one time he was the city's health commissioner. And all the while he was putting his money into the gas business, until, linking up with Standard Oil, he would become the first president of the Brooklyn Union Gas Company, the corporation under which William Rockefeller and H. H. Rogers consolidated all seven of Brooklyn's gas concerns.[50]

So the *Eagle* groused about politics mixing with police work, and, being the city's Democratic organ, was glad to take aim at General Jourdan, who had replaced its longtime publisher, Isaac Van Anden, on the police board.[51] Despite the general's proven competence and success—he was said to be widely considered the "smartest man in Brooklyn"—the newspaper was onto something. The Charles

Goodrich murder case would be the one episode in that long career in city and borough that would make him look foolish.

At the house where Charles had been killed, the police had found a dozen letters from one woman. The writing was large and neat, the grammar correct, the composition skillful. The last of them was dated February 27th, 1873. "I am sure," she had written then, "you did it without thinking, and, believing that, I am willing, as you often say, to 'let bygones be bygones' and commence all over again. Why should people who love each other as we do allow small things to separate them? It is not my disposition to do so, and I believe it is not yours."

This was the woman whom the *Eagle* assumed to be the murderess, and it had learned more about her: that she was from New England, that she had "earned her living by honest industry" in "one of the uptown stores in New York." The letters, however, were signed not by the "Kate Stoddard" who had been identified, but with another name, which was not yet revealed.[53]

Exactly a month after that letter had been written, Brooklyn police seized a woman in New York in connection with the murder of Charles Goodrich.

The two-horsed carriage in which Detectives Folk and Videto brought her arrived at headquarters at just past seven on the wet evening of March 27th, six days after the Goodrich killing. The officers stepped out first, and "with a politeness that would have done honor to a Chesterfield, handed a closely veiled lady to the sidewalk." Chief Campbell, who had been tipped off about this woman in a letter from a man who called himself "Beach," awaited her in his office, and offered her a seat when she was ushered in. She refused it, but, invited again, sat down. Folk and Videto withdrew, and she pulled aside her veil.

"What," she asked, "have you had me brought here for?"[54]

Campbell, 46, was short and stocky, with deep-set eyes and a full, graying, Lincolnesque beard. The New York police chief George W. Walling, in his memoir, would praise him as "one of the most skillful detectives in the country." He had once worked for the *Eagle* as a printing supervisor. Born in Charleston but raised mainly in

Brooklyn, he was an Irish Catholic and a Democrat, son of a political father, and brother of a Brooklyn Congressman. He'd had the common distinction with Nathaniel Hawthorne of having been appointed a customs inspector by President Franklin Pierce. His customary manner was genial.[55]

He followed the woman's question with his own.

"Do you know Mr. Goodrich?"

"Oh, yes, I knew Charlie well." That was almost the exact response elicited from the ringleted Adeline Palm.

"Were you ever in Brooklyn with him?"

"Yes, I was over in his houses in Degraw Street about the 20th of last month." She would add that she had been there three times.

He asked her then about a quarrel between Goodrich and some other men in her New York apartment. She granted that there had been such a quarrel, and added that she "took Charlie away from them and put him in another room."

Where had she been the previous Thursday night? She did not remember that, nor what she had done Friday night, nor why she had arrived late at work on Saturday.

Since she had been "so very intimate" with this man, he commented, "it seems very strange to me that you have never been to Brooklyn about this man's death."

She was quiet for some time before she responded, "I did not want to see him that way."

He was skeptical, telling her that he thought there was "another object that kept you away." He asked her to admit it, but she wouldn't.

"I do not want to keep you here five minutes more than is necessary," he told her, but "you do not give us any explanation for this thing. You do not seem inclined to talk except to answer questions put to you."

"Well, I cannot be any worse off than I am, and if I have got to stay here I will stay." [56]

The press, for all their diligence in discovering this conversation, did not know her name or where she'd been found. The latter they learned from the coachman, after they had "treated him to liquor and cigars." It was 22 Orchard Street on Manhattan's Lower East Side, where she worked as a shirtmaker. She had, he said—between puffs, perhaps—been "mighty unwilling" to come.[57]

"If I go I will give no information," she had remarked to Billy Folk, "for I am a parrot that never talks."[58]

Campbell and others pressed their mainly fruitless questioning till one a.m., after which the parrot was caged for the night in the janitor's room.[59]

At Brooklyn headquarters the following morning, 27 press representatives were working this story—six from the *Herald*, five from the *Times*. And the city of Brooklyn buzzed with news about the capture of Charles Goodrich's "mistress."[60] But was she? And, more important, was she his murderess, the "bad" woman whom he had housed at Degraw Street? To determine this a newsman who had interviewed Professor Boyle of Degraw Street looked him up again at his Brooklyn Institute studio downtown on Washington Street. Boyle agreed to walk the several blocks to police headquarters and ask to see the prisoner. He had to overcome the thick obstacle of Detective Van Wagner before he got Campbell to admit him, then took a "good look" at the woman sitting "silent and moody" in a cell. He met the reporter afterward at the corner of Court and Remsen Streets.

"I don't think it is the same woman," Boyle told him. "This is the same type of woman, I think, but it is not *the* woman, I am quite sure."

The same type. What type was that? Boyle had previously seen a Diana, but the reporter's own glimpse of the prisoner that morning revealed no goddess. He described a "tall, thin, black-haired woman" who "was neither stylishly, nor yet even well dressed. She had the appearance of a hard worked shop girl, or a female who had dissipated in one way or another to some degree." He may not have noticed, as others would, that she was missing some teeth. Another writer estimated her age at about 30,[61] several years more than the lady on the stoop was thought to be.

The Brooklyn police, already scorched by ridicule, seemed to have mixed up two of Charlie Goodrich's companions. And this woman they'd brought in was a bird rarely fashioned to make them pay for their mistake. What she knew or didn't know, and what the Brooklyn police believed or didn't believe about what she told them, would complicate the Goodrich murder case and the functioning of the department for months to come.

Campbell soon realized that this woman was not the killer that he was after,[62] but he believed that she could lead the way to him or her. "She's a Yankee woman," he commented, "and just as sharp, I tell you, as they make them. From what she did say, however, I am satisfied that she knows enough, and is trying to conceal a great deal more."

One thing she did say eventually was that she thought that Charles Goodrich had been killed by a man, and the chief seemed to take this possibility seriously. Perhaps she had been present when a jealous rival shot Goodrich, and it was she who then washed him and propped his head on his boots.

"I tell you," he said, "we are in possession of certain facts, and if they come out the people of this city will be astounded at the way the thing was done. Yes, sir, they will be thunderstruck!"[63]

With its own story of the murder now in doubt, the *Eagle*, determined to identify Campbell's captive, put a man on the ferry and into the apartment at 22 Orchard Street from which she had been taken. There he found "three or four females" working and chatting and "a handsome Jewess with olive cheeks, large dark eyes and teeth like pearls." This was Miss Levy, who ran the place with her mother. The woman now detained in downtown Brooklyn, she said, "gave her name as Lucette Myers," but had asked her to tell anyone who inquired that "no such person worked here." She was quiet and one of their "best hands," who often took work home to nearby 13 Stanton Street, where she lived with and supported her parents in conditions so mean that Miss Levy felt sorry for her. She had heard her tell the Brooklyn detectives the previous night "that Charlie Goodrich was her beau." Mrs. Levy then appeared and nudged her daughter to be silent.[64]

Adeline Palm, Kate Stoddard, Lucette Myers. And what was the name on those letters?

The *Eagle*'s man moved on to 13 Stanton Street, and learned that a woman known as Lucette Armstrong and her family had recently departed owing two months' rent and moved a block south to 46 Rivington Street. At that "brownstone tenement house" he knocked on the door that he was directed to, and a voice invited him to come in. He entered a small, clean room, in which sat "an old and feeble looking woman, her head bowed upon the back of a chair." She seemed to have been crying, and behind her stood two small boys. One volunteered his name as "William Gaylord Armstrong"—"yes," the old woman said, "Lucette's little fellow," five years old.

"Please, sir, don't 'oo know where my Loeden is?" the younger boy would ask, using a pet name for his mother. "Dey will let my Loeden tum back, won't dey?"

The old woman was Lucette's mother, Mrs. Hubbell, and she spoke in a marked rural accent, being "from the kentry—up from Bridgeport, Connecticut." Lucette Jane, she offered, had been married and widowed twice, first by Armstrong, then by Myers. As they spoke she was visited by Miss and Mrs. Levy, who asked if "those shirts" were ready. "Part of them," Mrs. Hubbell replied, and, as the shirts were counted, added: "I don't know when Lucette will finish the rest. Mebbe never; mebbe never."

The reporter's inquiry as to how much Lucette earned caused the old woman "to bolt upright in her chair." Her answer was three dollars a week, which was eked out by some pittances from a son-in-law. Then followed a lament for the downtrodden, presumably within hearing of the Levys: "I often say to myself has people got hearts? Sometimes I wonder how God lets 'em wring the hearts of the poor so. But he does an' we must toil on, starve away, an' no one knows the misery of the poor."[65]

Within a couple of days, the *Eagle*, the *Herald* and the *Graphic* began to collect donations for the Hubbells, amounting to many times Lucette's stated weekly salary. To one correspondent, the imprisoned daughter's travails evoked an English poem bemoaning the exploitation of seamstresses, "The Song of the Shirt," by Thomas Hood.[66]

At the County Court House, Coroner Whitehill was given use of a regular courtroom to accommodate the crowd that flowed to the inquest that began at mid-afternoon on Saturday, March 28th. General Jourdan and District Attorney Britton were present, and there were nine jurors. The first witness, William W. Goodrich, told the story of finding his brother's body,[67] and continued his testimony on April 1st. On that day Whitehill released the letter, dated February 15th, that had been sent to both William and his father by the woman who had lived in one of the houses on Degraw Street "for the past eight months . . . unknown to anyone but Charley"—or so she had presumed. "About one year ago," she added, "I was married to him secretly," but "had learned since then that the clergyman who married us was no minister at all, only a friend of his, Ruben Smith, a doctor, I think, who lives in the City." "The City" meant New York.

Whoever had previously leaked information to the *Eagle* had evidently read or been told the contents of this message. It continued: "In December last—two months ago—our baby was born. Before that and since then Charley has treated me with the utmost cruelty, disowning all ties between us."

Then, just days before writing, she had seen her lover with "a woman with ringlets," whom he afterward admitted was "his new love," and informed her that "there was no marriage between us" (that is, him and the letter-writer), and that they had to part. "My heart," she wrote, "is completely broken . . . It seems like some deadly nightmare." It was all lucidly phrased, and signed "Amy G."[68]

William Goodrich had learned that the woman also used the names Amy Snow, Amy Stone and Kate Stoddard. The last would be the name by which she would most commonly be known, although Chief Campbell would later indicate that it had been found in just one place in Charles's house—beneath "four lines of writing, written in a female hand" in a memorandum book. William stated that he had received his copy of the letter at his office by mail, but that his father had been handed the same letter by Kate herself in his jewelry-business office on John Street, New York. "This was," he added, "my first intimation of there being anything wrong or immoral in my brother's character. I was greatly shocked."[69]

Lucette took the stand for more than three hours on April 1ˢᵗ, and spoke of the man she had implicated in the murder. He was "a Spaniard," a former lover of hers who she believed had fled to Baltimore, where Chief Campbell had sent a dispatch asking the police to look for him. Although she had been acquainted with him six months, she knew him only as "Roscoe." His trade was counterfeiting, and he carried a pistol. When Whitehill asked what size it was, then presented the gun that had been found at Charles's side, she responded, "It was about the same size and character of the pistol now shown me"—which must have fallen as a *double entendre* on many ears. In a reluctant, indirect and at times inconsistent manner, she explained that Charlie had replaced Roscoe in her affection, that the two men had quarreled in her very busy Stanton Street apartment, and that Roscoe had afterward exclaimed to her, "God help the person that comes between you and me!"

Was this the thunderclap that Campbell had foretold? The *Eagle* was skeptical, cautioning that "experienced members of the bar say that the exact truth can never be drawn from a woman on the witness stand."

Charlie, she claimed, had first presented himself to her by stepping on the hem of her dress as she boarded a midday Brooklyn-to-New York ferry—a means of human connection that the observant ferry-passenger Walt Whitman had not imagined. He had asked her to excuse him, but she did not reply. During the trip, he approached her again and began to talk to her, but still she was quiet. Then he followed her home to Stanton Street. He found out that she took in boarders, and in the evening he came back and asked if he could be one of them. That would not happen, she stated, but she began seeing him, as much as four or five times a week, in the winter of 1873. She revealed that the last time she'd been with him was the last night of his life, when they had spent two hours together. She had previously told Campbell that she had no memory of that evening.

Well along in her testimony, Whitehill asked her to "look around this court and see if there is any person you recognize as Roscoe." She provoked some laughs when she pointed to a court clerk who, she said, bore a "marked resemblance" to him, but was "not he."[70] Lucette was playing with her captors.

After recess, the coroner called "Samuel Roscoe" to the stand, and all present looked about in astonishment to see who this might be. Stepping quickly forward was a short, dark-complexioned man with medium-length dark hair and a thick mustache. He was involved in soap-and-toiletry sales at 302 Broadway, New York, where in February Lucette had responded to an ad seeking salespersons. Since he lived downtown, that evening he dropped off a sample of liquid soap to her that they were interested in selling. Yes, he declared, he was Samuel Roscoe. No, he had never boarded with her. With understandable sarcasm, he stated that he was "from a place called 'America,' where I was born; it is on the Camden and Amboy Railroad"[71]—that is, in New Jersey.

Well, this was April Fool's Day. The police department's reaction to this upshot of the Roscoe story might have been to laugh along with the courthouse spectators and accept that they had been had. But Lucette already had them spinning about in search of Roscoe, and they couldn't seem to stop. One thing that may have kept them going was Mrs. Hubbell's saying that her dear, kind daughter did have a Spanish suitor, and a farcical pursuit of somebody looking like the soap-salesman was conducted in the cities where she mentioned that her counterfeiting lover did business. In successive days non-Roscoes (and non-Spaniards) were picked up in New York (a Frenchman named Dalzen), in Philadelphia, where the arrest of a fellow named Hoffmeyer "caused quite a sensation," and in Baltimore, where a drunken sailor, name unknown, was pursued and caught, but "turned out to be a totally different person from that described in the telegram from New York."[72]

Still, belief in a nefarious Spaniard persisted. On April 3rd the *New York Times* declared its certainty that Lucette's account of him was true. They knew his real name but could not reveal it. He was a Cuban by way of New Orleans, where he'd been a well-known counterfeiter. Cincinnati and Buffalo could now be added to his urban league of operations. It was "extremely likely that in a few days he will be arrested."[73]

Although Lucette was no longer a serious suspect herself, Whitehill did not release her, but sent her to the witness's quarters at Raymond Street.[74] Citizens objected. A lawyer who had been "enlisted by charitable persons" petitioned for her release, and a drunk stumbled into the courtroom, fell down, got up and offered to post her $1,000 bail.[75] But for many days she continued to board at Raymond Street, where, the coroner promised, everything would be done for her comfort.[76]

Her residence was described in a New York paper as a "barn-like" room with "four bare walls." And "in one corner . . . is an iron bedstead with a straw mattress, sheets, and a gray army blanket. . . . Leading to the hallway is a thick oaken door, with a small panel on hinges, which can be open or shut at the pleasure of the occupants. Through the barred windows may be seen the prison yard, with its row of dismal-looking cells on either side."[77]

By Other Names

When the Goodrich murder inquest resumed on the evening of April 4th, 1873, the attention again migrated to Kate Stoddard/Amy G and the details of her pregnancy, "marriage," and falling-out with her lover. The session began at seven and went on past midnight.

Frank Williams, a druggist at 104 Fifth Avenue, spoke of three transactions with Charles Goodrich over four-to-six weeks, beginning the previous November. Each time he bought a box of "Hooper's Pills," which were, said Williams, "used for disordered state of health in females." And, though he had "never known females to use them to produce a miscarriage, they are put up for that purpose undoubtedly." The "cool" Goodrich had not minded explaining that "his lady was troubled with irregularities," or informing the druggist that he "was keeping bachelor's hall"[78] on Degraw Street.

He was followed by Dr. Reuben Smith, the Goodrich friend and former roommate, who was now revealed to be "the mysterious stranger from New York" seen at police headquarters the day after the murder. He had known both the betrothed Miss Palm, who had visited him after Charlie's death, and the woman named "Snow" or "Green," whom he had met at Degraw Street. Charles, he revealed, had found her through a newspaper ad: "he was in the habit of inserting 'personals,' and he wanted me to join him in doing so, to get up a large female correspondence."

"I asked him where the woman came from, and who she was," Smith added, "but he said that he could not find out from her, as she was very reticent, and would not even tell the state where she was from."

In November 1872, Smith had examined her at his office and determined that she was pregnant. Goodrich asked him to perform an abortion, and Smith, bristling, "told him I was a regular physician, and there were plenty of charlatans." Charles looked up the same charlatan whom Sam Morris had pursued, Madame Van Buskirk, but decided that her fee was too steep. Then, sometime in December, he went to a man named "Bottles" or "Butts."

Smith's recorded words are so elliptical that it is impossible to be precise about what happened next. But it seems to have been something like this: the abortion was done, but Kate worked up some sort of pretense that it had not been. The lovers left the appointed place and "walked eight or ten blocks" to the apartment of a nurse, where Kate feigned labor pains. Goodrich gave Kate five dollars to give to the nurse and left. The morning after he returned and found a "full term" baby in bed with her, which she claimed to be theirs. But Smith knew that this was impossible, for she had been just three months pregnant when he'd examined her a month or so earlier. He believed she had resisted having the abortion because she feared dying from it, and also because she wanted the child born so that she would "have a hold" on Goodrich. From her letter of February 15th, it seemed that what she held after these events was a fantasy that she had given birth.

After her return to Degraw Street, she continued to act very strangely, and possessively. One wet evening, as Charles prepared to leave for New York, she demanded that he stay, then followed him into the street, grabbed him "and got into a pool of water up to her knees." In Smith's telling, the abortion episode and this aftermath made up Charles's mind to be rid of this "bad and dangerous woman."

"Amy G." had written that Dr. Smith had conducted her mock marriage to Charles, which Smith now called "a positive falsehood." But he revealed that he had lent Charles, his friend "up to the day of his death," a total of $3,000.[79]

The papers reacted to the evening's accounts with disgust and outrage. The *Eagle* was contemptuous of the "niggardly lover" who'd made a five-dollar contribution to his recuperating mistress. The *Graphic* and the *Times* both admonished papers that peddled personal ads, and, the latter added, had "another section for the purpose of advertising abortionists"—thus "trad[ing] in female honor and child-murder." The unidentified malefactor was the *Herald*, yet even that daily spoke of "the Degraw Street den of shame" and viewed the character of Charles Goodrich with "loathing and abhorrence."[80]

And W. W. Goodrich, who just months earlier had been a candidate for Congress on a ballot headed by presidential nominee Horace Greeley, wondered if he could ever run for office again.

The following day's featured informer was 22-year-old Charles Green, Charles Goodrich's quondam brother-in-law, who had worked for him at the lumberyard on East 18th Street. Goodrich had been quite as willing to call upon him for delicate services as he had Reuben Smith, and Green was a most material witness of the events of February 15th and subsequent evenings.

Goodrich had asked him "to help him out of a scrape with a woman," which would require his duty as a "watchman." The house in which Kate was staying was the one that his parents intended to move into, and Goodrich had removed her belongings to the house next door. He told Green that she had a job in New York, at Broadway and Prince or Spring Street, making straw hats. When she returned that evening, Green was to prevent her from entering No. 723, and to tell her she could examine her things in the other house, but that Charles wanted to meet her at the ferry at eight o'clock.

She stepped off the Fifth Avenue car between 6 and 7 p.m. and headed to what she supposed to be her door. Green described her as "tall, slender," with "a Roman nose, blonde complexion, light brown hair, firmly set lips," and "about 23 or 24 years of age." She bore "a resemblance in the nose, eyes and chin" to "Mrs. Armstrong"—Lucette.

When Green delivered his message, she responded, "I don't know why he treats me so." That was her calmest expression of the night. She then offered to pay him more than Charles was giving him if he would "let her go through the other houses," where she could cause hundreds-of-dollars' worth of damage, and when they had gone into the house next door, she demonstrated her point by trying to yank a piece of lead pipe from under the kitchen sink. She declared that she'd "get square" with him and wouldn't care if he was dead.

She sat on her trunk and wrote her letters until 9:30 or 10. Then Goodrich, having given up on the proposed riverside rendez-vous, showed up, and she greeted him with a blow to the chest, called him "a devil," and flung a smoothing-iron at him. After he left she produced an accordion and began playing and singing, interrupted by moments of crying. She announced that that she feared she would "go crazy."

Green recalled that Charles had planned to settle her in a hotel till Monday, then find a permanent room for her, even furnish it: "He told me he wanted to make a decent woman of her, and help her along." But she insisted on staying the night of the 15th in the unheated house at Degraw Street, sleeping on some pieces of carpet while Green sat on the cold kitchen range.

Goodrich asked Green to follow him and Kate the next after-noon as they traveled to New York. "He was afraid she might make some scene on the street." But they walked through lower Manhattan like any Sunday lovers, arm in arm, under an umbrella—up Fulton Street, to William, then to Chatham Street and Crook's Hotel, where they both registered—she as "Kate Stoddard." Goodrich would tell Green that he left her there and went to the room he still kept on 13th Street.

When Charles Green returned to Degraw Street on Monday night, Kate "was there again." He stayed the night, and after Tuesday morning he never more saw either one of them.[81]

The coroner adjourned the inquest, for there was no basis for a verdict. And the Degraw Street murder case, though still mysterious, began to loosen its grip on the cities in New York harbor—losing interest, wrote the *Eagle*, as it gained "offensiveness."[82] But that comment may have underestimated how compelled the population of the 1870s had become by the two throbbing elements of big-city life that Charles Goodrich's sordid death had revealed—sexual wantonness and spreading violence. The events that were described or implied, the words used, the arrangements made, were evidence that a recently urbanized nation was one in which natural desires and passions were more likely to turn base, and, having done so, to be more difficult to contain and impossible for even discreet persons to ignore. What the paper called "a coarse and commonplace life of economical lust,"[81] involving tacit exchanges of intimacy for money, involving cohabitation, pregnancy and abortion, abused emotions, conflict, rage and, finally, murder, was now in open, public view. The people were outraged; some were frightened; many may have been disgusted, but many would no longer have been shocked.

"By degrees there will be a better understanding," the *Herald* observed, in relation to the Goodrich murder, "of the great social undercurrent, which bears on its mysterious current so much that is good and evil in humanity."[83] Earlier that year, in the week after the killing occurred, George Templeton Strong had commented on a sermon delivered at Trinity Church, which "touched on the new school of erotic poetry (Swinburne & Co.), on the nasty illustrated flash weeklies that are sold at every newsstand, on fast women and fast men, on innocent flirtations among married folk, on increasing facilities for divorce, on our new race of women (like Mrs. Julia Ward Howe) who are not content with being different creatures from men and far nobler and better, but seek to become second-rate men, or bad imitations of men."[84]

Women who committed murder fascinated and perplexed the men who ran the newspapers, the courts, the governments, the professions—the world—and these men aligned against each other as they pondered anew the wonders, mysteries, and dangers of the female sex. As more and more women migrated unattended into great American cities to find work and lodging—and lovers—for themselves, the "woman question" penetrated the public consciousness, and the male consciousness particularly, more deeply than in any other age. In the 1870s the issue the issue of women's suffrage heated to a boil, and all the related issues of women's rights and "liberation" would never quite cool over the next century and longer. These feminist arguments, and the less respectable claim for unleashed female sexuality, along with related controversies about adultery and divorce, became very much focused in that decade on Brooklyn. But the question "what is woman?" spread everywhere. If she is meant to work like a man and earn a man's wages, a contributor to the *Brooklyn Union* wondered, why is she so frail and gentle?[86] The question he dared not ask was why, if she hoped to share men's responsibilities and authority, she had a body that was constantly in process for producing children. Questions about that awesome and mystifying function would, however, be asked repeatedly during the trials of women who had turned violent, and possibly mad. And while some editors, lawyers, and jurors commiserated with women who had emerged from a more confined and protected life to become victimized by predatory men, others railed against the sentimentality that excused their deadly crimes and noted that some women evinced a refined capacity for viciousness.

By the inquest's end, then, the Honorable W. W. Goodrich had been dishonored, and so, in another way, had been the police department of Brooklyn, whose reputation festered as the case lingered unsolved. They continued to insist that they were acting appropriately, and to bristle at their treatment in the press. One stratagem they conceived was to provide Lucette Myers with a companion in the witness's quarters at Raymond Street. But the New York parrot, it was said, spoke to this agent only "in monosyllables" and offered her no new intelligence.[87] Lucette was released, without bail, from the Brooklyn jail on April 14th. Yet policemen and editors still credited the stories she had told.

On that same day, the Board of Aldermen adopted a resolution to change the name of Degraw Street above Fifth Avenue, in the direction of Prospect Park, to "Lincoln Place"—although it was hard to deny the accuracy of one reaction, "that the butchery in Lincoln

Place" could not "seem less horrible than the butchery in Degraw Street."[88]

On April 28th, the date of another withering editorial concluding that "so far as the police force is concerned the Goodrich case is practically at an end," the department issued an order prohibiting any employee from publicizing any detail of a crime or of an investigation of a crime for which an arrest had not yet been made.[89]

This same week Kate Stoddard was mistakenly reported to be living in rural Connecticut,[90] and on the evening of the 29th, a man was held in New York on suspicion of being "Roscoe," but he produced a letter from Philadelphia's chief detective indicating that he had been stopped there for the same reason and found to be "some other person."[91]

On May 9th, an Irish gangster from West 16th Street, New York, known as "Pop" Tighe—he had once worked in a soda factory—was arrested in that city and detained at Brooklyn's First Precinct as a suspect in the murder. The connection was probably his involvement in the supposed Roscoe's supposed trade of counterfeiting. But Tighe claimed to know nothing of Goodrich, and apparently didn't.[92.]

And when summer arrived in Brooklyn, neither Roscoe nor Kate had been found, and W. W. Goodrich and District Attorney Winchester Britton were vacationing in Europe.[93]

Queer Crime, Queerer Woman

As the Brooklyn Common Council was approving a $1,000[94] reward for information leading to the conviction of Charles Goodrich's killer or killers, the cities were alarmed by another murder of a man with a well-known name. In the early morning of June 3rd, 1873, in a room at The Sturtevant House, Broadway and 29th Street, Manhattan, 19-year-old Frank H. Walworth, scion of a distinguished New York legal family, fired four bullets into his 43-year-old father, Mansfield, attorney and author of lurid novels, including *The Mission of Death*, Mansfield was an apparent madman; Frank was not. He killed his father because he had repeatedly abused and threatened Frank's mother, and would not let up.[95] But the peculiar question arose of whether or not the murderer had been tinged with insanity inherited from the person whom he had murdered.

"A most uncommonly shocking murder," George Templeton Strong commented. ". . . We shall have to make the carrying of concealed weapons a felony."[96]

The council's reward would supplement the $2,500 that W. W. Goodrich had offered in March. But at the same moment Coroner Whitehill was canceling a resumption of his inquest[97] into the case because there was nothing to investigate. Like Mr. Micawber, he would wait for something to "turn up." The police had also been waiting, but not because, as most journalists believed, they didn't know what to do. Their delay was caused by bad luck, and complicated by division within the department.

That division, political and operational, would lead to some very peculiar turns in a case already made peculiar by the circumstances of the killing and the befuddling presence and reportage of Lucette Myers.

Chief Patrick Campbell had focused his force on the woman known as Kate Stoddard. They had interviewed persons who had seen her, "and others who imagined they had seen her." And they had looked earnestly for even one person, other than the elusive Myers, who had known her well.[98]

They found one: Miss Mary Handley, of 198 Clinton Street, corner of East Broadway on New York's lower East Side. Detective Folk would say later that he and Videto had located her, but, just when they had, she had become severely ill, and for about six weeks was "laid up in bed," at least part of the time in a hospital. While the papers caviled and ridiculed, then, she was of little use to the police. And some noxious air must just then have been circulating around New York harbor, for, when she had recovered, Campbell also got sick, and another two weeks was lost. Finally, well into May, she became Campbell's hired agent, at a salary of two dollars a day.[99]

Guesses of her age varied, but she was likely in her 20s, and, judged one observer, "a handsome brunette." Another described her as "of medium height, firmly built, of graceful figure, brown hair, light blue eyes, sharp features and clear complexion." She spoke "rapidly—as most women do," with "a captivating mode of address."[100] Reporters liked her just fine, and so, in a professional way, did Patrick Campbell.

But Commissioner Jourdan didn't, if only because she was Campbell's woman. Jourdan, in fact, had wanted to dump the chief months earlier after he had revealed too much about Kate Stoddard in an interview with the *Herald*. But Briggs wouldn't consent.[101] And Campbell, when the time was right, would claim that Jourdan had his own preferred agent—Lucette Myers. That was an amazing revelation, but the *Eagle* backed it up, and offered more. Jourdan's sleuthing team, it contended, included Alderman William Richardson, that fellow who kept showing up in both the Hyde and Stoddard cases, and yet another outré female, an "Anna E. Park, M.D." of Atlantic Avenue, Brooklyn, who identified herself as a "medical electrician," but whom the *Eagle* also had down as a "clairvoyant." This bunch had supposedly continued to search for Roscoe.

It was not that Jourdan had no interest in pursuing Kate Stoddard. Indeed, he had a photograph of her, which he granted was a "poor" one. Campbell would declare that it was less than that; it was bogus. He had showed it to Handley, who had immediately gainsaid that it was Kate—"Oh my, no!" To begin with, the woman's style of dress was ten years out of date. This picture, added Campbell, had been given to Jourdan by Lucette.[102]

Mary Handley had lived with the woman she had known as Kate Stoddard during the first half of 1872 at 45 Elizabeth Street, just west of the Bowery in what is now Chinatown. They were both hat-makers—Kate, as was already known, had worked "in the straw business" at a place called Thompson's at Broadway and Spring Street. Mary had found her to be "impulsive, pleasant, eccentric," a "creature of moods" varying from "hilarity" to deep depressions in which she thought of suicide. She often walked around their room in the middle of the night, naked and playing "an old accordion." She had, Handley believed, been badly disappointed in love before she had come to New York. In June or July she had left Elizabeth Street and moved to the "Working Woman's Home."[103]

Agent Handley pursued Kate mainly in New York City, visiting every shop there that manufactured straw bonnets, in some of which Mary took jobs for a few days. No Kate. So Handley turned her attention to post offices, knowing her former friend's habit of corresponding with men through newspaper columns and postal boxes. Campbell tipped her, from some unknown source, that she had been using the P.O. on 12th Street, New York. There Mary went, and learned that the postmaster indeed recognized Kate as a woman named "Amy Marlow." She "waited for her, day after day, expecting her to come," for she "knew among her other peculiarities that she would walk . . . two or three miles to place a letter of that kind in a particular box, so that her correspondent would be sure to get it." Day-after-day became more than two weeks, until the same official told her that the lady had directed that her letters be forwarded to a post office in Philadelphia. Campbell sent Mary down there for a week, in the company of a policeman. Then he called her back. Kate's correspondence was again showing up at 12th Street.[104]

Spring had turned to summer. Jourdan now appointed his own detective to spy on the spy. In time this man would also speak up and reveal that he had met with Richardson, Park and Myers, and had "shadowed" Handley, just returned from Philadelphia, to her New York apartment on July 7th and back to Brooklyn headquarters on the morning of Tuesday, July 8th. She met with Campbell, and he went upstairs to tell Commissioners Jourdan and Briggs that she had discovered nothing on her trip. Jourdan told him to let her go. Shortly afterward, the board president's spy sent him a note from the street outside.

> General Jourdan raised the window and beckoned me to come upstairs. When I had obeyed he asked me what I meant by saying that Mary Handley was in the building, and I told him that she was down in the Chief's office then. He seemed to be astonished, and sent for the Chief. I was told that I was then withdrawn from the case. This was after the Commissioner had told the Chief to discharge Mary Handley.[105]

But Campbell hadn't. He had sent her back to 12th Street and handed her a five-dollar bill for expenses.[106] During what was about a 15-minute walk along Court and Fulton Streets to the ferry, she may have fallen into a reverie about that day's assignment, for, she would remember, she kept the money in her hand, "rolling it between my palms," as she went down Fulton:

> After going two or three blocks I discovered that I had lost the money. After looking about me I retraced my steps about two blocks, and strangely enough found the $5 bill

lying on the sidewalk, beneath passing feet. Now, this I call strange. After getting the bill, instead of walking, as I had intended, I got into a car. It was a close[d] car. I however was looking out the window. At the corner of High Street I saw a woman coming along with a cream colored veil and some other light colored material about her that attracted my attention. Looking a little closer, judge my astonishment that the woman was no other than Kate Stoddard.[107]

She bid the driver to stop the car, and hurried out. Kate, too, was headed to the ferry, along the east side of Fulton Street, a block or two ahead of Handley, who then crossed the street and pulled abreast of her.

It was close to noon.[108] Before them the Brooklyn tower of the East River Bridge rose to about two-thirds of its eventual height of 276 feet, and, in the heart of construction season, a team of laborers mounted the great granite blocks being lifted by three huge derricks.[109] Near the ferry-house, amid a stream of commuters in front of a tavern called the Franklin House, stood Officer Edward Doherty, and Handley called to him to arrest the woman before her. He balked at first, then, presumably after she had identified herself as an operative of his department, he complied.[110] In the view of a young fellow who had watched as he stood outside the Franklin House, Kate "looked as if she was goin' to faint first. Then she says, you needn't take hold of me, I'll go along with you."[111] On the way to the Second Precinct station at Jay and York Streets, Kate was silent, and Doherty, said Mary, "did not know until he got to the station house who he had arrested."[112]

Although Kate said nothing, she did something. As they walked to York Street, she pulled from her pocket two blue envelopes containing letters inscribed on matching paper and addressed to different men. She attempted to tear these apart, but they were snatched away by her attendants.

One, intended for a post-office box in Jersey City, read:

It is not convenient for me to enclose my photograph, and since you advertised with a view to matrimony I should not think you would wish your intended wife to send her picture to a gentleman she had never seen. I remain respectfully votre fiancée,

Jesse Willoughby,
Jersey City, N.J.

The ad to which she had previously responded, with its "view to matrimony," would then have been of the same sort as the one that had brought her and Charles Goodrich together.

The other letter was addressed to "Mr. F. T. Evans, 54 East 12th street, New York," and written with the same impeccable grammar:

> I regret that I have only just now received your letter of the 2d. I hope you will have returned from Saratoga by the time this reaches you. In my letter to you I expressed the wish that whatever letters I had sent you should be preserved, and I feel just a little bit grieved because you did not assure me that they would be. I remain, respectfully,

Jesse Willoughby

> P.S.—I consider "age," when it brings with it profitable experience, rather an advantage than otherwise to its possessor.[113]

"Willoughby" was the name of a downtown Brooklyn street, adjacent to Fulton—a street, in fact, that continued east and bordered the Kings County Jail at Raymond Street.

The commander of the Second Precinct was Captain John McConnell, who questioned the captive when Doherty and Handley brought her in. Ever mercurial, Kate now became garrulous, but he warned her that her statements could be used against her. Then, wanting her searched, he sent across the street for a woman named Mullins, who operated a dry-goods store.[114]

Kate's veil and dress had caught Mary Handley's eye, but Mrs. Mullins found her appareling to be pitiable.

"It did not take me long [to search her]," she remarked, "for the poor creature hadn't an article of value about her. . . . She had no underclothing. Her skirt, shawl and hat were all she possessed."[115]

And beneath those articles her figure had wasted. The guy who had watched the arrest from in front of the Franklin House was asked if he considered this young woman, once described as "Diana-like," to be good-looking.

"No, he answered. "She looked as if she didn't have a square meal in a month. She had a big chin on her like Governor Hoffman and a sharp nose. She was a bony lookin' woman."

McConnell telegraphed Chief Campbell at headquarters, and he rushed down to York Street.[116]

On at least three occasions over the next 33 years, this articulate, good-natured veteran would comment publicly on his encounter with this famous, desperately sought fugitive, and on the extraordinary police-work that he had ordered in its aftermath.

General Jourdan, once more examining his supposed photograph of Kate, doubted that the arrested woman was indeed she. "He laughed at me," said Campbell, who was sure he had her.[117]

But she would not give her name, nor where she lived, nor would she admit to the murder. And when he addressed her as "Kate," she snapped, "Don't call me that. Call me 'Amy G.'" The chief detained her overnight in McConnell's office.[118]

Neither Campbell's boss nor his prisoner offered him respect these days. "At last," he would remember, "she laughed in my face and confessed," proclaiming, "'I did it; I killed him—shot him down as I would a dog. He was untrue, false; yes, I killed him, and I am glad of it.'" She had indeed called to Charles and shot him while he was lighting the Baltimore heater.

Then she warned the chief that she would deny this admission at an inquest, and said that she had told him what she had just to stop his questioning.[119]

Forty years later one of the *Eagle*'s venerable writers or editors would reveal that a famous man who had briefly been an *Eagle* reporter had drawn information about the confession from Kate herself. The late revelation was included in a remembrance of New York Mayor William J. Gaynor, who had just died in office, in September 1913. In 1873 he had come to Brooklyn and been hired as a court reporter. It is likely, then, that its accounts of the Goodrich murder inquest were also provided by that 25-year-old man[120] who had not yet set out on his extraordinary legal and political career.

Was this newly arrested woman mad? The papers gave that impression. They liked a story that she had shot him, not on the Friday, March 21st, on which he had been discovered, but on Thursday morning, when his brother had first found the house silent. Then she was supposed to have remained with her victim all day and night, or to have gone to work, returned in the evening, performed her peculiar undertaking services, and sat with him all night before heading to work once more. On Friday, then, when she arrived again at the Brooklyn ferry-landing at the end of her day, she had allegedly heard newsboys hawking the report of the murder, reboarded the ferry to New York and taken lodgings in the vicinity of 42nd Street. There were also accounts that she had returned to Brooklyn on Sunday and appeared at Charles's funeral.[121]

But in the face of evidence—the several persons who had seen Charles that day and night, the blood at the scene on Friday still dripping into the cellar, and the gory Thursday evening paper—this scenario was improbable.

Then there was the episode of the gold locket. Campbell would mention that she wore it at their interview—an "article of value" that Mrs. Mullins had overlooked. Two sketches of Kate drawn at the inquest would clearly depict it, and the press reported that she had had it inscribed, "Done, Thursday, March 21st, 1873," which only aggravated the uncertainty because the 21st had been Friday. Moreover, it quickly become the focus of grisly newspaper stories. In one version, Campbell had asked her to hand him the locket, and when, after hesitating, she did so, he attempted to open it. And she exclaimed:

"Oh, be careful! Be careful! There is a mineral in that which I do not want to lose."

Yet a morsel of this "mineral" fell to the floor, and she stooped, picked it up, and put it in her mouth.

"What did you do that for?"

"That is Charles Goodrich's blood."[122]

Chief Campbell never described such a scene. But to the papers that depicted it, it was their clearest indication that she was crazy.

"A queer thing is crime," stated an *Eagle* editor. "A queerer thing is woman."[123]

Twenty-two years after Kate's arrest, Superintendent Campbell, on the day of his retirement, would also provide more information

about that week in 1873. Choking back emotion to address his officers, he would speak of only one case, the Goodrich murder, and of
one moment in particular. "I never asked you to perform a task that
was not performed to my perfect satisfaction," he would tell them.
"There is one case of loyalty to which I will refer. It was a test, an
extraordinary test of loyalty from subordinates to a superior."

Kate, or whoever she was, had described to Campbell the missing watch, wallet, and ring that had been taken from Goodrich's
house. But, although he "had tried every possible way" to get her
address from her, she still refused to direct him to these articles.
Like her presumed onetime rival, Lucette Myers, she played with
him, allowing him to feel the growing pressure of having no tangible
proof to present to the fast-approaching inquest. " 'If you ever find
out where I live,' " she told him, " 'you will discover that I have been
telling you the truth and you will find the property.' "

"I puzzled my head night and day," he would state, "how I could
discover where she had lived," and, after "long hours of thought,"
the way to do it "flashed" in his head: "I had made up my mind
that he only way to find the woman's residence was to search every
house in Brooklyn."

Every house? In a city nearing a half-million population?

It was the only course left [he continued], but it was a very
serious thing. It meant that we must search between sixty
and seventy thousand homes. I told the commissioners of
my intention and they told me that I must do just what
I deemed best. I sent out word to all the captains to send
for every man on the force and hold them in reserve and
wait for further orders. Then I sent word that I wanted
to see all the captains and I told them what I wanted,
knowing well what I was doing and knowing well the
responsibilities of my act. I told them that I had lost a
woman in my charge, that I had her in my keeping for
two days and that I wanted to find out if possible where
she lived. "Go back to your precincts," I said. "talk to the
men; cut up your precincts into districts as small as possible and inquire in every house if there has been a woman
missing since last Tuesday." That was on Thursday, you will
understand. I told the men that the responsibility rested

entirely with me, let it be a failure or a success. An order of that kind had never been issued in this country up to that time and it has not been issued since. Of course when the captains went back to their stations and told the men what was wanted, there was some grumbling, maybe. And all had some opinions to express. I never told the captains whom I was seeking. Three hours or three hours and a half after the order went out 300 people were reported to me as missing. Every servant who had changed her residence within two days, every wife who had gone to the country, every girl who had been sent out to boarding school was reported. The people were excited over the order. They wanted to know what it all meant and some came to me asking questions. Three hours and a half passed and along came a captain. "Chief," he said, "I think I know what you want. You want to locate Kate Stoddard." I said he was right and asked him what he knew of her. "Because," he replied, "I have found out where she resides. She lives on High Street." When Kate Stoddard was arrested, her keys were found in her possession and I had been carrying them around in my pocket for two days. I told the captain that I would go with him to the woman's house and I walked down there at once. The keys in my pocket fitted every door and we went in. When I entered her room I knew at once that she was the woman. There was writing all around, such as "Kate Stoddard and Charlie Goodrich." I sent for a locksmith and opened her trunks. There was all the property taken from Mr. Goodrich's house. Every word she had told me was true to the letter. There's where the loyalty of the captains came in. It would have been death to me to have made a failure. The community would have risen up against me for interference with personal rights. I don't think I could have lived in this city if it had been a non-success. This case is an example of your loyalty to me. I have tested your loyalty and I say to you that I will never forget you as long as I live.[124]

When he was interviewed again by the Brooklyn *Standard Union* eleven years later—and, as he would point out, just days after the death of W. W. Goodrich—it would also be the first case that he talked about, and he would add the detail that her refusal to reveal where she lived was made "persistently," and "in a cool, sneering way." [125]

In one of the two trunks in Kate's High Street room was Charles Goodrich's Danish-made gold watch, with a plain chain from which hung a seal incised with an old-English "G." Beside it was a gold ring that was set with a blood-red stone, and a pocket-book or wallet containing, by one count, $40, by another, just $16. [126]

Also here was what she was reported to have indicated was the murder weapon, a "plain, unnickeled revolver" with seven chambers, three of them said to be empty. As with the pistol that had lain beside the dead man's head, his father could not identify this one as his son's. [127] And the question of which gun, if either, had killed him would deepen in the coming days and would never be publicly resolved.

Every account seemed to add to the confusion. Captain McConnell was said to state that two pistols were in the trunk—and Kate would later repeat this. But it was again stated, as it had been on the week of the murder, that the gun found beside Goodrich was a match for his wounds, even though there had been no ballistic investigation. (An *Eagle* editorial, taking a poke at Coroner Whitehill for this, noted "the presence of the bullets yet in Charles Goodrich's head.") Then Kate told a reporter that the Degraw Street gun, now identified as a silver-plated Smith and Wesson, was indeed Charlie's gun, and that his father remembered an older one. [128]

In any case, there were also lots of letters in the trunk, some to or from men. It had been her habit, or compulsion, to correspond with strange men since she'd been in high school, when her preferred recipients had been soldiers. Eight of the letters now found were to, and five from, Charlie Goodrich, for whom her love was "so complete that I feel as if I were your own little child." And a diary, containing the story of her marriage to him in May 1872 and their subsequent stay at the Ashland House, New York. Her letters, which were partly in verse, sometimes addressed him as "my dearest husband." He wrote back that she should not call him that, and that "it is better for both that we should separate." [129]

Lover, poet, perhaps a lunatic.

There was a bunch of letters, too, from her 54-year-old mother in Plymouth, Massachusetts. The name of the daughter to whom they were addressed was Lizzie Lloyd King, born in Plymouth on May 27th, 1847.[130]

While Chief Campbell spoke publicly for that last time, in 1906, about Kate's extraordinary capture, High Street in the borough of Brooklyn was being all but obliterated to accommodate the extension of Flatbush Avenue as an approach to the proposed Manhattan Bridge. Today only one short block of High Street remains, between Adams and Jay Streets, and few New Yorkers would know that it exists were it not the name of the last stop on the "A" express subway line before it dips under the East River.

In 1873, No. 127 High Street was a building much like thousands that still stand in Brooklyn's northern and western neighborhoods—"a neat three story brick house, with basement and high stoop." It was on the next block from the one block that would survive, "between Jay and Bridge Streets, on the left hand side going down." East, that is, away from the river, and Kate's walk from there to the ferry had been just six-and-a half blocks along High and Fulton Streets.

The *Eagle*'s man walked up that stoop at midday on the day after her arrest became known, and found a silvery door-plate inscribed "A. Taylor." His ring was answered by "a tall handsome brunette"—these newspaper operatives had fortunate encounters with women. This was the landlady's daughter, Hanna Knight, who soon admitted him into "a neatly furnished parlor." The woman he had come to ask about was known to her was "Minnie Waltham," and she had lived there since mid-April, having apparently arrived as randomly as a stray cat: "My mother never let out any portion of the house before, and wouldn't have done so only to a lady as we thought she [was.]" And so they rented her a room for $2.50 a week. Just as the alias "Willoughby" had likely been borrowed from a street in Brooklyn, "Waltham" may well have been taken from a town in Massachusetts.

Their boarder had blended well into the household. Ms. Knight observed that she had dressed not expensively, but "with great taste," and "was always very clean; her room was always tidy." A "perfect lady in her manners," she had "evidently been brought up in good circumstances, from her speech and her deportment." She had rented and played a piano, and "she was fond of going to Beecher's church; she used to attend every Sunday regularly."

"We thought a good deal of her."

A popular brand of piano at the time was the Stoddard. And Elizabeth Drew Stoddard was a well-known New York novelist and poet, born in Mattapoisett, Massachusetts.

After having traveled to work each day for a month or six weeks, Kate had begun to take work home. She had never received a friend, or a letter. Mrs. Taylor, her daughter remembered, thought "that she had something on her mind, that she had seen trouble," but she had not talked about it. She had told them that her father lived in Trenton, New Jersey, and that her mother was dead.

"I remember a circumstance which we took no notice of at the time," added Ms. Knight, "but which has some bearing on the case now. My brother used to come occasionally and read for us. He is a good reader, and Miss Waltham liked to hear him. One day he was going to read about the Walworth murder, and she said: 'Oh, don't read that, I don't like to hear of murders!' On my mother wishing to hear it, and my brother to read it, she got up and left the room."[131]

As the trail of her life became known, it was found to be littered with "as many names as lovers." The "Amy G." that she had asked the chief to call her, and with which she had signed her letters to William and David Goodrich, could have stood for either "Goodrich" or "Gilmore." And this had become "Amy Marlowe"—"Amy" being favored, perhaps, for its root in "love." During a sad and wild stay in Attleboro Falls, Massachusetts in October 1867, she had presented herself as "Emma Chase."

She had left home suddenly the year before, as she was turning 19, and had arrived in that town looking worn and hard-up. She begged for work, and was hired as a domestic "out of pity for her destitute condition." Then she got a job in a braid factory, but left the town within a couple of months after she'd been caught stealing clothes from co-workers and a local store. She had claimed that she carried a pistol.[132]

She learned to make straw bonnets, and lived and worked at that and other jobs in a series of eastern cities: Philadelphia and neighboring Camden, New Jersey, where it was said she had taught school; Providence, Hartford, perhaps?[133] Then, at some uncertain date, New York. And Brooklyn.

Isaac and Harriet King did not know that their daughter was the long-sought Brooklyn murderess until July 15th, after the previous evening's train had carried this news to Plymouth. A *Herald* representative visited Mrs. King at her "tidy residence" just after she had heard. "The poor woman," who had already been suffering with neuralgia, lay groaning on the sofa and crying, "Oh, my poor Betsey! My poor Betsey!" Her daughter's first adventure in name-changing had been to opt for "Lizzie" over "Betsey," although it is clear that she had been named for her aunt Betsey W. King, who died in Plymouth, Massachusetts in 1846.

"Oh, I know she must have been crazy," said Harriet King at last. "I would rather have heard of her death than to know that she would do anything wrong if she knew it."

The Kings were regarded as "among the most respectable and honored citizens of the town," and the young Lizzie, or Betsey, had been "not only the belle, but the model of propriety." Mr. King, said to be employed as a mason, arrived home that evening and "was reluctant to believe it at first, but when he realized the terrible facts, he gave way entirely, and all efforts to administer comfort were in vain."[134]

An unnoticed irony attached to this jaunt to Plymouth was that W. W. Goodrich was a member of the Society of Mayflower Descendants.[135]

The Positions that They're In

When the long-interrupted Goodrich murder inquest resumed on July 12th, "a perspiring multitude" jammed the sidewalk on Joralemon Street to gain a glimpse at the prisoner alighting from a carriage beside Captain McConnell. Her care for her appearance being restored, she wore a plain, light-brown dress overfitted with a white bodice, and a straw bonnet that she might herself have made. Her "light, wavy" hair falling onto her shoulders, she "smiled pleasantly" at the sightseers. But to one reporter there was "a strange wild light beaming from her eyes" when she entered and sat in the coroner's office. Those eyes, according to another observer, were grey.

Moments later Billy Folk escorted into the room a tall woman whom the crowd recognized as Lucette Myers. "I don't think," she opined of the prisoner, "she is any more insane than I am, and I guess I'm sane enough."

General Jourdan was present, as were "nearly all the detective force, most of the sergeants and captains of the department . . . nearly every public official of the city or county, . . . a dozen of the best known lawyers in the city . . . numerous substantial men of business . . . three clergymen . . . half a dozen ladies," and, seated along two long tables, "one or more men" from "every published journal in either city." One of these writers supposed that this case was "discussed in every household in the land."

When Coroner Whitehill asked Kate—for so most commentators continued to call her—if she had counsel, she answered no, but insisted that she wanted "the best." He sent for the "handsome" Corporation Counsel William DeWitt, and the lady blushed when he spoke to her and agreed to represent her at the hearing.

Myers was the first witness, and she exchanged glares with Kate that were compared on both sides to those of a tigress. Kate's never subsided while Lucette remained on the stand.[136]

The moment was extraordinary, for the conjunction of these untrustworthy young women, bearing some facial resemblance, was an intriguing strain in this drawn-out murder story. It was not at all clear what, if any, the relationship between them had been, or how, if at all, it had involved the man who had died.

The newspapers, eager to sustain the mystery in the case, were trying to keep Lucette Myers's role in it alive. Three-and-a-half months after her theories about a shadowy crook called Roscoe had been exposed in this same courthouse as apparent inventions, the press still speculated about his involvement in the murder and his current whereabouts,[137] and reporters would continue to pursue him for months, as she continued to resurrect him. This day, when Alderman Richardson, the jury chairman, asked Lucette to lift her veil and see if she recognized one of the two pistols in the case, she complied and stated that she did, and that it was not Charles Goodrich's, but Roscoe's. Indeed.

Up stepped the anxious and tearful Miss Adeline Palm, known previously as the lady in ringlets, the presumed fiancée of Charles Goodrich. Collecting herself, she declared that she had seen the prisoner the year before, and that their common lover had told her that Kate was his sister from Brooklyn.[138]

Since Counselor DeWitt had prevailed upon his client to reveal nothing about her case, the only suspense in the room when the prisoner took the stand was what she would call herself.

"My name," she stated firmly, "is Lizzie Lloyd King."

The verdict tersely concluded that Charles Goodrich had been killed by "pistol-shot wounds in the head, inflicted by Lizzie Lloyd King, alias Kate Stoddard, with intent to cause death."[139]

Keeper Howard Conrady took her to Raymond Street, where at first she was calm, but soon reverted to her queer habit of singing and dancing about, then chatting "with much merriment" with the other women. The prevailing theory in the jail was that this prisoner, like Prince Hamlet in some views, was not mad but pretending to be.

Three inmates were assigned to watch her and head off any attempt at suicide. One of them was Fanny Hyde.[140]

Fanny, "looking better than ever," agreed to an interview.

"She seems careless," she said. "She doesn't seem to realize the position that she's in."

Fanny and Kate had sat and sung side-by-side at Sunday services, and, within a few days, would become fast friends who had "a fellow feeling" and walked and talked together "constantly" in the corridors and prison yard. Kate, it was said, "fairly loves Fanny," who told the press that Kate would not speak about her case, but had been writing a full account of it for her lawyers.[141]

Within a week, though, Kate turned abusive toward her young companion, and for Fanny's sake was removed to the witness room.[142]

Otherwise, the new inmate was remarkably well-treated, in part because donations had arrived to provide her with special provisions. A visitor to the jailhouse found one of the keepers carrying "a large watermelon under his arm," which, he explained, Kate had "expressed a wish" for, so he "went out and got her one." Her partiality to fresh milk was satisfied by the production of "the spotted cow in the yard."[143]

Although some commentators suspected the baneful influence of tawdry romantic fiction on her character-development, she apparently also had a taste for more salutary poetry, and to indulge this, Conrady dug up volumes of Shakespeare and Ossian from the prison library. The text she chose to read was a drama of passion, jealousy, and murder called *Othello*.[144]

While Kate read and prayed, the papers and the public battled about the state of her soul. Probably a majority of each was sympathetic to her. "A dozen newspapers," wrote the *Times*, "are endeavoring to sentimentalize away" her guilt, or "justifying murder as a means of redressing personal injuries." And, taking up the "gender" issues of the period, it added: "Most women know the difference between right and wrong, but in these days, when they are claiming all sort of rights, they should be willing to share also a few of the responsibilities of the wrong."[145] Again the *Herald* was attacked by other papers[146] as the purveyor of the front-page personal ads that brought together adventurers and dupes of both sexes.

Sympathizers, mostly female, mailed or carried letters to the prisoner and pressed at the prison gates in hope of seeing her. "Is she really pretty?" asked one, wanting to determine for herself. "A gang of small fry ward politicians presented themselves" and also bid to lay eyes on her. None was admitted. Others delivered money and bouquets, and someone a bunch of bananas. A Mr. Howard wrote to offer her books. "A. F. W." commiserated with her in atrocious verse.

Despite the attention, Kate "lost her buoyancy."

"Do you think they will hang me?" she asked a jailmate, and was assured that this was "hardly probable."[147]

On July 22nd, her father, Isaac King, came to her, accompanied by her older sister's husband and Mr. Orrin T. Gray, a lawyer based in Hyde Park, outside Boston. King was described as looking like "a respectable country gentleman, with partly gray hair and "a full, reddish beard." His daughter "fell on his neck and kissed him." They spoke alone for about three hours, and she played a tune for him on a melodeon. She sobbed about her "poor, poor mother."

King and his son-in-law returned to Boston on a five-o'clock boat, but Gray remained in Brooklyn and headed to the law offices of Lowe and Thompson in the Long Island Savings Bank building at Fulton Street and Boerum Place. Corporation Counsel DeWitt had handed the case to Enoch L. Lowe, while, it was said, taking responsibility for expenses.[148] Gray would assist them in gathering witnesses from Massachusetts.

Lowe was one leading Brooklyn attorney who did not wear a title earned in the Union army. A Democratic governor of Maryland in the early 1850s, he had later supported secession and fled to the South during the war. Afterward he'd returned to Maryland, but, unwilling to take the loyalty oath required to practice law there, he had moved in 1866 to Brooklyn, where he would live and work for the rest of his life.

An admired orator, Lowe had once delivered a lecture on "The Historical Destiny of Women." [149]

The withering relationship between the Republican, Irish-Protestant president of the Board of Police and Democratic, Irish-Catholic chief of police did not survive the Goodrich murder case. On August 21st, in an episode that was both very surprising and surprisingly amusing, the commissioners removed Campbell. But they did not exactly fire him. The terse note that he was handed that morning stated that his "services as Chief of Police would no longer be required, there being no such office existing in the City of Brooklyn." This was Newspeak 11 decades before 1984. The office no longer existed because the recently installed city charter had replaced the title of "chief" with that of "superintendent."

Campbell approached the commissioners with his usual equanimity. But when he stepped into their office he did not find Jourdan; only Daniel Briggs, Democrat, and the newly appointed Republican James Jensen, a Greenpoint porcelain-manufacturer whose knowledge of law-enforcement was nil. This contributed to the comic scene that followed.

The erstwhile chief asked Jensen if the order were immediately effective. "I believe it is," responded Jensen, who then asked Briggs to confirm this belief. But Briggs professed that he had "not the slightest idea," and he did not want "any part in the transaction."

Campbell, still addressing Jensen, conceded that, if the commission so wished, he was "prepared to go," but he wondered what should be done with "some very important information in my possession relative to the Goodrich and other cases. . . . Who will I give it to?"

An *Eagle* man who was present described Commissioner Jensen at this point as "rubbing his little Dutch head as if it were very much puzzled and exceedingly warm." (Jensen had actually been born in

Denmark, but there had always been more Dutchmen than Danes in Brooklyn.)

"'What are we to do?'" asked Jensen, "looking as if he had been caught in a remarkably tight corner."

"I am sure I don't know what you had better do," responded Briggs.

What Jensen decided to do was to withdraw the letter of dismissal, and "let this matter stand over until tomorrow, when General Jourdan will be here."[150]

And on that morrow a slightly longer letter was delivered to Campbell, removing him once more, informing him that "Uncle" John S. Folk was now acting superintendent. Jourdan was in the building, and willing to defend his motives. They were not, he began, political. "I always have," he insisted, "and do now consider him unequal to the position." Aside from mismanaging the Goodrich matter, he complained, Campbell had allowed gambling and prostitution to flourish in the city.[151]

The next day Commissioner Briggs was asked his opinion of Patrick Campbell and his "fitness for the office of Chief."

"I don't think," he replied emphatically, and as succinctly as Mr. Darcy proclaiming his admiration for Miss Bennett, "he has any superior in any city in the United States. He is especially adapted to the place."

Then followed a shuttling of opinions about the force's, and particularly, Campbell's, efficacy in capturing Kate Stoddard.

"A fortunate accident," stated Jourdan.

To which the deposed chief responded: "Now mark what an 'accident' this was. Mary Handley was hired by me to find Kate Stoddard, and was kept hunting for her until she found her. . . . Mary Handley had on that very day been pronounced useless by Commissioner Jourdan, and I had been told to discharge her. Suppose I had done so?"

Jourdan, he added, also had directed Detectives Folk, Videto and Corwin not to cooperate with Handley and himself. "The force," Campbell lamented, "had been set against me."[152]

Even the *Union* conceded that Campbell had been an "able, experienced and in many ways worthy public officer," as well as "courtesy incarnate." But it suggested that, as a politically active Democrat who had been appointed for that reason, he had nothing to complain about. Indeed he was "in no small measure responsible" for "the most frightful period of election frauds this city has ever known." And he had also "bungled" the case of Professor Panormo,[153.] the music instructor who'd been murdered on a Fort Greene street a few nights before Fanny Hyde had shot George Watson. Brooklyn police had locked up a wrong man as Panormo's attacker for six or seven weeks. And the crime would never be solved.

In September 1873, Charles Videto was also gone, a victim not of political bias but of an attack of jaundice that had struck him in the spring, the same season in which Handley and Campbell had been severely ill. The breakdown that led to his death at 43 was attributed by his family and co-workers to the wasting anguish and sleeplessness he had endured during the frustrating pursuit of the Goodrich killer, as well as the ridicule aroused by the delay and confusion in the process. The flags at Court and Livingston Streets were lowered to half-mast.[154]

E. W. MATSELL & CO., *TORS AND PROPRIETORS.*   NEW YORK, FEBRUARY 10, 1872.   Vol. XXVI---No. 1280   PRICE TEN CENT

THE CARNIVAL OF CRIME—FANNY HYDE, THE MURDERESS OF MR. WATSON, OF WILLIAMSBURGH, LONG ISLAND.

Figure 1. A portrait of 18-year-old Fanny Hyde, "murderess" of "Williams-burgh, Long Island," formed the full cover of The *National Police Gazette* on February 10th, 1872. (Courtesy of the New-York Historical Society)

Figure 2. A somewhat different depiction of Fanny Hyde. Why there are variant drawings of her, wearing the same clothes and poised in the same attitude, is a mystery. (Courtesy of murderbygaslight.com.)

George W. Watson

Figure 3. The only known image of George W. Watson, the hair-net manufacturer who was shot and killed on the stairway of his factory building where he worked, in Williamsburg, Brooklyn, on January 25th, 1872. This drawing appeared in a commercially published "Official Report of the Trial of Fanny Hyde." (Courtesy of Historical & Special Collections, Harvard Law School Library)

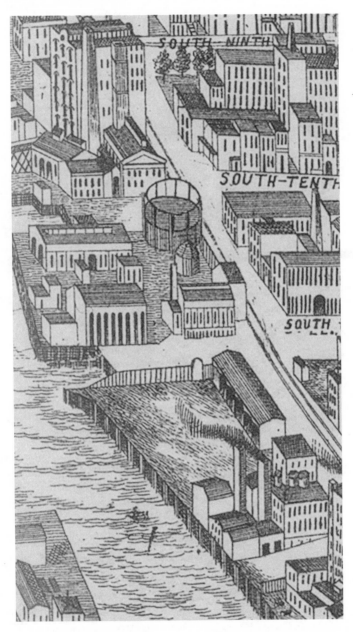

Figure 4. A close detail of an 1879 Galt and Hoy panoramic New York map (drafted by Will L. Taylor), showing an (imprecise) image of the Merrill Building at the corner of First and South 11th Streets (i.e., below South 10th), Williamsburg, Brooklyn, where George W. Watson was shot. Across the street are the works of the People's Gas Light Company. (Courtesy of the Library of Congress, Geography and Map Division)

THE HYDE-WATSON TRAGEDY IN BROOKLYN—SCENE IN THE FACTORY—THE TEMPTER AND THE SECRET RESOLUTION.

A FULTON STREET, NEW YORK, VICTIM WOUNDED AND GROPING HIS WAY IN THE DARK.
BROOKLYN HIGHWAYMEN AT WORK.

SUICIDE OF ALFRED EASTON, BROOKLYN.
THE MYSTERIOUS MURDER OF PANORMA—HE STAGGERS IN A STREET CAR, AFTER THE ATTACK ON HIM.

Figure 5. In February 1872, The *National Police Gazette* illustrated some recent deadly events in Brooklyn and New York. Among the scenes are, at center, George W. Watson, in the hours before his death, continuing his amorous pursuit of Fanny Hyde; at lower left, "Professor" John Panormo in a perilous state on a Brooklyn car after being attacked on the street; and, upper left, the suicide of Panormo's roommate, Alfred East. (Courtesy of the Collection of the New-York Historical Society)

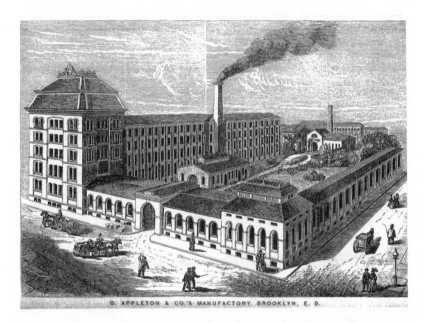

Figure 6. The Appleton & Co. book-bindery, where Henry Hyde, Fanny Hyde's husband, worked, at Kent Avenue and Hewes Street, Williamsburg. It was, *The New York Times* would write, "considered one of the most completely appointed binding and printing establishments in the world." (Courtesy of the Brooklyn Public Library, Brooklyn Collection)

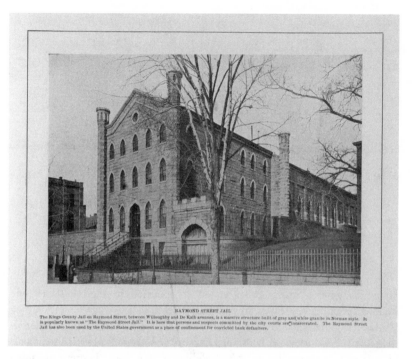

RAYMOND STREET JAIL

The Kings County Jail on Raymond Street, between Willoughby and De Kalb avenues, is a massive structure built of gray and white granite in Norman style. It is popularly known as "The Raymond Street Jail." It is here that persons and suspects committed by the city courts are incarcerated. The Raymond Street Jail has also been used by the United States government as a place of confinement for convicted bank defaulters.

Figure 7. The Kings County Jail in Brooklyn, known always as "The Raymond Street Jail," where "The Three Graces" were kept as they awaited their trials. This was how it looked before its expansion in the early 20th century. (Courtesy of Milstein Division of United States History, Local History & Genealogy, The New York Public Library, Astor, Lenox and Tilden Foundations)

Figure 8. Fulton Street, Brooklyn, as it appeared in the 1870s to one
walking or riding southwest toward City Hall and the Kings County Court
House, both designed by Gamaliel King. Oyster houses were popular in
the vicinity. (Courtesy of Milstein Division of United States History, Local
History & Genealogy, The New York Public Library, Astor, Lenox and Tilden
Foundations)

THE TRIAL OF MR. BEECHER—MR. MORRIS OPENING THE CASE FOR THE PLAINTIFF.

Figure 9. Samuel D. Morris defended Fanny Hyde against Winchester Britton, who had just replaced him as Kings County district attorney. In following months he headed a successful campaign to have Britton removed from office. He is depicted here, in the New York *Daily Graphic* of January 15th, 1875, presenting the opening argument for Theodore Tilton (behind him at left) in his adultery suit against Rev. Henry Ward Beecher (in second row at his right). (Courtesy of The New York Public Library and fultonhistory.com)

THE LATE WINCHESTER BRITTON.

Figure 10. Winchester Britton, the district attorney for Brooklyn who was elected, removed by the governor, and re-elected in the 1870s. He was involved in the cases of all the "Three Graces of Raymond Street." (Courtesy of fultonhistory.com)

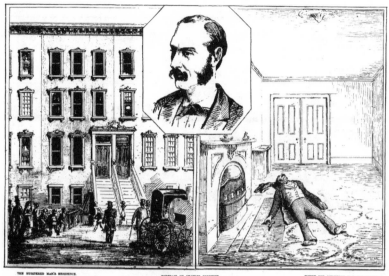

THE MURDERED MAN'S RESIDENCE.
PORTRAIT OF CHARLES GOODRICH.
WHERE THE MURDERED MAN WAS FOUND.

THE MYSTERIOUS MURDER IN BROOKLYN.

Figure 11. A *Daily Graphic* portrait of the late Charles Goodrich loomed over drawings of his brownstone house at 731 Degraw Street, South Brooklyn, and the basement room in which he was killed on March 21st, 1873. The case "occasioned more excitement in the city [of Brooklyn] than any thing of the kind reported in many years," and in the days following the discovery of the body a stream of curious citizens visited the scene. (Courtesy of The New York Public Library and fultonhistory.com)

A SUGGESTION FOR THE TIMES.

Figure 12. On March 26th, 1873, five days after Charles Goodrich was found murdered, The *Daily Graphic* commented pictorially and satirically about guns and violence in New York and Brooklyn. (Courtesy of The New York Public Library and fultonhistory.com)

PORTRAIT OF LUCETTE MYERS,

THE PRINCIPAL WITNESS IN THE GOODRICH MURDER CASE.

Figure 13. The *Daily Graphic*'s drawing of Lucette Myers, mischievous gadfly of the police. Some thought she resembled the woman known as "Kate Stoddard," the chief suspect in the murder of Charles Goodrich. (Courtesy of The New York Public Library and fultonhistory.com)

THE DAILY GRAPHIC, NEW YORK,

THE DWELLING PLACE OF LUCETTE MYERS THE WITNESS IN THE GOODRICH MURDER CASE

Figure 14. A Brooklyn reporter found the incarcerated Lucette Myers's family in a tenement building on Rivington Street in lower New York. Her five-year-old son asked the visitor if he knew where the boy's mother was and Lucette's mother complained that "no one knows the misery of the poor." This illustration is also from the *Daily Graphic*. (Courtesy of The New York Public Library and fultonhistory.com)

PATRICK CAMPBELL,
THE POPULAR, CAPABLE AND EFFICIENT POLICE SUPERINTENDENT OF THE CITY
OF CHURCHES, BROOKLYN, N. Y.

Figure 15. Brooklyn Police Chief Patrick Campbell was pictured in The *National Police Gazette* in 1889. His resourceful pursuit of the killer of Charles Goodrich and discovery of the evidence to indict her was unappreciated by the president of the police commission, who dismissed him. But Campbell would return to serve as, in the *Gazette*'s words, "the popular, capable and efficient police superintendent of the city of churches." (Courtesy of fultonhistory.com)

Figure 16. Brooklyn's ornate Fulton Ferry House was just two years old when it was photographed here in the summer of 1873, the season when Brooklyn's special police-agent Mary Handley, riding on a horsecar such as those depicted here, spotted and arranged the arrest of the woman she had known as Kate Stoddard. Under construction in the rear is the Brooklyn tower of "The Great East River Bridge." (Courtesy of Merlis/Brooklynpix.com)

LIZZIE LLOYD KING, ALIAS KATE STODDARD, "AMY G.," MINNIE WALTHAM, JESSIE WILLOUGHBY, THE CONFESSED MURDERESS OF "CHARLIE" GOODRICH, OF BROOKLYN, N. Y.

Figure 17. This portrait of Lizzie Lloyd King, known as "Kate Stoddard" and by many other names, appeared in *Frank Leslie's Illustrated Newspaper* on July 26th, 1873, and is likely the most accurate image of her. It shows the locket in which she was supposed to have saved Charles Goodrich's blood. (Courtesy of General Research Division, The New York Public Library, Astor, Lenox and Tilden Foundations)

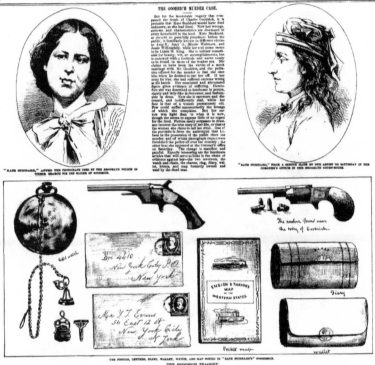

Figure 18. After Kate Stoddard's arrest, the *Daily Graphic* assembled this tableau, including: top right, an artist's rendition of her made during the coroner's inquiry; top left, a pen-and-ink reproduction of the bogus photograph of Kate Stoddard that Police Commissioner James Jourdan believed to be genuine; and, bottom, articles found on her person when she was arrested, and in her trunk at High Street, downtown Brooklyn. They include letters to two potential paramours, Charles Goodrich's ring, watch and wallet. The map of Western states and the gun at the right were found at the scene of his killing. (Courtesy of the New York Public Library and fultonhistory.com)

Figure 19. Thomas Kinsella, Irish-born editor of *The Brooklyn Daily Eagle* and a one-term Congressman. While he commented on "coarse and commonplace lust," in his city, he was himself deeply immersed in an adulterous liaison. (Courtesy of the Brooklyn Public Library, Brooklyn Collection)

Figure 20. Henry C. Bowen, publisher of *The Brooklyn Daily Union* and the Congregational Protestant *Independent*. He was a bitter political and religious ally of *Eagle* editor Thomas Kinsella and a close observer of the moral behavior of Kinsella and Henry Ward Beecher, at whose trial he is shown here. (Courtesy of Milstein Division of United States History, Local History & Genealogy, The New York Public Library, Astor, Lenox and Tilden Foundations)

MRS. SARAH MERRIGAN, THE ALLEGED MURDERESS OF MAGGIE HAMILL.

[FROM A SKETCH BY OUR ARTIST.]

Figure 21. The pleasant-featured and pleasant-natured Sarah Merrigan, as depicted in the *Daily Graphic*. "Few would recognize" her, it was written, as the woman who had been "tried for one of the most dreadful crimes on record." (Courtesy of the New York Public Library and fultonhistory.com)

THE DAILY GRAPHIC

AN ILLUSTRATED EVENING NEWSPAPER.
39 & 41 PARK PLACE.

VOL. VII.   All the News.   NEW YORK, TUESDAY, MARCH 2, 1875. $12 Per Year in Advance.   NO. 617.
Four Editions Daily.   Single Copies, Five Cents.

THE TRIAL OF REV. HENRY WARD BEECHER.
GENERAL B. F. TRACY OPENING FOR THE DEFENDANT.

Figure 22. Ex-U.S. Attorney, Republican leader, Medal-of-Honor-winner and future Navy Secretary, Benjamin Franklin Tracy was one of the City of Brooklyn's most distinguished citizens. He is pictured here as a defender of Henry Ward Beecher, who appears at the right. At the same time Tracy was preparing his second defense of Sarah Merrigan. The drawing, on the front page of the *Graphic*, was by Thomas Nast. (Courtesy of the New York Public Library and fultonhistory.com)

JUDGE CALVIN E. PRATT.

Figure 23. Judge Calvin E. Pratt, who presided over Sarah Merrigan's second trial. He was one of several significant Brooklyn legal figures in the last third of the nineteenth century who had served as Civil War generals. (Courtesy of the Brooklyn Public Library, Brooklyn Collection)

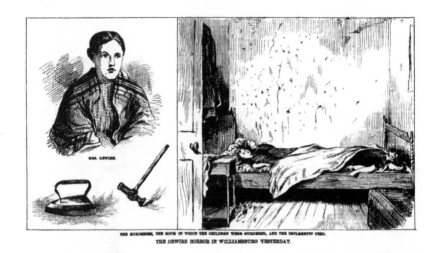

THE MURDERESS, THE ROOM IN WHICH THE CHILDREN WERE MURDERED, AND THE IMPLEMENTS USED.

THE DEWIRE HORROR IN WILLIAMSBURG YESTERDAY.

Figure 24. Mary Ann Dwyer, her weapons and the scene of the slaughter at North Eight Street on June 3rd, 1874. Her insanity was never in doubt. (Courtesy of fultonhistory.com)

4

Three Graces

Sarah and Maggie: A Very Strange Ending

Late on a warm September morning four days before the death of Charles Videto, Margaret Hamill made a fateful visit to her great friend Sarah Merrigan and her two small children at her apartment several blocks inland from the scene of George Watson's killing.

The women had met when the adolescent Sarah Dougherty, considering a religious vocation, had traveled to what is now Bronx Borough to consult with a nun at a boarding-school of the Ursuline Sisters, and was impressed by Margaret, who was about ten years her senior and studying to enter that order. When Sarah learned that Margaret had left the Ursulines, she enrolled instead at the Convent of Our Lady of Charity of the Good Shepherd at the foot of E. 90th Street in New York. And there again she found "Maggie," once more a novice nun. This would be called a coincidence; something seemed to bind them, and Maggie, Sarah would say, became the only "confidential friend . . . I ever had in my life."[1]

In the late summer of 1873 they were years removed from convent life. Sarah was married to James Merrigan and the mother of two small children. Margaret, who lived at 236 West 48th Street, New York, had inherited money from her father, and drew an income from rents on residential property that he had left to her and her brothers.[2] She was named godmother of Sarah's boy who had been born around November of 1872, and the women regularly visited each other, Maggie sometimes bringing gifts of baby-clothes. They browsed together at New York's Broadway picture-galleries,[3] and they discovered a new enthusiasm to fill the gap of religious piety that they had lost. It was an interest connected to the superstition that haunted the edges of Irish-Catholic devotion, particularly after the famine. Anxious about their futures, they became disciples of fortunetelling, and their fervor for it intensified as the year 1873 wore on.[4]

One day that summer a gypsy named Bertha, without apparent knowledge of Sarah's preoccupations, came to her door at 199 Ninth Street—now Rodney Street—Williamsburg, "selling fancy pincushions." When Sarah declined to buy, Bertha offered to tell her fortune. Sarah agreed, and was presented with a performance such as she had never imagined. The woman directed her to stand on a chair, then "measured my head with a tape measure, also my forehead, the length of my temples, around my neck, my feet, and across the muscles of my arm; I removed part of my clothing; she marked the measurements down on a piece of paper . . . she measured my toes, and looked at them, on each foot; the feet were measured last, if I remember. . . ."

The peculiarity of this method was not as important as the outcome: "I felt that she had told me more of the truth than the others had done."[5] Bertha told her that she was very intelligent and that, despite facing such troubles as would kill another person, she would live to be very old, for she had the disposition to overcome them. She was not one who concerned herself with the things of this world.[6] The gypsy also told her that she was pregnant, which Sarah did not think she was.[7] But it was true.

Bertha came a second time to perform this fantastic ritual, and Sarah told Maggie Hamill about it while they were on their way to visit another fortuneteller in Manhattan. It was on Maggie's mind the next time she came to 199 Ninth Street, at about eleven o'clock on the morning of Tuesday, September 2nd.

Sarah prepared a light lunch. They talked about the "children, about fortune tellers and about Bertha . . . Miss Hamill said she had spent so much money on fortune tellers, and was not satisfied; she asked me to tell how Bertha told fortunes." So Sarah repeated the procedure as best she could remember it, intending to write down the measurements and give the results to Bertha. She had no tape-measure, so she took a clothesline out of a laundry-basket. Maggie removed her shoes and stood on a chair before the door leading to the inner room, and Sarah, beginning, as Bertha had, at the subject's head, marked the measurements on the rope with pins. For some reason, Maggie determined that the best way to keep the rope steady, or to keep the two sides of it that hung down from interfering with each other, was to tie it around her neck and fling it over the door.

She was just about to finish—measuring Maggie's feet—when they heard someone at the apartment door. Matilda Knowles would confirm that she came by on that day; what would not be certain was that she had arrived at just this moment. When she did appear, Maggie was alarmed, and whispered, "Don't let anyone see how foolish we are."[8] So Sarah stepped outside onto the landing and, in Mrs. Knowles's memory, "excused herself for not admitting me into the apartment, as she said Miss Hamill was there, overcome with grief, as her brothers wanted to cheat her out of $5,000." Mrs. Knowles's daughter had had some photos taken and had just returned with them, and the visitor asked Sarah to come look at them.[9] Sarah agreed, and would state, with notable specificity, that she was gone from her apartment for "about 17 minutes." She told Mrs. Knowles that she was concerned that she was leaving her friend wait for too long.[10]

Here clarity ebbs into mystery. What happened during that supposed interval—and whether or not, indeed, Maggie had stayed in that very odd position for that length of time—is impossible to know.

Mrs. Knowles next saw Sarah that night about ten, when Sarah came to her door and mentioned that "Miss Hamill had gone, and she [Sarah] was lonely." The following morning, Wednesday, Sarah stopped by again, bearing a red morocco reticule that she wanted to give to Mrs. Knowles's daughter. This seemed to be the same bag that Sarah Kipp, the Merrigans' downstairs neighbor, had seen Maggie Hamill carrying into the building the previous morning. Mrs. Kipp also saw Sarah several times that Wednesday, coming and going from their building. Once, when they met in the yard, Sarah told her that she was feeling very sick, and she sat down and vomited. "She seemed very nervous, and in perspiration," added Mrs. Kipp. Another time Sarah mentioned that she intended to move downstairs, into an apartment across from the Kipps', because she "wanted more room and better company . . . more company." That night the Merrigans stayed at Sarah's parents' house.[11]

David Coe, "a musician with DeWitt's band," was engaged to Mrs. Kipp's daughter and at that time living with them. Coe saw Sarah Merrigan on Thursday morning, sitting on the front steps of their building. She complained again of being sick, and "looked pale and distressed." On Thursday evening Sarah approached two boys in the street and asked if they would help her move some things from the second- to the first-floor apartment. They came by half-an-hour later and brought down some boxes, chairs, a sewing machine and a few other things. It was a warm night. She asked if they drank beer; not surprisingly, they said they did, and she sent one of them out to buy three pints—one for each of them. She told the boys that her husband was at "the lodge," and she didn't like to be alone, that "she was afraid and the priest at the Mission told her not to be so." She paid the boys 75 cents.[12]

Coe came home that night about nine o'clock, "sat down to write," and "heard something fall in Mrs. Merrigan's room." He then heard Sarah rushing down the stairs. Mrs. Guldner, the German land-lady who lived in the front building, looked out the window and noticed Sarah coming across the yard, with her baby in her arms, and, at about the same time, smoke coming out of the Merrigans' window. She took Sarah's key, and Sarah, who had been screaming, shouted to her, and to Mrs. Kipp and Mr. Coe, who had also appeared, "Don't go in; there is kerosene burning there!" She put her hand on Coe's shoulder. The fall he had heard may have been a kerosene lamp.

He had drawn a pail of water from a hydrant, and replied, "I will go in!"

"I went up and tried the door and it was locked. Mrs. Guldner brought the key and unlocked the door; I could not see the blaze except in the next room; I poured the water on the blaze and went out again; the third time I could not go into the room because of the smoke; I took a ladder and went in by the window; the blinds were tied with a piece of clothes line; I tore them off and threw them down in the yard and got in; then I saw the bed burning; I pulled it [the mattress] off and threw it out of the window."

On the exposed slats at the bottom the of the bed was the body of a woman, nearly naked, her head hanging from the side of the bed near the door. The head and the upper portion of the torso were blackened; and "below it was as white as snow." Around her neck, a doctor who was called found "a rope, apparently a piece of clothes line"; it was "doubled in the middle, and the ends passed through forming a loop." The rope had been newly cut with a sharp instrument, and "was drawn tight."[13]

A Sealed Confession?

She had been a child of the Irish-famine diaspora, born Sarah Cecilia Dougherty in 1850 in what was still the Village of Williamsburgh.[14] The great potato-blight had lasted then for five hellish years, and had driven the hungry in hundreds of thousands to American ports from places like Donegal, her parents' hard, beautiful county in the northwest corner of the country.

Eighteen-fifty is also the year at which the historian Emmet Larkin placed the beginning of Ireland's "devotional revolution," a phenomenon driven in part by a national search for solace and deliverance in the wake of the famine's horror. This period, which extended to about 1875, was marked by a sharp growth in religious observance and practice, made possible by an extraordinary increase in the number of Catholic priests and nuns—especially nuns, whose presence more than doubled during the 1860s and 1870s.[15]

That was in Ireland. But Ireland was also in America now, especially in New York. By 1870, nearly 300,000 residents of New York and Brooklyn were Irish-born.[16] The dioceses of both cities were led by native-Irish bishops, and well-served by Irish priests and by the nuns and brothers who operated orphanages, hospitals and schools.

Sarah Dougherty attended one of those schools, Saints Peter and Paul, run by a parish that still functions in Williamsburg, and where the long-serving pastor in her day was the well-known and controversial champion of the poor, Father Sylvester Malone. Daughter of illiterate parents, she was a very well-educated Catholic girl for her time, studying there and at St. Joseph's Academy in the same neighborhood until she was 17.[17] Neighbors would remember her as a mild-mannered, well-behaved girl, but she became so devout that her parents were alarmed, particularly her father, Daniel, who would tell of her "religious delusions," of her spending "one-third of her time" praying, reading holy books, visiting churches and serving at a Catholic hospital. In Hoboken, New Jersey, she discovered a church that she thought "resembled the church the Virgin Mary worshiped in." She borrowed money from her mother and gave it to charity, and "she took the shoes off her feet one day and gave them to a poor woman."[18] She was destined to enlist in those prolific ranks of sisters.

The convent she and Margaret Hamill entered was the New York home of a French-based international order of sisters whose mission, according to an old *Catholic Encyclopedia*, was "to provide a shelter for girls and women of dissolute habits, who wish to do penance for their iniquities and lead a truly Christian life."[19] But some seed falls on shallow ground and withers away, and some falls among thorns. Although she had taken the vows that professed her as a nun, Margaret Hamill left about two years later, after her father, Peter, an iron merchant, had died. It was said that she wanted to marry, and, with her inheritance and income, she would have had prospects.

She went to work for the family, gathering rents. But she missed Sarah, and sent her letters that were delivered secretly by visitors to the convent. She exhorted her great friend also to leave, and within about six months Sarah did. She had not yet sworn her vows, and she told the mother superior that she did not feel fit for the sisterhood.[20]

The period that followed was the first of several in which Sarah was known to have been sick. There is no report of what the ailment was, and at that time few would have considered it "psychosomatic." But it was called severe, and, while it lasted, she was visited repeatedly by James Merrigan, an Irish-born ship's carpenter and stair-builder. On October 17th, 1870, she married him, and they took rooms on the same street, North Fourth, on which she had been born. She was 20; he was 21.

By winter she was pregnant, and during the early months became what she would call "delicate." At about ten o'clock on the night of May 27th, 1871, she was found wandering and distracted in the street by a policeman, who took her to the Sixth Precinct station-house, where the interviewing officer described her as "in a state of stupor, unable to walk," with "a vacancy of look and a wild stare." A similar episode occurred during either that or a second pregnancy, when she again strayed out and got lost in the Williamsburg streets. Her father found her a few blocks from home about half-past-two one morning. "I don't know where I'm going," she told him, and she was still "senseless" after he got her home. On a Sunday morning in the spring of 1872, when another patrolman approached her on a corner of Grand Street, she fell into his arms and was unconscious for 15 minutes. One cop described what happened to her as a "fit." She was indeed epileptic, for Daniel Dougherty remembered another day when she fell off a chair, "grinding her teeth and froth[ing] on one side of her mouth." She also suffered severe headaches.[21]

It was odd that Maggie did not attend the Merrigans' wedding, but at some point her and Sarah's relationship fully resumed. Maggie had money but was unmarried. Sarah was married, but, despite her husband's mastery of a useful trade, complained of being poor. Indeed, more than one person who knew the Merrigans commented that Sarah nagged her husband about the meanness of their condition compared to Maggie's.

The apartment at 199 Ninth Street, was the Merrigans' third—two-rooms for nine dollars a month[22] on the second floor of a frame, rear tenement-building near North Second Street, now Metropolitan Avenue. At that site today the Brooklyn-Queens Expressway rushes by.

Matilda Knowles, a neighbor on Ninth Street, also had a taste for fortunetelling and shared Sarah's interest in playing policy-numbers and consulting supposed psychics who could predict results. "Policy and money," said Mrs. Knowles of Sarah, "seemed to be her ideal."[23] One August day they consulted for this purpose "Madame La Rosa" on Canal Street, New York.

The madame would remember Sarah clearly:

> She was anxious to win money in playing policy; she seemed very much excited and nervous; I talked with her and advised her not to play; she asked me if a friend would leave her any money, and told me about her family affairs; she was very much affected in mind, and affected me . . . I advised her to pray; I observed that she was in a peculiar mental condition; I was never so affected before. . . .
>
> "Mrs. Merrigan," she added, "expressed a strong desire to be in better circumstances, to go in good society."[24]

Sarah agreed that she had been "greatly frightened"[25] that day, and, with Matilda Knowles beside her, she did find a church and prayed. But, Mrs. Knowles would remember, this was just one episode in an a disturbing summer-long drama:

> After she went to live in the rear of No. 199, I noticed a change in Mrs. Merrigan's appearance. She became more

untidy in her dress, so much so that the landlord asked me not to let her stand at my door; she was also morose and silent, so much so that my daughter remarked it and the neighbors spoke of it.[26]

A drawing of Sarah Merrigan at this period[27] shows a profile of a dark-haired young woman whose face is full, pleasant, but unexceptional, with soft nose and lips. But several months later a reporter found her more impressive than the artist had:

> She is a well built woman, perhaps weighing 140 pounds, and her figure is neatly proportioned, the only inconsistency being the size of her head, which is not quite in proper ratio to the rest of her physique. Her face is a remarkably prepossessing one, and it wears a shifting succession of smiles. Her forehead is rather low, but quite broad, and her hair and eyes are black as those of a Spaniard. Her teeth are exceptionally good, and as she laughs and talks, she shows them very pleasantly."[28]

"Prepossessing" was also the term that another journalist used to describe a ferrotype portrait of Margaret Hamill. In it she was smartly dressed in dark silk and linen, and wore a straw hat trimmed in velvet. Her "large, dark, dreamy eyes, delicate nose, and rather large mouth, chin slightly square and firm, indicate the owner to have been a woman of character."[29]

If Sarah Merrigan had set the fire beneath the corpse of Margaret Hamill, it had failed in its purpose. David Coe's little pail of water had sufficed to quench the bit of it that remained in the bedroom. Another pailful took care of a blaze in the closet, and there was nothing for the firemen to put out when they arrived minutes later. By then Coe had returned downstairs, where he met James Merrigan, who was concerned about the condition of his tool-chest.

"The fire is all out now," Coe told him. And then: "There is a dead person up there—burnt to death."

James told him that he was "mistaken—that there was nobody up in his rooms."

Mary Jane Knowles, Matilda's daughter, met Sarah, "very much excited" on the sidewalk. She gave Mary Jane her baby boy to hold, and picked him up later at the Knowles's apartment.[30] In no place is there a mention of the whereabouts of the child's older sister.

Police Officer Edmund Brown arrived about 9:30, saw the body, and an hour later, in the company of Captain Cornelius Woglom, arrested James and Sarah Merrigan at the apartment of James's sister, Margaret Walsh, across Ninth Street at the corner of North Second. On the way to the Fourth Street station-house Sarah told him a story. Maggie Hamill, she explained, had arrived at her house drunk and had asked for coffee. Sarah went out to get some, and "she supposed Miss Hamill had upset the kerosene lamp."[31] It was a tale she would tell some version of again.

A local doctor, the same Samuel Brady who had been summoned to attend to George Watson, and coroner John Parker were called to the death scene. Brady confirmed that there had been two "distinct" fires. Why? And if, as Sarah claimed, Maggie had set one, who had set the other? He believed, from the swelling he observed on the body's face and neck, and from foaming about the mouth, that the victim had been dead before the fire. Her full tongue protruded, and the only clothing he mentioned were "portions" of her dress remaining on her right arm. Parker, even with Brady present and exhorting him to be cautious, removed the rope from the neck "with some little effort," laid the body in a coffin and delivered it to his premises on Union Avenue. The next morning Brady found the rope from which the noose had been cut, but, although the rooms still reeked of kerosene, there was no sign of a broken lamp.

Dr. Joseph Creamer, the police surgeon, performed a postmortem that morning at Parker's. He judged Maggie Hamill to have been dead then for about three-and-a-half days, or since Tuesday afternoon, and he swore "most positively" that she had been strangled. It could have been done by a person of ordinary strength, and even "a woman of somewhat delicate health" could have lifted the body onto the bed. He did "not think it at all possible that deceased had committed suicide."[32]

Captain Woglom also heard Sarah's story of Maggie's arrival, and would remember that, after her arrest Thursday night, Sarah was "in a terrible state; could hardly walk and was very white," absent-minded, vacant. "When I talked to her, sometimes she would not know what I was saying to her." In her cell later, though, she did provide him with a bunch of keys, which included those to Maggie's apartment and her trunks. "She did not," he said, "say where she got them," and she would not or could not tell him where Maggie had lived. There was talk that she had stolen things from Maggie, and perhaps others, in the past,[33] and he wanted to know if she had taken jewelry from her friend's body, or from her rooms after her death.

On Saturday, although she was still "very feeble and sick" he interviewed her in his office for several hours. She stuck to her story about Thursday, adding that Maggie had come to Ninth Street about four o'clock that afternoon, and would tell him nothing else. Woglom, whom a journalist would years later remember as a man who "would give a beggar a quarter rather than arrest him," told Sarah that he "would do what [he] could for her," that he "had a family and knew what a father's feelings were; I might have said that I would be a father to her." This would be considered an improper inducement. Moreover, there was no witness to their discussion, so what she told him thereafter would not be admitted as testimony. This seemed a serious oversight by the old Chief of Williamsburg, for several papers reported she had confessed to the killing. He could reveal, though, that she finally gave him Maggie's address, and that he went over to West 48th Street and opened her trunks, a dresser and "other things." There was jewelry there,[34] which proved that Sarah had not taken everything. But it was not proof that she had not taken anything.

On that Saturday the scorched remains of Margaret Hamill were laid to rest in Calvary Cemetery, a Catholic burial-ground just across the Brooklyn border in Queens County. But there had been no church service, no priest to bless the body of the one-time nun. Her two brothers occupied the only coach that followed her hearse, and an inscription on her rosewood casket stated that she had died at age 33.[35]

The Merrigans would be tried separately and had different lawyers. Sarah's was Patrick Keady, who had also been first at the side of Fanny Hyde a year-and-a-half earlier. His interest in the case, and in Sarah particularly, was personal—in part, no doubt, because he, like the Doughertys, had been born in the west of Ireland. Having lived through the famine as a child and come to New York in the 1850s, he was now 33, a bachelor who had been Brooklyn's fire marshal, a rather ironic position under the circumstances. He had been a reporter for the original New York *Daily News*, a two-term Democratic assemblyman and a lawyer only since 1869.[36] He believed that Sarah was innocent, and would not only defend her for free but also put "hundreds of dollars" of his own into the cause.[37]

And what of James? Dr. Creamer had indicated that the crime could have been accomplished without his involvement. But the *Eagle*, after ruminating about the way that a woman, "whom an errant spider throws into convulsions," can nonetheless "commit the most thorough and complete murders," wondered how this "unusually hideous" killing could have been perpetrated by Sarah alone.[38] And the inquest that began in the district courtroom on the evening of Monday, September 8th, raised lingering questions about his possible role. The downstairs neighbor, Sarah Kipp, the sort of neighbor who notices much, testified that at about three o'clock she heard a man's voice exclaim, "Stand back, damn you!" and the female response, "It's mine—mine."[39] Her repeat of this recollection and her additional testimony would bear strongly on the case.

Matilda Knowles also heard a female voice when she came by on Tuesday, saying, "We must have" or "will have a separation."[40]

But a following session would provide James with alibis. A parade of workingmen with Irish names testified to having been with him on Tuesday afternoon and Thursday evening. He was employed that week on various stair-building jobs in the neighborhood, and two men swore that he was by their side until after four on Tuesday. Four more had been in his company at the monthly meeting of the St. Patrick's Mutual Alliance at a local Masonic temple—what Sarah had called "the lodge"—from just past eight to just past nine on Thursday.

James declared on the stand that he had worked ten hours on Tuesday and got home at 20 minutes past 7. He took supper, and noticed nothing amiss. The bedroom door was open, but he did not go in. His story, however, opened some vulnerable ground regarding his possible compliance in a cover-up. He would insist that for 48 hours he had been unaware that a decaying corpse lay beneath the mattress of his own bed, and that he had agreed, without suspicion, to stay with his wife two nights during that period in other people's homes.

On Tuesday evening, after supper, the Merrigans had gone to Sarah's parents' house. When they returned to their own building at about 10:30, she told James that she had left her keys behind, which may have been part of a scheme to keep her husband out of their grimly laden bed. Sarah suggested staying with the Walshes, across the street, rather than retrieving the key at the Doughertys, a few blocks away. Unlikely? Margaret Walsh stated: "Mr. Merrigan was very much vexed about it, saying he was so tired, he had a good mind to lie down in the lots."[41] Regarding the next night, Mrs. Cecilia Dougherty testified: "She remained at my house with her husband all night on Wednesday night only; she was sick and had Dr. Van Bradie attending upon her; Merrigan expressed a desire to go home that night but my daughter refused to go on account of her sickness." Given the inconsistency of name-recording in the newspapers of the day, this again was probably Dr. Samuel (or Sam) Brady.

Even if Maggie had caused her own death, accidentally or intentionally, it is clear that Sarah feared that if the grisly evidence was discovered, she would be suspected of murder. It is feasible that she schemed to prevent her husband's finding it, but hard to believe that when, as he testified, he finally entered his bedroom on Thursday night, he found "no change whatever" from its usual state, and had no idea "that a dead body was in the room"[42]—it was two days dead, and likely by then to stink like Lazarus. In fact, a foul smell was plainly detected shortly afterward by both the moving-boys that Sarah hired. When one of them remarked on it, she explained that her cat had carried a piece of meat in there. The other remembered that she had said that she had decided to move because she had come home and discovered that smell after being away for some days.[43]

At the inquest's end on the night of September 11th, Coroner Whitehill discharged James Merrigan, and his jury found that Sarah had strangled Margaret Hamill to death on Tuesday, September 2nd. Brooklyn's latest female murder suspect, while she and her lawyer still claimed her innocence, was returned to the Kings County Jail.[44]

Under the heading "The Three Graces of Raymond Street," the *Brooklyn Eagle* commented:

It is a matter not altogether unworthy of a little consideration that there are in this single city of Brooklyn, in peril of judicial strangulation, three delicate and feeble women, all under charge of willful murder. Mrs. Fanny Hyde, who in a moment of that emotional insanity so eloquently and so similarly diagnosed by the Hon. Daniel Voorhis and the Hon. Samuel Morris, perforated her quondam affinity, Mr. George Watson; Miss Kate Stoddard, Minnie Waltham, Jesse Willoughby, Amy Snow, Amy G., Lizzie Lloyd King, or whatever her actual name may be, who summarily evicted Mr. Charles Goodrich from certain fleshly and residential premises on Degraw Street; and finally Mrs. Merrigan, who, in the most approved style, relieved her friend, Miss Hamill, of that dipsomaniac appetite which surprisingly facilitated the operation—all these three fair slayers of their kind run the risk of being turned over by some unsympathetic jury to the strangulatory offices of the hangman. There is not another city of our size in all these United States which can rival this unique showing. There is probably no other community of eight hundred thousand [?] souls in the world which can exhibit, as the perpetrators of three extraordinarily revolting homicides, three of the meagrest and meekest looking women in the country. . . .[45]

Sarah, Kate, and Lucette of Raymond Street

In fact, the Three Graces never quite resided at Raymond Street at the same time, for on the day between Maggie Hamill's arrival at 199 Ninth Street and the discovery of her blackened corpse Fanny Hyde was released on bail. The judge had decided after all that she had shuffled off to Washington on Sam Morris's advice.[46] And the *Eagle* had commented on this development in its keenest tones of sarcasm. It now awaited the day "not far distant" when "the devil will get his due" and receive sympathy "as a much abused, greatly misunderstood and long suffering saint." It also expected that Kate Stoddard would only "have to linger yet a little before the time of her full compensation will come."[47] Meanwhile, the deficiency of one female resident would be supplied.

During her first month or so in prison, Kate, that able word-smith, had completed her "pamphlet" recounting the death of Charles

Goodrich. The title with which she labeled it, "What I Know About the Goodrich Tragedy," was a clear hint to the world that she hadn't caused it.

Her first adjustment of previously provided facts was that Charles was indeed alive on the stormy night of March 20th when she came "home" to 731 Degraw Street. After they dined together, he left for a nearby business meeting and returned at 10 o'clock. Leaving him reading the *New York Times*, she went to bed, slept for a couple of hours, and was awakened by gunshots. When she rushed downstairs, "Charlie was lying upon the floor with his own silver plated revolver near his feet. . . . I took his head immediately in my arms. I pressed my lips to his. His mouth was quite warm. . . . As I held him in my arms his face grew chilled and cold as marble. I never saw anyone die, and did not know it when he was dead."

She placed his boots, which he had removed, under his head. It was 2 a.m.:

> I sat down by his side and talked to him for hours, and sang in a low, contented murmur, "Now may the grace, mercy and peace of Our Lord and Saviour Jesus Christ remain and abide with you forever. Amen." Although he was lying there dead, and cold as marble, yet I think he heard every word I said to him. He looked happy. The room seemed filled with a deep peace. The quiet of the house was to me a holy quiet. Outside the rain fell heavily. I felt protected by the storm. The skies wept for me when I could not weep.

And so on. She collected his blood in a cup "that [she] had always drank [her] chocolate out of," washed his face, took his ring, watch and wallet as mementoes of him, and left in the bright dawn of six o'clock. When she returned that evening to the New York side of the Fulton Ferry, she became suspicious that cops were looking there for her. So she went back to a room she had at 204 E. 42nd Street. She "knew he had killed himself,"[48] she concluded, but she did not seem to know why. And she neglected to mention that she had laid him out in fine clothing.

Kate did not receive Sarah at all well at Raymond Street. When, on the night she arrived, Sarah offered her a cup of tea, Kate "curled her lips and turned away from" her. Sarah "tried to be pleasant with her after that, but it was no use. When I would call her Kate she would turn around sharply and say, 'I want you to understand that my name is Mrs. Goodrich, and I'll thank you to call me that and nothing else.' Then she would walk away and begin talking to herself."

Sarah, as the rope-wielding Bertha had determined, was pregnant when she entered the jail, but she miscarried about six weeks later. All the while, her baby boy stayed with her, and one night when it was teething and crying, Kate "sprang from her bed and shouted, 'Mrs. Merrigan, Mrs. Merrigan, have I got to be disturbed by that brat?'" But for that she did apologize.

Keeper Stinson would recall that Kate continually addressed Sarah "You contemptible Irish plague."

"Oh, you've no idea," Sarah would report, "of the scenes that we have had together. They would fill a good sized book, and make quite interesting reading."

To Stinson, Sarah was "the best behaved prisoner in the jail." She did not "give the slightest trouble," and was "grateful for what she receive[d]."

"We are all treated well here," Sarah explained. "I have nothing to complain about and neither has she, only she wants to put on airs and give the keepers trouble."[49] Although Kate reserved her fiercest animus for Sarah, demanding to be sent to another floor to be away from her, she was also "disturbing and insulting" to the other inmates. And she was haunted by night terrors, once upsetting the whole jail with her early-morning shrieks.[50]

One of the other inmates was Lucette Myers, back for a return engagement, occupying the witness cell lately vacated by her nemesis, and displaying a similar surliness, while the nemesis expressed resentment.[51] A visitor stated that Lucette was kept there "in solitary confinement," seeing no one but the person who brought her meals.[52]

She had been detained again because the grand jury that would indict Kate Stoddard had assembled, and Lucette, to the astonishment of some observers, was still regarded seriously as an informant. Her response to this treatment was a new burst of creativity that further flummoxed and embarrassed Brooklyn's guardians. The day after resettling at Raymond Street she gave her full account to a man from the *Graphic* of what really happened on Degraw Street. She now developed the character "Beach," who had signed the original letter about her to Chief Campbell, and was a buddy of Roscoe's who had hovered with him around her apartment. On the Monday before the murder Lucette had overheard Roscoe and Kate plotting to "fix matters" with Goodrich, who had offended them both, on Thursday night. The resourceful Agent Myers went to Brooklyn, made an impression of Charlie's lock, and on Thursday, having warned him to no avail, donned men's clothes (and smoked a cigar to complete the effect) and enlisted Beach to head with her back to Degraw Street, enter with her new key and hide in a downstairs closet. There she heard the Kate-Charlie quarrel—"This is the last time you'll leave me to visit any ———!"—then two shots, then someone entering the room, then a third shot. The last had been delivered by Roscoe, who, after Lucette, unable to stay still, had emerged from hiding, threatened to perforate her if she squealed.[53] She really was a pretty good dime-novelist.

More: The *Union* scored a long interview Dr. Park, to whom Lucette had given the same story, with variations. (While in drag, she picked up a woman and escorted her to a midtown saloon, where Lucette smoked the cigar and got sick.)

Park had re-emerged to participate in the climax and dénouement of the Lucette Myers story. Lucette in fact did become ill in jail, and in mid-October Park convinced Jourdan to release her so that, one, the good doctor could take care of her, and, two, Lucette could renew the pursuit of Roscoe and Beach—which, she had told the credulous Park, she had new means of managing. It was said that Park even provided her with new teeth. So out she came, and a week or so later got a fellow collared who was no more Beach than the soap-salesman at the inquest had been the wicked Roscoe.[54] After two more non-Beaches had been brought into headquarters, and another non-Roscoe had been fingered at Blackwell's Island Penitentiary, the scales at last dropped from Dr. Park's and General Jourdan's eyes.

"Lucette's story of the murder," she told the paper, "and the circumstances which led to it, was told with such an air of truth that no one could doubt it who heard it, and if it was false she is the most consummate actress that ever lived. But I cannot imagine what motive she could have for making up such a story, as it could only cause her trouble. . . . I must confess that she is a mystery to me."[55]

The drolly deceived General Jourdan now had no doubt about her falsity, and supposed that she had "expected when arrested to make some money. In that, however, she miscalculated, though she has cost us something."[56] She had also cost something to more than a few compassionate citizens who had donated various sums to her and her hard-up parents. He then called her "the biggest liar I ever met." And from the other side of the political divide the *Eagle* dipped, as it often did, into Shakespeare's *dramatis personae* and labeled the commissioner and board president "Dogberry."[57]

She answered, "Oh, dear no! (laughing and smoothing her dress), I know no more about it than old General Jourdan does." (Jourdan was 41.)

Why, then, had she spun those tales?

"You see, I'm fond of fun. I'm full of deviltry at times, and I feel as though I must get rid of it."

She giggled again when he asked about Roscoe. She knew a man by that name—the toiletry-merchant, apparently—"But, bless you, he knows nothing about the Goodrich case."

Beach? She hadn't seen him in years. And she knew nothing about a man who had been falsely identified as him. She explained that, having become tired of the detectives hounding her to produce someone, "I said to myself, 'I'll point out a man to you, my gentlemen!' and I did." Her amusement overflowed when she was told that this man "is going to take out an action for false imprisonment, or to have the detectives arrested for assault and battery."

" 'Is he? Oh, how funny!' and she laughed with great glee."

She said that she knew she had been wrong, and was "very sorry" for what she had done, but she continued in a tone of delight, revealing that she had planned her own role in the affair.

"I myself wrote the letter which attracted the attention of the authorities. I wrote, saying that if they wanted to find the murderer in the Goodrich case they must find one Lucette Myers, living at such a place. I thought it would be good fun and stir things up. I never intended to carry it so far."

She claimed then, most likely retreating into her habitual inventiveness, that Dr. Park had encouraged her to weave stories for Richardson and Jourdan to help stimulate interest in her medical-cum-electrical practice.

Jourdan? " 'He's a fussy old fool, and don't amount to anything. I can't help laughing at their going to prosecute him for having the man I pointed out as Beach arrested.' (She put her hand to her face and laughed for half a minute.)"

How long had she known Kate Stoddard?

"I never saw her in my life until I saw her in the Station House, after she was arrested."

"Did you ever see Charles Goodrich?"

"I never saw him, that I know of."

She wrote a letter to D.A. Britton, appealing for her release, and he recognized the handwriting as the same as that in the original letter about her signed by "Beach." Britton declared that he had never believed her, but it had been his responsibility to keep her as a witness when she stood by her story even after he charged her with deception. He conceded, though, that she was one of a kind:

> She lied for the mere love of lying, and I think with her it may be the mania of a mind oddly constructed, unbalanced by a love of notoriety, and unchecked by any moral principle whatever. . . . I trust I will never see her or another like her during the rest of my professional life.

On November 20th he moved that the court release her, and it did. As she left the judge's room, heading for the Greene and Gates Avenue line to Fulton Ferry, "she was laughing immoderately."[58]

On October 5th, James Merrigan had been re-arrested[59] and scheduled to be tried, after all. He, Sarah and Kate were all arraigned on October 7th, along with Cortland Sprague, the city treasurer accused of embezzlement. When an officer directed Kate to get dressed quickly for court, she informed him that she would need two hours, and appeared in an indigo dress with bow and white ruffles, a blue-velvet hat and lavender kid gloves. Sarah wore a black dress observed to be "rusty and much worn," a gray shawl and a straw hat. She held her little girl, just turning two, in her arms, and the child, while her parents pled "not guilty," looked about and smiled at the large audience. Governor Lowe, standing for Kate, explained that he was still waiting for his colleagues in Boston to pull together defense testimony, so he and his partner, D. B. Thompson, were not ready for trial.[60]

A crowd followed Sarah and Kate back to Raymond Street. They were interested mainly in Kate, who remained a criminal celebrity, and "whose face everybody desired to look at."[61]

The two alleged fair slayers would wait and wait to be turned over to a jury. Kate's lawyers had received a commission from the court to search for witnesses not only in Massachusetts but also in Connecticut. And it became known that humble Sarah Merrigan had won the services of an attorney as distinguished as the former Maryland governor, and more so—Benjamin Franklin Tracy, who had agreed to join Patrick Keady in Sarah's defense. He told the court that the little studying he had been able to do had impressed him that further investigation was warranted and quite possibly would establish that no crime had been committed at the Merrigan apartment.[62] Britton was patient with these appeals, but got the court to schedule both trials for the first half of December. Neither would begin that month.

On that same day, Judge Jasper W. Gilbert, with Britton's assent, granted a motion to admit James Merrigan once more to bail. The price was $2,500, the same as for Fanny Hyde.[63]

Kate granted an interview to the *Union* in November, in which she stated quite lucidly that she had never confessed to the murder of the man she continued to call her husband, and revealed that the wedding date had been her 25th birthday—May 27th, 1872. She rhapsodized again about the hours she had spent beside her beloved's corpse, his open eyes aglow with a "heavenly look." And yes, she had attended his funeral, and "was the last to leave the sidewalk when his coffin was placed in the hearse."[64]

Tall, slim, and trimly bearded, Benjamin F. Tracy at 43 was in the very middle of a greatly achieved life. Born and raised in the upstate town in Owego, he had in his 20s been one of the founders—or *the* founder, he liked to claim—of New York State's Republican Party. His distinction as a brigadier general and regiment leader in the Wilderness Campaign would earn him a belated Congressional Medal of Honor. After the war, still in his mid-30s, he had been appointed U.S. attorney for New York's Eastern District, and he developed political clout as one of those "Three Graces" of the Kings County Republican party. After being nominated, then withdrawing as his party's candidate for Brooklyn mayor in 1881, he would become a justice of the Court of Appeals, New York State's highest bench. Then in 1889 President Benjamin Harrison would appoint him secretary of the navy. He may have seemed an unlikely candidate, but he would be one of the most influential holders of the post in the country's history. He built the first steel battle-fleet, in a partnership with business magnates that was effectively the start of the military-industrial complex. The modernization and reform he and his allies achieved lifted the United States to the status of a world naval power, proven shortly after his term by convincing victories in the Spanish-American war. Those triumphs helped to earn him the accolade of "father of the fighting navy."[65]

For Sarah Merrigan's sake, though, it was more important that it was said of his legal acumen "he was seldom defeated in a case which he fully and maturely prepared." And as he prepared to defend her, the Democratic *Eagle* called him "a worker, a man of great ability, and a lawyer of learning."[66] But his workload would cost Sarah more time. Such was his prestige that Winchester Britton, as he prepared the case against Sarah, employed him to defend against Samuel Morris's impeachment plot.

The district attorney's political ordeal lasted all year. In March 1873 Governor Dix asked him to respond to the list of charges against him, and he denied them all.[67] Dix, in no hurry to act, eventually appointed a referee, who held hearings in December above a restaurant on Washington Street, Brooklyn. They went on for two weeks, and there were some lively moments when Morris himself stood up to interrogate Britton.[68] As charges and counter-charges were batted back and forth, the *Eagle* became fed up with it all, and actually embarrassed for its city: "the men from Albany . . . laugh at our folly in thus exposing our domestic differences and internal disagreements."[69]

Was it funny, though, when two boys visited Morris at his home and presented him with a box of cigars, a supposed New Year present, that concealed an "infernal machine" (a nineteenth-century circumlocution for "bomb")? The recipient claimed that he prevented its detonation by drowning it in his bathtub, but others, including Britton, judged it to be dead on arrival because it had been manufactured in Morris's own camp.[70]

The ruling came at last on February 20th. Governor Dix removed Britton only on the basis of failing to investigate embezzlement charges against the city collector.[71] Most lawyers in the city considered this to be, in Morris's favorite phrase, "too thin,"[72] and the political historian

Harold Syrett's best guess about Dix's decision was that he "probably fear[ed] that a civil war was about to break out in Kings County."[73]

Morris's ally, A. C. Davis, whom Britton portrayed as a lush, approached Sam Morris in a county courtroom, whispered to him, and Morris "arose with a radiant smile on his face." He asked the judge for an adjournment, and said to Davis: "I could no more try a case today, after the joyful news, than I could fly." Then they left the courthouse together, leaving the strong implication that they were headed to a saloon.[74]

More delay. The man whom Dix appointed to succeed Britton broke down physically during his failing prosecution of the city treasurer and resigned, to be replaced in May by Republican John Winslow,[75] who at last would try Sarah Merrigan. But the postscript of the story would be written in November 1874, when Britton was re-elected by a wider margin than in the tainted and endlessly controversial year of 1871.[76]

Both Raymond Street prisoners complained of their long detention, and it became known in early March that Kate was upset about more than that. She had fired all her lawyers.

Her particular animus was against the Boston lawyer, O. T. Gray, whom her father had hired, and who Kate suspected was gathering evidence that she was insane. She had composed a blistering letter to her father in December:

> If you have been so foolish as to pay O. F. [sic] Gray four hundred dollars for his services, you will have the satisfaction of knowing that you might as well have thrown the money into the fire for all the benefit it will ever do me. . . . My case does not require any witnesses from Massachusetts to testify on my behalf. My own statements will clear me if anything can. . . . You say you will not come to trial unless you are compelled to come to court. . . . If you, or Augusta, [her sister] or her husband, or any of my relations come to the trial, I hope you will all break your necks getting here if you attempt getting here after what I had said. . . . I hope you will never have another word

to say to Mr. Gray, I will never speak to him again unless it is to insult him.

A few weeks later she wrote to "Counsellors Lowe and Thompson," and stated that she was parting with them "with the deepest regret," because they had not written two letters she had asked them to write, to her father and to Gray, directing his dismissal. In early January she wrote to them again, rescinding her decision to let them go, but on March 3rd, D. B. Thompson appealed to Judge Gilbert to allow his firm to withdraw from the case, "because since that time she has continued a course of conduct which has greatly embarrassed us."

"Oh, I cannot let you do that," Gilbert responded. ". . . Why not have a preliminary investigation to decide whether she is in a condition to be tried. If she is a sane woman, then she may be tried. You will therefore consider yourselves as acting for this woman by order of the Court."

"The defense," explained Thompson, "is not that she is insane at the present time, but that she was at the time of the offense, if any was committed by her."[77]

Temporary insanity, once again.

That spring, while Kate took up artwork and predicted she would soon be free, Sarah's sufferings reached an awful new patch. Her 16-month-old boy, her "only comfort" in the jailhouse, died in April. She was not allowed to attend his funeral.

"It seems to me I would not feel so bad as I do," she told a visitor, "if I could have been there to see it when it died." And, "Oh, if I could have been there to see its little body laid in the grave!"[78]

She did not mention that she had just endured another seizure, which had been witnessed by a keeper. "There were convulsions," this woman reported, "twitching of the arms and legs; it took three or four people to hold her on the bed; she was unconscious for some time; her eyes looked wild; it was two hours before she came to; and she was weak."[79]

A few days after this attack, Dr. Charles Corey, the well-remembered witness in the Fanny Hyde trial, arrived at Raymond Street again to interview Sarah and Kate. Corey, being cautious, would not reveal his findings, and would wait to compare his observations with those of others.[80] Sarah bristled when asked if she intended to plead that she was mentally ill:

"Why, the idea! I'm not insane at all, and never was. The only thing that I've done that's been insane is waiting here so long without a trial; I ought just to have made a row about it and demanded a trial before this, that's what I ought to have done."[81]

Kate? What had been revealed about her tortured life indicated an unsound mind to some, but employees at the jail continued to suspect that her wild behavior there was a "dodge."[82]

Both trials were expected to begin at last in June, but only Sarah got to court that month. And when she did, on the 19th, General Tracy was in Albany, arguing a case in the Court of Appeals, and Keady was accompanied now by Tracy's brother-in law, Isaac Catlin. D.A. Winslow reacted with sarcasm, remarking that it appeared that "unless General Tracy is in town, justice must stop." The equally annoyed judge was Calvin E. Pratt—no close relation to Charles Pratt, but yet another Civil War general, wounded during the Seven Days—who directed that Tracy be telegraphed for.

When he arrived at last the next morning, Tracy petitioned for further delay. He explained that, despite Mrs. Merrigan's recent protestations, he intended to mount an insanity defense, and an important medical witness was out of state and could not be located. He had also learned that "several of the men relatives of the defendant have been confined in a lunatic asylum, in Londonderry, Ireland," and he needed to arrange for persons with knowledge of this fact to arrive from other states.

"This is getting to be a very solemn scene," lamented Winslow. The judge agreed to postpone the trial until October.[83]

Meanwhile, a significant legislative development was occurring that would alter the futures of many troubled New Yorkers and bear on the fate of Lizzie Lloyd King, also known as Kate Stoddard.

≈

Brooklyn's Lesser Scandal, Continued

The opening question of the year, therefore, not alone for Brooklyn, but for the whole United States, is a question of sexual immorality!

—The *Brooklyn Sunday Sun*, January 3rd, 1875

Although hardly an editor in the country dared to avoid the Beecher-Tilton controversy, there was a clear parting of minds regarding the coverage of other sexual scandals, such as the divorce of Thomas and Emeline Field and the continuation of Emeline's romance with Thomas Kinsella. New York's *Times* and *Herald* barely touched these developments, and the three established Brooklyn papers, Kinsella's included, handled them gingerly. That would not have been the case if Henry Bowen, whose *Union* had blown the lid off the Field-Kinsella affair, had not sold the paper in October 1873 to a group of fellow Republicans, including Benjamin Tracy and Controller Frederick Schroeder.[84] But the new *Union* expressed "regret that a former proprietor of the paper saw fit to make public details in reference to the case under consideration which should never have been printed."[85]

The New York *Sun*, however, deemed the Field-Kinsella news as fit to print, and, dubbing it "Brooklyn's Lesser Scandal,"[86] was glad to soak up the juice of Thomas Field's suits of divorce against his wife and against Kinsella for damages. The cases came simultaneously before City Court Judge Joseph Neilson in December 1874, just as he was also preparing to hear Tilton versus Beecher.

Kinsella agreed to pay $15,000 to Field, which would be used for the benefit of Emeline, and he would not contest his nomination as co-respondent in the divorce case.[87] But, showing once more that everyone in Brooklyn had an ax to grind, Field stipulated that she would receive the interest and any other income from the money while she lived, but that after her death the principal would be donated to a public charity known as the "Kinsella Fund," which Field declared would be "an enduring monument to the man's infamy," and, by one report, would be dedicated to "the reclamation of fallen women."[88]

Observing all this, Emeline didn't want the money. And that was the least of it. Kinsella's new paper, The *Brooklyn Sunday Sun*, published the scorching letter that she sent to her husband when she learned of his intention.

> I have again and again told you, as explicitly as was necessary, that Mr. Kinsella never seduced me. . . . I would, as you very well know, starve in the public streets before I touch a dollar of money gained under such circumstances. . . . Since nothing is left that you *can deprive* me of, leave me the poor satisfaction of believing that I have

not spent the best years of my girlhood and youth with a man lost to all sense of manhood.[89]

It is likely that Kinsella had his hand in this composition, for, whoever had seduced whom, the love-affair continued. And some tasty details of its history were produced at a December 29th hearing, at which Field testified that, when he visited his wife in November 1873 at a cottage in Lake George, New York, he discovered "a number of letters from Kinsella, making appointments and containing many expressions of love and devotion."[90]

Field hired a detective, who learned that several hotel managers and employees around the resort towns of Lake George and Glens Falls had spotted Tom and Emeline. On more than one register Kinsella had mischievously written himself down as "Kingsley"—as in William C. Kingsley, a rich Brooklyn contractor, beneficiary of its Democratic party, major promoter of and profiteer from the East River Bridge, and Kinsella's partner in both the *Eagle* and *Sunday Sun*. And the recorded name of a woman traveling with the couple, "Mrs. Henry R. Stiles," seemed to have been another inside joke, since that would have been the wife of the distinguished Brooklyn physician and editor of a multi-volume history of the city. But it actually was she. One of Kinsella's letters mentioned his acquaintance with her at this time, and the Stileses had a home in Lake George for years.

Wherever they stopped they ordered refreshments such as milk punches, brandy, and pints of Piper-Heidsieck champagne.[91]

The *Sun* later published excerpts from the Kinsella letters that Field had extracted from his wife's trunk:

And you want me to tell you that I love you. Don't it spoil it to be asked to? . . . I do love you, and there is no way of stopping it, despite the fact that every gossip who meddles with our affairs, thinks there is.

. . . I hate to have you out of Brooklyn, and yet I am free to say I dread what may follow your return, if affairs remain where they are, and we attempt to see each other.

. . . Then I got angry [at Field], and wound up by asserting that in the opinion of all men, my life was worth a hundred such as his, and that it was not for me to get out of the way.

He wrote about the mixing of their liaison with the miasma of scandal and litigation that was blowing around the Brooklyn of their day, including Henry Bowen's libel suit against him and the *Eagle*, and Bowen's role in the Beecher-Tilton matter:

> It need give you no trouble. . . . Bowen loves money so well that he would hardly spend it in this way. . . . The suit can be settled. Bowen is only too anxious. I have got him on the hip. Beecher has had an interview with me, and showed me Bowen's denial of the charges against him. It is complete and emphatic. With this in my possession, I can show that Bowen is a self-confessed slanderer. I have not done with him. He must sell his paper and get out of sight in Brooklyn; and I think that he has come to that conclusion. . . .

Indeed he had. Elsewhere Kinsella returned to "that wretched day at Olmstead's," and blamed the spilling of events there on the Republican politician William Booth, who had been present in the hotel parlor.[92]

The decision of Referee Greenwood, to whom Judge Neilson had assigned the "criminal conversation" suit, stated, in part:

> I . . . find that the defendant debauched and carnally knew and had illicit intercourse with said Emeline Field . . . and alienated and destroyed the affection of the said Emeline for her husband, the said plaintiff; and thereby destroyed the peace and comfort of the said plaintiff and deprived him of the comfort, society and assistance of his said wife.

And the plaintiff, as agreed, was entitled to receive $15,000 from the defendant.[93] In a courtroom around the corner, the Beecher-Tilton jury was being impaneled.

Kinsella revealed that he intended to appeal the case and gain a public trial.[94] But that didn't happen.

The divorce did, but not before a nasty quarrel erupted between the parties regarding the custody of their child. When they conferred in Greenwood's office, Thomas demanded that the girl would live with him. Her mother would be allowed to see her, but not at his home. Nor did he want Ada to be taken anywhere where Emeline's lover was present.

"Is that your decision then?" she asked.

"It is."

"Then, sir, I will kill you!"[95]

That didn't happen, either.

Women and The Law

... but why will you say that I am mad?

—Edgar Allan Poe

A Fourth Grace

About Mary Ann Dwyer's madness there was never any doubt. "A Crazy Mother"[1] was one of the headlines that introduced her to the public. And the day after her arrest a medical doctor who interviewed her in her precinct cell concluded that she had "been insane for some time," that "she had no definite or rational idea of the crime or its nature" when it was committed, and was "not legally responsible."[2]

Born in Ireland probably in 1846, as the famine grew blackest, she arrived in New York at 17 and, in October 1866, married Michael Dwyer, a Williamsburg cooper about 20 years her elder. In six years she bore four children, three of whom—Maggie, seven; Jimmy, four, and Timothy, a year and nine months—were alive at the start of June 1874.[3]

Michael was a member of the United Association of Coopers, who that spring, as the depression that followed "The Panic of 1873" gripped hard, had been locked out by the principal oil-refiners in New York and New Jersey. Williamsburg was one of the hubs of this industry, being home to Charles Pratt's famous Astral Oil Works, which was about to be incorporated into the Standard Oil Company. The neighborhood was also the country's largest sugar-refining area, another industry that packed its product in barrels.

On the night of Monday, June 1ˢᵗ, Michael Dwyer attended a union meeting in Williamsburg,[4] and—depending on whether one credited the *New York Times* or the Irish-edited *Eagle*—either stayed out and got drunk and returned home in the morning, or went home and got up early. Home was three rooms on the second floor of a three-story brick tenement at 35 North Eighth Street, hard by the river, amid the smells of coal gas and oil smoke, across the street from the Dick and Meyer sugar refinery and a block north of a massive cooperage. There he sat reading a paper in the early light before 6 a.m. when a co-worker named Owen Murphy knocked on the door. Murphy was bucking the union and going to work, and expected his friend to come with him. Michael had told his wife that he would go, but now he said no, not yet—maybe in a few days.[5]

Mary Ann was also up; Murphy, who knew her well, could hear her moving about.[6] She was thought to be generally placid and easy-natured. "She was very kind to her children," a neighbor, Mrs. Slavin, said of her, "and used to keep them as clean as wax dolls. They never cried or anything like that."[7] A "better woman never lived,"[8] said her husband.

Yet there were storms amid the calm, and this June morning she grew furious at her husband. She would give reporters a sample of what she said to him: "Do you think my children and me could all starve to death just because [of] his plagued old societies and unions and tomfoolery of that sort? If other people are willing to starve, I'm not, and that is all there is about it, now I tell you."[9]

The Slavins, an older couple, lived on the same floor as the Dwyers, in adjoining rooms. Thomas Slavin was eating his breakfast at 6:30 when he heard a man shout. Mary, his wife, opened the door between the apartments, and Dwyer, still in his underwear, "rushed into the room. His head was bleeding, and he said: 'Oh, murder, Mrs. Slavin, I'm killed!' And he stooped down his head and I saw that he had been mashed at the back of his head."

Mary Ann had struck him twice with his cooper's hammer, and soon followed him through the door, ready to swing it again. As she lifted her weapon, Slavin "ran at her and gave the hammer a sudden twist, and it fell to the ground, and I pushed her to the door, and got my knee against the door and pushed her out."

" 'If you want to hit people,' " he shouted at her, " 'you must stay where you belong.' "

Mary Slavin wrapped a cloth around his head, and Thomas was anxious to get him to a doctor, but concerned about his scanty covering—"he had a pair of red drawers on and his shirt; he had no pantaloons on." So he went next door and yelled, "For God's sake, Mrs. Dwyer, give me a pair of pants and don't let your husband go into the street in his drawers." She "got a pair from somewhere and pitched them on the floor." But Michael never put them on, for Sergeant Fielding of the Fifth Precinct soon found him "coming up North Sixth Street, in his drawers and shirt, bareheaded."

Nothing amusing happened after that.

Fielding sent him to a doctor on the next block, and hurried to the address that Dwyer had given him. He caught Mary Ann just as she was about to leave, dressed for the late spring morning in a shawl and a red woolen hat. He asked if she were Mrs. Dwyer.

"Yes."

"Do you know that you've hurt your husband badly?"

"Yes, and it serves him right. He won't work and we will get put out for non-payment of rent."

"Where are your children?"

"In there asleep," she answered. She was "pointing to the dark bed room."

"Where are you going?"

"I'm going off."

"You will have to come with me to the station house."

"All right."

He escorted her outside and, as they walked away, he asked her if she had any friends who could mind the kids.

"No," she said, "they do not want any minding; they are in heaven, where I hope I am going to meet them."

He had been joined by an Officer Landry, whom he told "to take the woman a minute, and I ran upstairs to see the children. In the bedroom I pulled off the quilt which was partially covering them . . . and saw their heads all covered with blood; I felt for their pulse and could find none."

He asked her what she had done it with. "Smoothing irons," she said. He found one of them on a table, and Captain Woglom the other on the stove. She told Fielding that "one of the children, Maggie, spoke when she struck it. She said that it said, 'Oh, mamma.' "[10]

In her precinct cell she recounted to the press that she had attacked the baby first, and that she thought "he cried quite hard, but it didn't last long." Maggie was second—"She told me many times she wanted to go to heaven. . . . Then I took Jimmy. He woke up and moaned, so I turned him over and let the blood run out of his head faster. They were good children."

I can honestly say," she explained, "that I feel a comfort to know that my children are in heaven. Wasn't it the Lord who sent down His only Son to die? Well, I took the lives of my children, but it was for their souls' sake. . . . I have often felt like killing myself, and I knew that if I went first, and left them behind me, they would never reach heaven. You see, Sir, my husband wouldn't go to work. I warned him to go, and yet he persisted. And my brain is not quite right sometimes, and that's the way it happened."[11]

Outside the police station a crowd of hundreds, including "women with babies in their arms," gathered and vainly sought to get a look at the prisoner. "It was remarked in conversation," wrote the *Graphic*, which printed a drawing of a youthful, oval-faced Mary Ann Dwyer in her shawl, "that it seemed as if Brooklyn had given birth to a race of female murderers."[12]

Again a woman's madness was attributed to the wanton effects of reproduction. When he examined her the next day, Dr. William DeLong found that her first deranged episode had occurred "after the birth of her second child, when she was said to have had the typhus fever and was sent to the Flatbush Hospital." Over three months she had quarreled "with everybody" and "flung bottles at nurses' heads." So she was placed in the adjacent asylum. But he believed that what really affected her was not typhus but "puerperal fever" (caused by post-partum placental infection), "attended with mania." Over the six months before the killings, symptoms of insanity had returned. She would wake in the night and see "imaginary men, devils, etc., who were there to injure her and her children." Michael tried to laugh these illusions away, but "this idea of starvation, induced by her husband's refusal to seek employment, caused a sudden and violent reaction."[13]

The inquest began in the presence of the children's bodies at Parker's Union Avenue funeral parlor, where Maggie Hamill had also lain, and continued the next day at Coroner Whitehill's office, in the presence of the hammer and flatirons. The children were buried in one casket, the two younger ones lying on Maggie's arms, on Thursday, June 4th, at Calvary Cemetery. The expense was paid by Charles Pratt, the oilman for whom Michael Dwyer would not work without his union's blessing.[14]

Michael had been admitted to the Fourth Street Hospital, where he was attended by the omnipresent Dr. Samuel Brady. His skull fractured, Michael had at first not been expected to survive, and was administered the last rites of the Church, but on the morning of the burial Brady spoke optimistically of his recovery.[15]

When the inquest was adjourned that afternoon, the case of Mary Ann Dwyer was delivered to "the commission on lunacy,"[16] which had never happened before in New York State.

Since 1872 the New York State Legislature had been weighing proposals to strengthen the law establishing the conditions under which a person could be admitted to and detained in an insane asylum. The impetus for reform was said to have spread from England, where it had been galvanized by Charles Reade's vivid novel *Very Hard Cash*. In '73 a bill to this effect passed the Assembly but was voted down in the Senate, and the initiative's failure was attributed to opposition by proprietors of private asylums. In January '74, Queens Assemblyman L. Bradford Prince introduced the bill that would finally become law.[17]

The primary intent of the bill was to ensure that persons committed and kept for insanity were really insane, but it also provided for criminals to be assigned to asylums without being found insane in jury trials. Prince was concerned about a process so loosely regulated that physicians were being bribed 25 or 50 dollars, often by family-members of those assigned, to sign certificates of commitment.[18] With the endorsement of two state-licensed physicians, a person could have someone committed by swearing before two justices of the peace that he or she had observed certain conditions of insanity in that person. And once one got locked inside, it was much more difficult to get him or her out.

The new law still required the sworn statements of two physicians, but stiffened their necessary credentials, in regard to character, education, experience, and expertise in mental health. They would be required to examine the appointed person and to state on a formal certificate to the state commission of lunacy the grounds for their conclusions. This evidence would be presented within ten days to a "justice of a court of record" of a given county or district, who could then conduct his own inquiry.[19]

These guidelines then extended to the criminal courts in cases of persons accused of arson, murder, or attempted murder, including those under indictment who were thought to be insane and those who had been acquitted on the ground of insanity. The county judge could call witnesses and a jury and enlist the aid of the district attorney, "and if it is satisfactorily proved that such person is insane, said judge may discharge such person from imprisonment and order his safe custody and removal to one of the State lunatic asylums . . . where such person shall remain until restored to his right mind."[20]

The law did not take effect until weeks after its passage in May 1874, apparently because Governor Dix did not immediately sign it, and the Kings County clerk received his official copy on June 21st.[21] So the Dwyer proceedings had actually begun under the old rules and would resume under the new ones.

At Raymond Street, Kate reacted even more strongly to Mary Ann than she had to that Irish plague Sarah Merrigan. When the Fourth Grace took her place in Kate's corridor, the latter "became almost convulsed with rage" and soon became so sick, or apparently so, that a doctor was called to her.[22]

Whitehill reopened the inquest on July 8th, and the two medical experts who testified were the familiar Dr. Charles Corey and Dr. Carlos MacDonald, who had determined that the prisoner "was suffering from puerperal insanity, induced by a low diet and giving too much nourishment to her third child." She still believed that she had done "a creditable thing" in slaughtering her children and sending them to heaven. Moreover, she had inherited her madness from her mother.

That news had just come from Ireland, brought by Essie Cahill, Mary Ann's sister, who'd had the misfortune of arriving in Brooklyn just a month before the massacre of her niece and nephews, and had lived for a while with the Dwyers. She took the stand and described her mother's delusional behavior and her "insane" religious devotion. Michael Dwyer spoke not only of his wife's already known episode of dementia after the birth of their second child, but also of her being "out of her mind when her last child was born."

The jury took but a few minutes to conclude that Mary Ann Dwyer had killed her children. Then they added what might theretofore have been determined by a trial jury: "we are of the opinion that she was insane at the time of the commission of the act."[23]

She would come back to the courthouse the following Monday to hear her fate from a county judge, and Kate Stoddard would come with her.

Last Words

"Do you think I'm insane?"

Kate wore a yellow gown, and the reporter thought she looked better than when she'd first arrived at Raymond Street nearly a year earlier.

"I do not," he answered, although he was not at all convinced of that.

"No, certainly not; and no one else would."

In states of tantrum she would break things, and it was revealed that three female attendants had struck for higher wages to endure and subdue her "almost unruly temper."[24]

Under the insanity law of 1874 the medical doctors would have their say about her condition in the Kings County Court House on Monday, July 13th, 1874. And so would many others.

That morning was warm, and the *Times* found Judge Henry A. Moore's crowded courtroom—"one of the worst ventilated apartments used for public purposes, either in New-York or Brooklyn"—to be "unendurable." In the audience nonetheless were many lawyers who wanted to observe an historic hearing, and the deposed Patrick Campbell was also there. Lizzie Lloyd King and Mary Ann Dwyer entered together and sat beside each other behind the jury-box. Lizzie, or Kate, wore a silk dress of black and blue stripes, a beribboned and feathered "jaunty" dark hat, a sacque and veil of black lace, and kid gloves. She fanned herself "energetically." It may have surprised the spectators that she talked freely to Mary Ann, who wore a black silk dress and her accustomed plaid shawl and knit head-covering. She looked about vacantly when her bereft husband also spoke to her.

Kate, whose case was taken up first, never lifted her veil during the proceeding. It was rumored that behind it her hair and eyebrows had been dyed black with shoe-polish, and that she had hoped to escape during her carriage-ride to court—as, it would be learned, she had some practice in doing. She had expected, it was said, to travel that morning in the phaeton of a Mrs. Remsen, her benefactress and a descendant of a Dutch Brooklyn family for whom a street and avenue are named. That good lady had showed up in her vehicle, but the prisoner had not been allowed to go with her.[25] This disappointment would not have improved Kate's ever changeable mood.

Some doubted the story of her disguise, but one newsman detected traces of the blacking in her hair the next day.[26] It was stated later that Sarah Merrigan had brought the stuff to her.[27]

District Attorney Winslow explained how the new law applied to Lizzie Lloyd King. But the proceedings began with evidence exceeding what the law required: testimony about her past gathered by her *bête noir*, O. T. Gray of Boston.

As soon as he lifted his papers to read, Kate bolted from her chair, charged at him and attempted to wrench the documents from his hands. When a court officer grabbed her arm, she struck his face repeatedly with her fan. He had to struggle to get her back to her seat.

"This man is not my counsel!" she yelled. "He shan't read that! He is a liar!"

Judge Moore asked the guard to bring her forward, and not to be rough with her. "Flushed," "a wild light playing in her eyes," "all trembling with excitement," she approached the bench.

"Now," the judge said mildly to her, "you must be quiet. You were brought here this morning that you might be aware of what was going on—"

"I should think it was proper that I should be present," she interrupted, and her voice rose. "What right has anyone to be my counsel? Mr. Gray don't know anything about it when I was fourteen years old or any other time."

"It is essential that you should conduct yourself properly to stay here."

"Hum! I don't consider it any privilege to stay here, I can tell you. I don't want to stay here and hear such a rigmarole read."

"You must keep quiet, or I shall have to send you somewhere else."

"I don't care where you send me. You can't send me to any worse place than I am now. I regard Mr. Gray as the meanest man that ever breathed the breath of life."

"Now sit down," Moore concluded, and she was quietly led back to her chair.[28]

As Kate obviously knew, Gray had been about to read the deposition of her mother, Harriet A. King. It was a sad tale:

> She was with me all the time up to the age of thirteen. She was a good child, always kind and dutiful . . . good company and real interesting . . . a pure-minded girl always. . . . She always attended the Sabbath School and liked it. [But then] she began to take in strange ways; she appeared odd. The beginning of her strangeness was not going to Sabbath School any longer. She was retiring in her manners, wanted to be by herself; her state of health was not good then. She ate a great many cloves and pickles at that time, and seemed to have an unnatural craving for such things. She grew more and more unnatural and unreasonable. She had an intimate friend who was taken sick, and she did not go to see her when she died, she did not go to the funeral, did not inquire for her, did not take any interest in her. . . . There were times when she would not speak to any of us; she was then fifteen or sixteen years old; she was changeable in her ways, very; she would appear kind or dull, and then would end in very bright, too much so altogether; she seemed to be imagining. When she was between sixteen and seventeen she left the high school and said she was going to the butting mill to work; she dressed herself for that as shabbily as she could, which was a contrast to her general desire about dress. Then she stopped these ways and dressed differently and wanted to go back to high school; she stayed round home nearly two years and there was no comfort in her; her strange ways continued during this time; she would rock for hours together and was so imaginary. It seemed as if she was all imagination. . . . Once that I remember, I went out to spend the day, and when I returned, I met her on the street, and crossed over to speak to her, but

she carried her head up, and had a lofty way, as though she looked on me with contempt, would not look at me nor speak.

Here Kate called out, "It's a lie! It's all a lie! I'll bring my mother here to prove him a liar. My mother never wrote anything like that, and I will not sit here and have my mother or myself insulted in such a manner."

"Never mind now," said Judge Moore, "You shall have your chance to talk. I can't hear both at once, you know. By and by, I'll hear you." Gray picked up Harriet King's painful remembrances:

I recall one instance when she was about seventeen years old. She wished her father a bad wish; I said to her, "You frightened me," and she said, "You need not think anything of that; if wishing would do any good, you would all be dead before morning." . . . When she was eighteen she commenced to go to school again. I know that she studied very hard . . . graduating at the head of her class of about twelve or fourteen. . . . She was to take part in the exhibition but took a notion not to go and would not go although they came for her. . . . During the vacation she was very strange in her ways. . . . [One afternoon] she turned her back to me, and I said, "Betty, what do your actions mean? I cannot stand it any longer." . . . She left the room without saying a word . . . at about six o'clock she came into the room; she had changed her dress; she went to the sink and washed her face and appeared to be very much excited but did not say a word; then she put on her waterproof and left the house. . . . It was a misty night. She came back at nine o'clock and went directly upstairs; she had no supper. . . . It was a Friday night . . . and she did not come down until Sunday. . . . Monday morning . . . I went into her room and I found written on her table, "Friday night I went up to the Little Pond with the intention of drowning myself. I plunged myself into the water and I found it was too hard for me; I floated on the water three hours; oh, it was blissful!" . . . after that some little time she came into the room with her writing materials . . . and I said to her, "Betty, you are writing what you had not ought to, it will kill me." She said if I ever gave her a word of advice again, she would knock me down dead, and she had just as lief do it as not.

Very soon after that she left home . . . it was on the 15th day of April, 1866 . . . she left saying she was going downtown, and did not return; she took with her a valise, unbeknown to us. She has not been home since, except for a single night in the Fall of 1867.[29]

Betty. Even her actual name took three forms: Lizzie, Betsey, Betty.

She was not yet 19 when she took off from Plymouth to Boston. The following year word got back that she was in a hospital there. Her father, Isaac King, went up to look for her and found that she had been admitted to a "lunatic asylum" in Taunton.[30]

The place still exists, as Taunton State Hospital, and it was from there that she had arrived at nearby Attleboro Falls. She had been assigned to Taunton by a judge's order just before she turned 20, and released after five months. While there she had used the name of "Alice Howard."[31]

Her case appears to have been a common, though ever heart-breaking, instance of mental illness—schizophrenia—erupting in adolescence. At Attleboro she told the story that she had run away from the hospital—had jumped out the window of a carriage, then trekked through woods for two days before arriving in that town "ragged, dirty and haggard."[32] (Would the pseudonym she used there, "Emma Chase," have had special significance?) Kate would repeat the story, and a coachman at Taunton would credit it. It was, he would state, at least the third time she had tried to escape.[33]

Salting her wounds now, one of her Brooklyn attorneys, D. B. Thompson, stepped up and read other affidavits about her behavior in years past. One woman from Attleboro remembered that her conduct had "alarmed" the woman's family, particularly when she boasted of her escape from Taunton. Another testified that Kate had asked her "where she could purchase a pistol, saying that she wanted to shoot birds, but would as soon shoot a man."

"That's another lie!" Kate yelled. "That is pretty counsel I have! What chance would I have before a jury with such counsel. They are a disgrace to Brooklyn!"[34]

A man who had rented a room to her in Providence remembered that she had poured kerosene on her cat to rid it of fleas, and had thereby rid it of all its fur. And "because it was sick she shoved buns into its mouth, and because it could not swallow them she turned the cat out to die."

"That's a lie!" cried Kate. "It didn't die. That cat was the smartest cat in the neighborhood." This amused many in the room.

He remembered other queer things, that she would swing from fury to calmness, that she worked a rocking-chair so long and so hard in the night that she wore its rockers off. Several other depositions followed, including one from her Aunt Susan and another from a schoolmate stating that she had been peculiar even as a child. A letter was read from Dr. W. W. Godding, superintendent of the Taunton Asylum, briefly attesting to her admission to that hospital. He also knew that she had been medically treated in Boston in the spring of 1867.[35]

Dr. Charles Corey took the stand and was questioned by Winslow. He had, he testified, visited Kate in jail four times, twice by himself and twice with Dr. D. Tilden Brown of Bloomingdale Asylum. His first interview had lasted four hours. He had read her account of Charles Goodrich's death, and particularly noted her admission that she had preserved his blood in her locket and eaten it. She confirmed to him that she had done so. "These things," he said, "would not be consistent with sanity."

He had "no doubt that she is insane and dangerous in every respect and a dangerous person to be at large. . . . I have made a thorough investigation in every possible way. It is not probable that there will ever be a marked improvement in her; on the contrary, she would grow worse: it is an indication, this homicide, of what she would do if she were permitted to go at large."[36]

Dr. Brown agreed that her mind had long been and continued to be "unsound."[37] With his testimony the terms of the insanity law were fulfilled, yet more evidence about Lizzie King was expected the following day. In the meantime, the judge would hear the case of Mary Ann Dwyer.

It didn't take long. Dr. MacDonald, former head of the Flatbush Insane Asylum, appeared first and offered the new information that Mary Ann's mother had been sent to a mental hospital. He had no doubt that Mary Ann had been insane at the time of the murders and was insane now. Corey now called her condition "puerperal melancholia." She told him, he said, that she would rather be beheaded than hung, for hanging would be disgraceful.

"I have no doubt," Judge Moore then concluded, "as to what is proper to be done in Mrs. Dwyer's case." There was only the matter of which "lunatic asylum" he would send her to.[38]

At the end of that day, as on other days, many in the crowd followed Kate onto the sidewalk; she was surrounded and trailed by an estimated 500 people.[39] The next morning, still in a feral state, she was brought back to hear the deposition of Taunton's Dr. Folsom. He named the disease he had treated in Kate as "mania," and believed its form was "peculiar to females." Because she had been considered violent and destructive, she had been fitted in a straitjacket. Although she had improved at the asylum, he believed that she had been still insane when she "ran away."[40]

This was quite enough. Moore stated that he would write an order committing Lizzie King to a state asylum. The designated place for sending the afflicted of Kings County was Poughkeepsie, in the Hudson Valley, but it was not yet clear that they were prepared to receive the current two prisoners. He would wait to hear.

Now Kate asked to speak to the judge, as he had told her she would be allowed to do. But this was a different woman from the one to whom he had made that promise two days before. This was the intelligent, reasoning, articulate person who had graduated at the head of her high-school class.

"I understand from the testimony of one of the physicians," she said to him, "Dr. Brown, I think [it was Corey], that he says I committed a homicide, and that I am a dangerous person to be at large. I want to know whether that question has been decided, and by what authority you or anyone else pronounces me guilty of homicide."

"That question was not passed upon at all. I do not say whether you are guilty of the charge against you or not. . . . We do not decide that question now. That would have no weight with me."

"But the jury, or whoever have me in charge, seem to think that it is true. I wish to remove that impression."

"It was not a jury. It was my duty to pass on your case."

"The public think that I am guilty, from that testimony that appeared in the papers. I wish to remove this impression, until it has been proved true."

"You have not been decided here guilty of homicide. What I have decided is that you are not in a mental condition to be tried."

"Oh! If I am willing to take that risk, I think the rest ought to be."

"When the question of your mental condition is decided—when it is decided that you are in a fit condition to be tried, then perhaps a jury will pass on the question of your guilt or innocence. Until then we must make a different disposition of you."

She turned away with annoyance.

"I don't think the truth will have much weight in such a court as this anyway."

Moore's response to this was remarkable: "Perhaps not."

The officers escorted her toward the door, but, still "scornful," she turned back. She complained that several articles, including two looking-glasses, as well as some money, had not been returned to her. Moore told her that they would be.

She had heard that the mirrors had been auctioned, and, with "tremendous sarcasm," she said that she was anxious "to get what was left before another auction takes place."

"Whereupon," concluded the Brooklyn Eagle, "Kate Stoddard and her famous case disappeared from public view."[41] The last word had been hers.

Judge Moore's formal commitment of Kate and Mary Ann, delivered to the sheriff the next day, named their destination as "the State Lunatic Asylum for insane criminals at Auburn,"[42] a small city 35 miles west of Syracuse, in the Finger Lakes region where Charles Goodrich was born. Opened in 1859 as an attachment to the original state prison, this hospital had been the first institution in America designated for that purpose.[43]

At Raymond Street Kate protested that she was not insane and "ought not to be sent to an asylum. I have been to one once, and I know what it is." She allegedly had once stated that she would "rather be hanged."[44]

The Eagle tried to interview her, but found her to be protected from intrusion by various visitors, chiefly the woman previously identified as Hannah Knight, the landlady's daughter at High Street. The visitor then settled for a talk with the complaisant Sarah Merrigan, who had resumed relations with her fellow prisoner. Kate, she said, had taken the insanity judgment "terribly to heart," and had wept for hours after returning to the jail. She felt that she should be tried, but would not be because her lawyers had been "bought" by the Goodrich family.

"She says that the Goodrich family do not want her trial to go on, that they know if it did there would be lots of ugly things come out." If she had honest lawyers, she believed that she would be acquitted. But another visitor, a Protestant counselor called Sister Elizabeth, advised her "to go quietly to your destination," and Kate, remembering that she would be tried if she would later be found to be sane, at last determined to do so.[45] But not before addressing another concern to Judge Moore, again with a clarity and precision that might have been envied by many a sound-minded correspondent:

Friday, July 17th, 1874

To Henry A. Moore, County Judge of Kings County:

Your Honor's attention I wish to call to the wording of your commitment of me in yesterday's papers. It reads that I was indicted for having "feloniously and willfully, and of her malice aforethought, killed and murdered Chas. Goodrich." Please, your Honor, I was present when the indictment was read, July, 1873, and it read "that Chas. Goodrich came to his death by pistol shot wounds in the head, inflicted with intent to cause death."

Your Honor has introduced the words "feloniously and willfully, and of her malice aforethought." By what authority, I ask, have you introduced them? These qualifications of the charge which it has pleased your Honor to originate are likely to do me a vast deal of harm in the opinion of that public from which my jurors are to be taken. I feel that your Honor has "feloniously and willfully, and of your malice aforethought," so worded your commitment of me that I am irreparably injured thereby, and I wish to call the attention of the public to the circumstance.

Lizzie L. King
Raymond Street Jail, Brooklyn, L. I.[46]

No wonder that many still considered that she was sane, or perhaps had been only temporarily demented. "It is thought," wrote the editors of the *Rochester Democrat*, "that having to talk so much with such hopeless lunatics as the Brooklyn detectives unsettled her mind."[47]

Moving day for Kate and Mary Ann was July 21st, a Tuesday. Kate began the day by hurrying out a letter to the editor of the *Eagle*, her favorite, or least contemned, newspaper. She did not use Mr. Kinsella's name.

"I have the great honor of going to Auburn," she began, ". . . the first victim of the "new Lunacy law."

She felt that this distinction (never mind her companion) qualified her to choose which asylum she would be sent to, and, of course, being Kate, she did not want to go where she was being sent, but, for reasons not stated, preferred Poughkeepsie. She had been told that the facility there was not yet complete, and wanted to express her wish that she remain at Raymond Street until she could be sent there. And she was still miffed about not having had her property returned, now said to include "two mirrors, two pairs of opera glasses, silver ring, card plate, gold pencil, my music box, satchel, crotchet tidies, about $45 in bank notes, umbrella, and numerous other articles, as well as my two revolvers." She understood that the last would have to be kept until her trial, "although those revolvers had no more to do with the death of Charles Goodrich than they had to do with the burning of Moscow—not a bit more."

The *Times*, which also printed the letter, commented that she was fibbing about this, as she had so often about other things. She had, it said, eight or nine dollars on her when she was arrested, and nearly all the articles were Goodrich's.[48]

A special correspondent for the *Eagle*, who cryptically signed his dispatches "Mul," met the prisoners and their escorts about 9:30 a.m. at the Grand Central Depot. It was another draining July morning, and Kate again was wearing a "masklike" veil—he did not say what else. "Stouter" Mary Ann, with a plump, oval face, seemed "the very picture of good nature." Sheriff Aras Williams, "short, stout, pleasant-faced," appeared to him "as if he might be a jolly Methodist divine about leaving the hot city for a vacation." Keeper Thomas Stinson, "as mild a mannered a man as ever turned a key on a criminal," was described as "tall, wiry" and "young . . . with a very black mustache and very determined cast of countenance." They quickly entered a train, and "were joined by a very ladylike looking woman, who shook hands heartily with the veiled female." This very likely was Sister Elizabeth.

The train left at 10. At 152nd Street, Kate spoke her first words, to Elizabeth. They touched a familiar theme:

"Do you think it would kill me if I jumped out now?"

"Indeed it would."

"I don't know," replied Kate with a hysterical laugh, "When I was out at Taunton Lunatic Asylum, I escaped through a smaller window than this."

"How?"

"I was out riding with three patients from the asylum, and we were in a carriage with both doors locked, but the window was down. Just as we got back near the asylum, I jumped clean through the window and ran for dear life. The three who were left behind commenced to scream, and so the driver was afraid to leave them and I escaped."

"Where did you go?"

"It was dark and instead of running far from the asylum I just ran to the woods close by, because I knew they wouldn't expect to find me *near* the asylum That night I slept in the woods. I was very cold, and in the morning my dress was soaked with the dew. I waited all that day until night without a morsel to eat, and then I walked by moonlight. The first house I stopped at I met a woman. She gave me something to eat, and I asked her if I could stay all night. But she wouldn't let me; and she sent my heart way up in my throat when she said, 'Maybe you come from the asylum.' I said then that I must go on, and I did, footsore, wet and friendless. I suffered enough, I tell you, but I would rather have died than gone back."

The sheriff asked if she had been captured again, and she explained that she had got to the village and found work. Elizabeth asked why she had escaped.

"Ah," said Kate, "you don't know how I suffered there." She claimed that she recovered from her "brain fever," but was placed repeatedly in a straitjacket because she would not "do the work of a servant." They left her alone and scantily dressed in a cold room. "Ah," she lamented, "God knows it was a terrible place!"

When a small child sat down near her, her thoughts moved with self-pity to her own childhood. "My home," she complained, "was never made pleasant for me; if it had been I might not have been here. If only I had a few years of my life to live over again, if—" and she broke off. As they traveled up the broad and gleaming Hudson, she recalled "going up once on a day just like this with Charley. We had a splendid time." At Albany she remarked, "I'm homesick, and I wish I were back in Raymond Street Jail."

They made a connection for Syracuse, and while they waited there for their final train west, "Mul" had a chance to question her. She chafed again about not having been able to choose her own counsel, who would have proceeded to a trial rather than attempt to prove her insane. And again her mind gravitated to the fixed idea of escape, ever a hope for her to proclaim her independence from a world that insisted falsely that there was something wrong with her, that she did not have full right to her proud, noble, wise and significant self.

"I don't think it was fair to refer in court to my escape from Taunton," she told the correspondent.

"Why?"

"'Because it may prevent any attempt to escape from Auburn,' she replied with a laugh."

The reporter got to an unresolved question:

"Was any marriage ceremony ever performed between you and Goodrich?"

She looked at him "very earnestly."

"I was married to Charles Goodrich, and I had a certificate given me. It was in my possession until about three weeks before his death. At that time he took his picture, several letters and the marriage certificate and burned them."

"When your troubles with him commenced, did he threaten you?"

"He said that I had been in a lunatic asylum once, and he would put me there again. But I loved him for all that."

She would rather die, she said, than be going there now.

"Has your father been to see you?"

"'Father? Yes, *once*,'" and her lip curled scornfully." Mul was sympathetic with her bitterness about having been neglected by her family.

They noticed, in this spot 250 miles from the city where she had committed her crime, that they had drawn the attention of a group of locals.

"These people are listening to our conversation," said Kate. "I do not care to talk for the edification of such a crowd."

On the Auburn train she grew nervous—"moved uneasily in her seat and shot quick glances in every direction, as if looking for an avenue of escape." She gazed out at the twilit woods and fields, sighed and wondered if she would "ever be free again to enjoy such a sight." Mul grew, in his word, more "sentimental" about her, sharing the feelings over the past two-plus years of thousands of other men and women toward the Degraw Street murderess.

She turned to Sister Elizabeth, and said, "Do you know, if it were not for you I would be tempted to do something wrong?" But she promised "to go quietly to—to my home."

Whatever Mary Ann Dwyer may have said during the long trip, which landed them at Auburn station at 9:25 p.m., was not reported. But Kate continued to chatter, and quipped about the handsome carriage that brought them to the asylum, "We are going in style anyway." Then, as the "heavy door" of the hospital closed behind her, she made one last reference to the thought that obsessed her: "There is no use in trying to escape now." They were assigned adjoining rooms.

Their travel-companions returned in the morning, and Dr. Wilkes, the superintendent, allowed them to visit Kate in her room, which she had refused to leave for breakfast, insisting that the meal should be brought to her. Williams asked her how she had slept. Hardly at all, she answered, because a woman in a nearby room had yelled and howled through the night. The room, though, was large and airy, with a window that looked through bars onto a "beautiful garden." She conceded that it was "so much nicer than Taunton, but I would rather be in Raymond Street Jail." The "genial superintendent" assured her that she was free to receive newspapers and books, and the "kind-hearted sheriff" left some money for both women.

They also spoke to Mary Ann, who "said she was perfectly contented, that the place seemed like a gentleman's mansion, and then retired to her room to read a prayer book." After Wilkes had given them a tour, and they had met "several lunatics from Brooklyn," they said farewell to the woman best known as Kate Stoddard, who began to cry.

"I do not know that I shall ever see you again," she said. "Good by." And she hurried away.

As they walked through the garden below her window, they saw her face between the bars, and she called to them:

"It is very pretty here—but oh, if I could only go back with you—If I could only go back!"

"She clasped her hands over her face," wrote the compassionate Mul, "and as we walked away we heard her sobbing like a child."[49]

Seems Like a Dream

After the postponement of Sarah Merrigan's trial in June 1874, Benjamin F. Tracy, vestryman of Henry Ward Beecher's Plymouth Congregational Church, became occupied as his pastor's advisor in a church trial that Beecher himself had called for. The result, delivered by a special committee at the end of August, was his full exoneration on charges of intimacy with the wife of Theodore Tilton. She had testified against her husband and for the pastor, and before the judgment was reached, Tilton filed a civil suit against Beecher, seeking $100,000 for the loss of Elizabeth's company and services. "Tracy's connection with the case," wrote the *Eagle*, "has only just begun."[50]

Mrs. Merrigan, dressed in black, with a plumed hat, appeared for trial at last in the Oyer and Terminer courtroom of Justice Abraham B. Tappen at 10 o'clock on the morning of Tuesday, October 27th, 1874. Accompanied by her mother and her mother's namesake, 3-year-old Cecilia, by a clergyman and two women associated with the Raymond Street Jail, she took her seat behind the jury-box. She was charged with first-degree murder.

Curly-headed, like her mother, the "very prettily dressed" little girl charmed the room, playing with pieces of paper that had fallen from the lawyers' tables and interacting with the onlookers. When a band of musicians passed outside, Cecilia ran to the window, and a court officer lifted her to give her a better view.

Two of the jurors were, like Kate's friend Mrs. Remsen, members of old Dutch families for whom Brooklyn streets are named: Peter Rapelye and Adrian Van Sinderen. In another courtroom that week, a jury was being chosen for the embezzlement trial of Isaac Badeau, City Collector of Taxes. Spectators shuttled between the events.

In his opening statement to the Merrigan jury, District Attorney John Winslow reinforced the point that Sarah was aware that Margaret Hamill collected rents at the beginning of each month, and that the murder was committed on the second day of September.[51] A witness would testify that she had paid Hamill $66 in rent on September 1st, and two policemen would state that they found more than $50 in a "pocket-book" in James Merrigan's tool-chest. There was no evidence, however, that these two sums were related, for James was in the habit of keeping money in the chest.[52] But also in the chest was a "hair anchor" or "anchor charm" that Maggie's brother would testify looked like one he had seen her wear. He would also say that one of the keys found in Sarah's possession was to Maggie's safe-deposit box.

Sarah Kipp, the first witness, repeated that she believed that on that Tuesday, September 2nd, she had heard a man upstairs yell, "Stand back, damn you!," and she added that she now thought she had heard not one but two women's voices.[53] At about the same time there was "a sort of scuffle"—"like two or three persons having a scuffle." Then "somebody was thrown down heavy on the floor and dragged across the floor . . . heard a smothered, distressed noise, as if of someone crying and moaning; this continued a quarter of an hour or so, and afterward I heard it again about 11 o'clock at night." She also stated that she had noticed James Merrigan "go out and in at various times during the day." And on the night of the fire, she recalled, Sarah told her that "poor Maggie Hamill is up there"—a remark that would have been inconsistent with the supposed intention to destroy the corpse.

David Coe, who was now Mrs. Kipp's son-in law, had also heard the sound of feet scuffling in the room above," lasting "a few minutes," about 2 p.m. on Tuesday, but made no mention of other sounds and voices. That night, Eva, his wife, "heard a kind of crying in the room overhead like a baby crying"—which indeed it could have been. Matilda Knowles, the neighbor who shared Sarah's taste for fortunetelling, said that what she heard on the landing as she approached the Merrigan apartment that Tuesday was "two women arguing," and the words she had heard as she "passed through the yard" were " 'There must be a separation' or something like that." She did not indicate who she thought had spoken them. That night, added Knowles, Sarah had told her that she thought Maggie had been burned in the fire.[54]

The Merrigans' former landlady testified that Sarah had often spoken of Margaret Hamill, telling her that she was wealthy and would include Sarah in her will.[55]

The critical testimony then was Sarah Kipp's, but it was dubious. Only she had heard a man's voice and something like a body falling. Why hadn't David Coe? Mrs. Knowles's report of two women arguing was significant but hardly conclusive, and the remark about a separation, besides being heard from outside the building, left the question, "between whom?" Sarah and Maggie, with the implication, more suggestive in our time than theirs, particularly in regard to two convent-mates, of an amorous relationship? Sarah and James? Or Maggie and her brothers?

Patrick Keady opened for the defense, and told the story of Sarah Dougherty Merrigan's life up to the moment of the seizure she had suffered earlier that year at Raymond Street. As he spoke, Sarah was observed to "watch the proceedings carefully," and "her looks and manner were all gentleness," as she smoothed back the curls from her daughter's forehead. In a reporter's view, it did "not seem possible that she could be guilty" of the "deed of blood of which she stands accused."[56] Nor did she seem to be crazy, which her counsel hoped to establish that she was.

The defense, in fact, was in two parts: Margaret Hamill's death was an accident, and Sarah had been insane. So even if the jury believed what was not true, that she had killed her best friend, it should believe she was not morally responsible. And whichever they believed, they should understand that the subsequent setting of the fire was the work of a madwoman.

The doctors who had examined Sarah under the recent lunacy law had not concluded that she was insane, for she was lucid when they interviewed her.[57] They would have much to say about her mental life nonetheless.

Keady offered exactly ten evidences of his client's lunacy;[58] then he and General Tracy produced the witnesses who would prove it was so. They called on four physicians, two of whom, John Byrne and Charles Corey, had testified on behalf of Fanny Hyde. Byrne, who now identified himself as president of the New York Obstetrical Society, and Alexander Skene of Long Island College Hospital (a bust of whom can be found today in Brooklyn's Grand Army Plaza), were there to tell about the potential influence of pregnancy on a woman's mental state. If she be vulnerable to mental weakness, including epilepsy, Byrne stated, it is more likely to appear at that time. Skene agreed. Carlos MacDonald declared that "there is a kind of insanity called epileptic insanity"—"considered one of the most dangerous kinds of mania." It could be "first manifested by violent excitement and mania," and "most writers, in fact, nearly all, agree that epileptics are not responsible during the paroxysm, and both before and after the attack, particularly after." He added that "the chief characteristic of epilepsy is loss of consciousness for a greater or less period; they may recollect what took place as one remembers a horrible dream. From what I have heard, my impression is that she is an epileptic." Corey agreed that epilepsy "is a cause of insanity, and is frequently connected with it. . . . It may take the form of the destruction of life, property or suicide; there are cases recorded when the mania developed suddenly, the person caused the death of some person or friend, and after the attack was found to be epileptic. . . . at the time of Miss Hamill's death [Mrs. Merrigan] may have been suffering an attack of epilepsy," especially "if she was in the early stages of pregnancy."

Both of the "mind doctors" considered heredity to be a telling factor in insanity, and found the wandering and blacking-out episodes Sarah had endured, and that would be described at the trial, to be consistent with a certain form of epilepsy.[59]

Epilepsy as a basis for defense was unusual, or even, as the *Eagle* considered, unprecedented. Very likely, at least, it had never been as thoroughly presented as an argument for acquittal in an American court. Although it had been used conspicuously the previous year in the insanity defense of Frank Walworth, the New York patricide, the expert who had appeared there had not gone quite as far as Corey had in considering the dead person to be a possible victim of an epileptic attack.[60] (The Walworth jury had found him guilty of second-degree murder, but Governor Lucius Robinson would pardon him, concluding that he had indeed been epileptically demented.)

Testimony followed from Williamsburg policemen and Daniel Dougherty, Sarah's father, about her nocturnal rambles, and Dougherty also spoke of his wife's brother, whom he himself had had committed to the Kings County Lunatic Asylum: "when he became insane he insisted that his name was Fairview; his delusion was that he was the President of the United States, that God had told him so." The defenders then called up three witnesses who knew about the mad McCarrons of Donegal, cousins of Cecilia Dougherty. They told of three members of one family who had been dispatched to the asylum in neighboring County Derry. One of the women was said to be "inclined to be violent."[61]

On the morning of October 30th, 1874, General Tracy quietly announced Sarah C. Merrigan as his witness. To one observer she seemed "somewhat pale, but collected," and would respond "in a low, quiet voice, occasionally a little tremulous."

She articulately described the things she remembered, but there was much that she did not:

> . . . the rope was too large to be held together by a pin. And it kept slipping; Maggie made the noose, and asked me to hand her the bunch of rope; she put it through the loop and over the top of the bedroom door . . . after I had measured the other parts she had to stand on a chair that I might measure the soles of her feet . . . with the other end I was in the act of measuring her feet, when the noise came . . . After I had gone out and returned she was suspended by the rope as described; her artificial teeth were starting out and her eyes were growing large . . . the rope [was] looped to the door handle; the chair was lying on its side; I looked for a scissors to cut her down, and then got a small carving knife; I can't remember whether I cut the rope before or after I took her down, only that her eyes and teeth were all the time looking at me; her toes might be a foot from the floor; I don't think she was dead when I got her to the floor . . . I don't know how she got into the bedroom; I knelt down by her and said,

"Maggie, what can I do to help you?"; then I prayed and felt for her heart beats; the baby began to cry . . . I can't say how long it was before I knew she was dead . . . I can't remember what I did after I knew she was dead . . . I was in great trouble to get rid of her clothes and reticule; that troubled me more than the body . . . the whole thing seems to me like a dream, or like something that happened in very early childhood. . . .[62]

Like a dream. That was precisely what Dr. MacDonald had described. And yet the precision and intensity of her recollection had a sharp ring of reality. She went on then to say more about what she had no memory of: "I don't know whether I remained at my sister-in-law's that night; I have since been informed that I did . . . I can't say when I first saw her body on the bed; I can't say I ever saw her there; I don't remember."

Oddly, although she could not recall anything about Maggie's body, she remembered that James had been in the apartment after her death, that he had supper there, and that she did not eat. And she added: "I don't know whether the body was then in sight; if it were he would have seen it; I believe my husband wanted to remain indoors, but I learn since that I asked him to go out for a walk." Nor did she remember where she "stopped the night of the fire; think that I tried to concoct a plan; thought that evening that a fire would keep me and my husband away from home."

There, a ring of honesty. But she could not recall moving things downstairs, nor hiring the two boys. She did not remember the fire except that she had realized the closet must have been aflame when she had looked up at her window from the yard. Nor did she have a memory of holding her little boy, or of handing him to Mary Jane Knowles. Or going to jail, or of having a fit and fainting spells there.[63]

Commenting on this "extraordinary case," the *Eagle* found the combination of events so amazingly aligned that it "irresistibly forces on the mind Poe's tree behind the house in the Rue Morgue . . . exactly at the right distance from the window of the fatal room, whose shutter slanted in just the right direction for the ape to climb and enter, while the iron nail on the open sash fitted so nicely as to baffle the police as to the murderer's mode of entrance."[64]

The testimony wound down on October 30th, when there were conflicting reports as to whether or not there was an indentation on the top of the door at 199 Ninth Street, such as might have been made by a rope and the gravity of a hanging body. Then, just after three o'clock, two hours of Benjamin Franklin Tracy.

The first question for the jurors to consider, he stated, was whether or not they believed that Sarah Merrigan had killed Maggie Hamill: "If she did, you would have to convict one of murdering the best, the dearest, and, in fact, the only friend she had on earth." But there was no sufficient motive for this, although the prosecution had attempted to establish the motive of robbery: "that the defendant caused the death of Miss Hamill for gaining possession of the few dollars which she had upon her person."

"We say and believe that the defendant did not cause the death of her friend, and that if she did, it was done under the influence of a paroxysm of epilepsy. In either event she is not responsible for the death of Miss Hamill." Not for first-degree murder, "with malice aforethought," nor of second-degree murder, nor manslaughter.

He read from medical sources on the relationship between epilepsy and violence. A man named Audsley had posited that "when a murder is committed without an apparent motive, epilepsy is to be looked for." Tracy then cited a killing by an epileptic Frenchman and an instance of an 18-year-old girl with the disease who had cut her own throat. He referred to the Walworth case and others in which persons who had acted violently were later proven to be epileptic. And now, "Here is a case where no motive is shown. The defendant is an ignorant Irish girl, living among an ignorant class of people, where even repeated attacks of the disease would not be noticed, and only until this great tragedy was the attention of the world and the medical fraternity directed to her case."

Her attacks had of course been noticed, as his own defense had established, and her class of people remembered that those attacks had occurred when she was pregnant. Tracy too remembered that they had, and reminded the jury that she was also pregnant in September 1873. And her family, he insisted, were not only ignorant, but also "saturated with insanity."

In the prosecution of Fanny Hyde, Winchester Britton had warned the jury against an inclination to "mawkish sensibility" and "sympathy" for the female defendant. John Winslow told this jury that they "must not yield to sickly sentimentalism," and informed them, if they did not already know it, that "the most diabolical of murders are committed by women." The evidence of Sarah's guilt was clear, and it was for them to decide only whether or not the murder had been premeditated—first or second degree. The money and the hair-anchor found in James's tool-chest had been Maggie's. The story that Sarah had told on the stand was "the idle tale of a desperate woman," and "her conduct was only to be attributed to a guilty conscience. All her steps were steps of stealth and concealment . . . reeking with falsehood." There was no proof of her epilepsy, and the insanity of her relatives did not establish that she was insane. "To his mind," a reporter summarized, "it was one of the clearest cases of premeditated murder ever tried in a court of justice," and "the trial was the most painful one he had ever been engaged in."

Indeed, said A. B. Tappen when his turn came to charge the panel, "it is a peculiar and painful case," but advised them that "the law makes no distinction in sex or age." The testimony, he told them "tends to show that the deceased came to her death by strangulation. Did the prisoner draw the cord? . . . In this case there appears to be no declaration of hate, and the prosecution has relied upon the motive of gain. . . . Also was it possible for the accused to have caused the death? It is shown that Margaret Hamill was of equal strength and muscle development. There are then two defenses—one a denial and the other of insanity."

Tappen directed the jury that if they had reasonable doubt about the responsibility of the prisoner, it "should go to the prisoner's benefit," and they must vote to acquit. Also, Sarah's character must be considered, along with testimony that she had revealed to her neighbors, both before and after Maggie's death, that she was in Sarah's apartment. His implication was that someone who was planning or had committed a murder would not reveal that. And, during the bizarre episode of the fire, she had again told of Maggie's presence. That might indicate Sarah's confusion about her intention. He was moving the jury away from first-degree murder and offering them room for acquittal.

It was 7:30 p.m. At a quarter past ten they returned to the courtroom to re-hear the testimony of Sarah Kipp and David Coe about the noises they had heard above them on the night of

September 2nd. At the same they time informed the judge that they had "little hope" of reaching a verdict. He sent them back.

At nine the next day, Saturday, the 31st, they filed in and declared again that they could not agree. Their last vote, it was learned, had been eight for conviction of second-degree murder, and four for acquittal. Tappen discharged them.

Sarah Merrigan "received the announcement of the result without the movement of a muscle."[65]

A peculiar and painful case. And distinctive in the history of epileptic disability as a basis for the temporary-insanity defense. As the defense testimony demonstrated, there was great interest in the disease at the time, and there had been valuable advances in knowledge about it. There were many misconceptions, as well. In Italy a neurologist and pioneer in the field of criminology, Cesare Lombroso, was preparing to write the book *L'uomo delinquente*, or *Criminal Man*, in which epilepsy would be defined as one of the principal causes of moral insanity.[66] Lombroso was a skewed and prejudiced thinker who hatched crackpot theories about the physical properties of born criminals; yet the more sober local physicians who had testified on Sarah's behalf had made similar observations about epilepsy. And their views hold up surprisingly well.

Dozens of scholarly studies in recent decades have recognized the overlapping of epilepsy and psychosis, and, in particular, the relation of epilepsy to violent behavior. The disease has a dizzying number of forms and variations,[67] and for well over a century it has been understood that epileptic episodes in the temporal lobes of the brain may have particular psychic characteristics.[68] Some experts have downplayed the incidence of violence, but others have shown clearly that the connection exists, even if it is not frequently manifested. In 1969, Dr. Pierre Flor-Henry published an article in which he concluded that "temporal lobe epilepsy of the dominant hemisphere predisposes to psychotic manifestations,"[69] and further investigations distinguished between psychotic violent episodes that occurred during, after and between epileptic attacks.[70] One neurologist, who in his paper pointed to two murders known to have been committed by epileptic children, observed that, "Many episodes of violent behavior are incompletely remembered, remembered incorrectly, associated with strange feelings of unreality. . . ."[71] A more recent study determined that psychosis occurs up to seven days after a seizure (postictal psychosis) in two-to-eight percent of epilepsy patients, and is marked by "gross abnormalities of" or "irritable and aggressive behavior, and hallucinatory experiences."[72] And a chart of criminal offenses "related to epileptic automisms" in England and Wales between 1975 and 2001 reveals several acts reminiscent of the charges against Sarah Merrigan: two throttlings—one with a telephone cord; three fires—one "to a flat, oblivious of flames," another an attempt to set fire to a person. There were also an "unpremeditated assault on a brother-in-law," a deadly attack with a hard tool, and stabbing a wife and locking a daughter in a cupboard.[73]

Apropos of Sarah, as well, is the association of (particularly) temporal-lobe epilepsy with hyper-religiosity. "Aggression," wrote Drs. Borum and Appelbaum, "has also sometimes been reported as part of an 'interictal [between seizures] behavioral syndrome, which includes, among other features, . . . religious preoccupation. . . ."[74] Other researchers compared this to what William James, author of *The Varieties of Religious Experience*, called "an acute fever.' "[75] Indeed, James declared that St. Paul, when he tumbled from his horse on the Damascus road, "certainly had an epileptoid, if not an epileptic seizure."[76]

There is an uncommon form of epilepsy known as "gravidarium," in which "the attacks occur mainly or entirely when the patient is pregnant," as well as "catamenial" epilepsy, in which they "arise in relation to menstrual periods."[77] And there is ambulatory epilepsy, also associated with the temporal lobes and characterized by " 'sleepwalking' and postictal wandering and confusion."[78]

Sarah Merrigan was certainly an epileptic, with repeated and complicated symptoms, and District Attorney John Winslow was altogether wrong when he dismissed evidence of the disease and its influence on mental derangement. Jurors in 1874 might not have trusted medical opinions about such phenomena; still, as Judge Tappen hinted to them, there was more than sufficient room in the case for reasonable doubt. It was uncertain that she had acted without her husband's aid, or that his motive of greed was not as strong as or stronger than hers. Nor was it certain that Maggie Hamill was not of such fragile temperament that she could have taken her own life, particularly on a day when she was evidently upset about her family relations and a supposed attempt to cheat her out of a great deal of money. And it was less certain that if her close friend did kill her, she did so in sane consciousness. It seems quite likely that in the very strange course of events on September 2nd, 1873, Sarah strangled Maggie, and quite possible that she did not know she had. It is also possible that she didn't kill her, but feared she had, and therefore, in her addled state, burned her house in an attempt to obliterate the unfortunate woman's corpse. Whatever she did, it would not have been with "sufficient reflection and full consent of the will," which her Catholic mentors had taught her were necessary conditions for a mortal sin.

Tappen would not admit her to bail, siding with Winslow that to do so would be inappropriate in a case where eight jurors had voted for conviction.[79] So back to Raymond Street she went, where, in contrast to the gruesome behavior of which she was still suspected, she resumed her role as a benign and gracious prisoner. Months later she spoke again of receiving the "kindest of treatment" there, and indeed, that she owed "the preservation of her life" to Sheriff Williams. At another time she talked gratefully of the sheriff's wife and daughter, for having frequently visited and comforted her.[80]

James seemed now to be out of that life. "She says she will never live with him again,"[81] the *Eagle* reported.

Benjamin Tracy became detained at The Trial of the Century, the Tilton-Beecher suit that began at Brooklyn City Court on January 11th, 1875. Patrick Keady was also on the preacher's payroll, working offstage, but Tracy was a principal actor in the trial. It was an outsized event, not only in the attention and publicity it attracted across the country and beyond, but also in its duration—nearly half a year, through the sweltering morning of July 2nd. One-hundred-and-seven witnesses would be called by three august lawyers for the plaintiff—including Samuel D. Morris, who delivered the opening argument—and six for the defendant. Tracy was rushed into duty in the second week to cross-examine one of the most critical witnesses, Tilton's confidant Frank Moulton. And in March the general opened Beecher's defense with a presentation lasting four days. "Its effect," wrote a legal contemporary, "was remarkable, both in the rapidity and the extent of the change made in public sentiment." The proceedings ended with yet another split vote, nine to three in Beecher's favor.[82]

But the reputation of a celebrated moral leader had been permanently diminished.

Tracy could still be found in the Tilton-Beecher courtroom in June as Sarah Merrigan's second trial approached, but he managed to slip away for its opening on the 16th. The presiding judge was now Calvin Pratt. Winchester Britton had returned as district attorney, but because, while out of office, he had consulted with Keady about the first trial, he assigned the prosecution to his first assistant, Thomas S. Moore.[83] Once again the two Cecilias, Sarah's mother and her daughter, now three-and-a-half and "bright and pretty," accompanied her. Sarah was said to look thinner than she had in the fall, and to have been through further illness,[84] which may have been what she was referring to when she credited Sheriff Williams for saving her life.

The witnesses repeated their previous testimony, led again by Sarah Kipp. But new details jumbled her story. She now thought she might have heard similar sounds on the day of Maggie's death and on the day before. Other testimony then compounded the confusion about when Maggie had left her home and about what time disturbing noises, including a woman's screams, had been heard from the Merrigans' apartment.[85]

But it was not these inconsistencies that most interested Tracy. Everyone in court wondered what was on his mind when, as soon as the prosecution rested, he motioned the bench for an acquittal. The prosecution, Tracy contended, was bound to the testimony of its own witnesses, and what Kipp had stated about hearing a belligerent male voice and seeing James Merrigan leave the building afterward had implicated husband more than wife. It was also more likely that a man, not a woman, had dragged a body across a floor and lifted it onto a bed.

At issue also were the precedents regarding a wife's responsibility if she either committed a crime jointly with her husband or was present when he alone committed a crime. "It is generally supposed," said Tracy, "that when the wife acts in the presence of the husband, she acts under his coercion." And in a case where the man is the sole offender, "Wives are not compelled to run away from or expose their husband's crime. If they remain passive, they are held innocent."

Judge Pratt announced a recess to study the matter, and announced when he returned that, so far as he could determine, "the theory of coercion does not apply to the crime of murder." In that case Tracy hoped the judge would charge the jury that Sarah's guilt depended on her participation, not just her presence. But hold on, said Moore, we've been surprised, and we should be allowed to bring in the witnesses who had stated long ago at the inquest that James had been at work all day on September 2nd. But this, Pratt noted, meant that Moore wanted to prove that one of his own witnesses was mistaken. The judge needed to think some more.[86]

The determination he expressed the next morning was that such an important case "should be tried on its merits," and he would admit the new testimony. Back then came two of the stair-builders to recall that they had seen James at work at various times on Tuesday, so it was at least very unlikely that he could have got away long enough to go home and kill somebody.[87]

"Is the case now closed?" Pratt asked Moore.

"Yes, sir," answered Moore.

"Finally?" asked Tracy, and a ripple of laughs went through the crowd.[88]

Tracy boldly brought forth no witnesses, and opened and closed his defense in one address in which he attempted to convince the jury that the prosecution had not proven its case. After the return of James Merrigan's co-workers, this became especially risky.

But the People, he insisted, had left much room for reasonable doubt. "Save only a dead body being found in the house," Tracy stated, "there is no other fact that is favored with any clearness. . . . The secret of the death will never be known until the secrets of all hearts are revealed."[89]

True enough; it is still not known. But the most likely agent remained Sarah, and without certainty about her mental irresponsibility she was quite vulnerable to conviction. Moore, granted a second closing speech, argued that the circumstantial case against Sarah was strong enough to convict her.[90]

The jurors retired at half-past three on June 21st and deliberated for the remainder of that longest day of the year. At eight o'clock they returned and told him that agreement was unlikely. He sent them back. Less than an hour later they announced that a verdict was impossible, although the extra time they had taken reportedly wrought two more guilty votes for second-degree murder. That made ten, versus two for acquittal—a narrow escape for Sarah Merrigan.[91]

Despite the confusion in the case, there was much less sympathy for her in Brooklyn than for the sexually active teenager Fanny Hyde who had obviously shot her lover dead.

The *Eagle*, judging that the prosecution's contradicting witnesses had left their case "in a muddle," and giving credit to Tracy for his strategy, referred to Daniel Webster's "assertion that if there be anything known to the Almighty it is the verdict of [a] petty jury."

"It is not likely," it concluded, "that Mrs. Merrigan will ever be tried again."[92]

Remembered and Forgotten

No, Sarah Merrigan was not tried again, nor were the other graces of Raymond Street. But their cases, especially Fanny Hyde's and Kate Stoddard's, were remembered in New York and Brooklyn for decades and used as points of reference whenever a woman lifted a deadly weapon, or a killer's defenders argued that he or she was insane. And for many newspaper editors, *The Brooklyn Eagle*'s chiefly, Fanny and Kate continued to be ready implements of sarcasm when the people's sympathy flowed for wronged women who satisfied their hellish fury with murder. More than once that paper assigned such feelings to the "airy science" of psychology.

By what curious psychological jugglery," it asked, "does assassination lose its hideous colors when practiced by a woman?"[93] And again: "The amount of compassion lavished upon" Fanny and Kate "would, if properly used, have sweetened all the cannibals in Carriba."[94] It also told its readers in 1897 that Sarah had killed Maggie Hamill "for money."[95]

Aside from the seismic Tilton-Beecher trial, no legal events were more closely watched during the 64-year life of the City of Brooklyn. "The history of American criminal law," wrote L. B. Proctor in Dr. Stiles's 1884 history, "has nothing more interesting in it than the case of *The People vs. Fanny Hyde*."[96] A few years later the *Eagle* described the murder of Charles Goodrich as "the most sensational and mysterious [tragedy] in the criminal history of Brooklyn."[97]

Fanny, like Kate, seemed to harbor nostalgia for Raymond Street. After her bailing-out in September 1873, she was next seen making a social visit to her old quarters in the women's jail, accompanied by a woman who had been housed there for smuggling burglar's tools to her husband in the other wing. That was in December, and Kate "appeared to be pleased"[98] to see her former sidekick. Then, in May 1874, the *Eagle* referred cryptically to what today might be called Fanny's "lifestyle." Not only had she not been punished for the elimination of George Watson, but also "it was the means of her being introduced to 'good society,' and she is now ten times more comfortably situated than she could ever have hoped to be had she relied on virtue and frugality for advancement."[99] There were no further details.

The noose and gibbet, however, may still have haunted Fanny's dreams, for the people expected her to be tried again. Occasionally a reader would write the *Eagle* to ask why she was not. The last time, a man who claimed to be named Watson asked if a *nolle prosequi*, ending the case, had been entered by the district attorney. He was told that none had been, but "the probabilities are entirely against" her being re-tried. "There seems to be a general impression," the paper could not resist adding, "that a woman who kills a man cannot be convicted, if their relations have only been guilty enough."[100]

She would appear in court again, though not on so grave a charge as murder. In August 1878, while living near the Navy Yard on Ryerson Street, she was arrested, according to one report, at the behest of a neighbor whom she had pasted with "violent, abusive and indecent language." Her relations with "good society" apparently had not lasted, for the victim had been upset by Fanny's "drinking and carousing" with other women, which, the account indicated, had become habitual since her husband had deserted her two weeks earlier. She was dismissed with a warning,[101] but a different judge sent her back to Raymond Street for five days when she came before him in February 1880 on another complaint of "raising a disturbance," back in Williamsburg. This penalty was imposed when she either would not or could not pay a five-dollar fine.[102]

How far this downward spiral reached is unknown, but it is clear that Henry Hyde was gone for good. He is listed in the 1880 U.S. census as an unmarried bookbinder boarding at 193 Franklin Avenue,[103] a few blocks east of where he had last lived with Fanny. One benefit of the breakup for her was that she could shed her infamous name, and indeed she was last heard of as Mary F. Windley, "alias Fanny Hyde," when a carriage in which she and a male companion were riding crashed on Wythe Avenue in December 1881, and they were tossed onto the pavement. Her only injury was "a slight scalp wound."[104]

Since the split juries were weighed against Sarah Merrigan, she was more likely than Fanny to be tried once more. At the end of her second trial, in June 1875, she remained at Raymond Street, now in her 22nd month, unable to make Judge Pratt's $7,500 bail. But she was released in July after he had reduced it by a third.[105] Retrial was scheduled for December, then for March 1876. Sarah, however, was sick again, with an "inflammation of the lungs" so severe that her recovery was said to be doubted.[106] In November of that year her defense, still consisting of Tracy and Keady, submitted that they could not proceed because important witnesses were in Ireland and unavailable. And Sarah was observed to be still "sickly and weak."

In his last year as district attorney, Winchester Britton lost patience with the case, which looked to him as though it would be put off "ad infinitum."[107] He was succeeded in 1878 by Isaac Catlin, and before the month of January was out, a much improved Sarah, "whom few would recognize" as the woman who had been "tried for one of the most dreadful crimes on record," showed up at his office and told his assistants that she wanted to start a new life in California. Could her case be closed at last, if not by trial, then with a *nolle prosequi*?[108] Although Pratt denied her,[109] her very strange case had ended, and its many uncertainties floated out of sight.

The new life that she had planned would not have included James Merrigan, for, as she had indicated in jail, their marriage was doomed,[110] and it ended even sooner than the Hydes'. Their parting revived suspicions that her husband had been complicit in the killing for which she had been tried twice and detained for nearly two years while he had remained free and unthreatened. But in 1877, when a lawyer suing him for unpaid fees described the killing as "the biggest piece of brutality I ever heard of," Merrigan "rejoined that he recognized it as his right to prove his innocence of such a horrible crime."[111]

His wife became Sarah Dougherty again, and she and Cecilia, also Dougherty, moved in with Sarah's parents on Bushwick Avenue.

Living there in 1880, Sarah, well-educated Catholic woman that she was, had become a schoolteacher.[112]

In the Auburn asylum Kate Stoddard's obsession about her lost possessions still burned. A month after her admittance she wrote to D.A. Winslow, via the *Eagle*, again demanding their return and expanding the inventory to include such items as a bible, "four volumes on physiology," and tickets to the Fulton Ferry and the Fifth-Avenue–Green-Wood-Cemetery horsecar. She went on in an incensed tone for hundreds of words, complaining again about her unjust treatment, her hostile representation, and the malicious Goodriches, and she refocused on the two guns, which "were never used to injure anyone." If she could get them back, though, she might apply one to herself for she was "weary of life" and preferred "death to incarceration in a madhouse."[113]

Kate was next heard from in October when Governor John Dix, then 75 and running for re-election, visited Auburn Prison and toured the asylum. The old warrior shook her hand and asked her how she liked her residence. She answered that time hung heavily upon her, but she was doing as well as could be expected.[114]

The name of Mary Handley, Chief Campbell's amateur agent who had fingered Kate at Fulton Ferry, was back in the news. The City's $1,000 reward to the person whose action led to her conviction was challenged by Detective Billy Folk, who insisted that all the information Handley had acted upon had come from him and his partner, the late Charles Videto, and that Videto's widow should get a portion of the money. Handley finally got her full payment,[115] but W. W. Goodrich would not produce the $2,500 he had offered, because Kate had not been convicted. He was playing the dog in the manger he had himself supplied, for he did think, he would say, that she had killed his brother.[116]

Now and again over the next few years Kate was able to publicize her lingering complaint about being confined. In 1880, not being allowed to handle a pen, she composed a letter to the state prison superintendent by sewing together characters from a bible. She hoped through him to appeal to "the Congress of the United States" to "repeal the State law authorizing persons indicted, but not convicted of a crime, sent to an insane asylum." Such a law, she charged was "*ex post facto*." The following year, a Syracuse reporter who visited the hospital, considered her "once handsome" looks to be "fading"—"although she retains traces of her former beauty." She spent "most of her time reading."[117]

Thomas Kinsella continued to lead the *Eagle* with force and fire into the 1880s, thrusting verbal encouragement toward the long, ethically and technically vexed completion of the East River Bridge, the name of which history would eventually grant to his beloved Brooklyn. Once denounced as a "Ring" Democrat, he would win points for his reputation by fiercely opposing the tactics of the great bosses of two counties, Tweed and McLaughlin, after having advocated the Liberal Republican candidacy of Horace Greeley.[118]

Thomas Field, after winning his divorce from his straying wife Emeline, married for the fourth time at the end of the same year. The newest Mrs. Field, considered as pretty as the previous three, was a 30-year-old former public-school principal,[119] who would live in the Bushwick neighborhood with him and his three children, including Emeline's Ada, until his death at 61 in 1881.[120]

Kinsella had a more difficult time divorcing the feisty Catholic Elizabeth, and did not marry Emeline Van Siclen until May 19th, 1880. His divorce was said to have been recently "obtained in some other state than New York."[121] Upset over these events and reported to be ill, Elizabeth removed for a time to the "quiet little town" of Stamford, Connecticut with her eldest daughter, Hannah, 24 and "very attractive." There a distracted young fellow named Theron Holly became obsessed with her and fired a shot at the head of a male visitor to her home, who ducked and returned a bullet into Holly's chest. The stalker survived, and Hannah, who had jumped out a window and engaged a policeman, observed the irony of such an episode occurring many miles from her perilous hometown.

"I came to Stamford," she lamented, "to hide myself, and I have been annoyed in this town more than I ever was in Brooklyn."[122]

In the months after The Great Bridge opened to New York and the world on May 23rd, 1883, Kinsella sailed with Emeline to England and, probably for the first time, his native Ireland.[123] It was a trip intended to improve his health, which was racked by gout and kidney disease, but it didn't cure him. By winter he was confined to bed, suffering from jaundice and finally pneumonia, and he died at age 51 in his Clinton Street home on the afternoon of February 11th, 1884.[124]

The *Eagle* lined its columns in crepe, and 200 employees gathered to honor him, as the *New York Times* noted how distinctly American a story it was for a "poor Irish printer" to become the editor of one of his new country's leading newspapers—which would have been "almost unthinkable" in London. The *Union*, now well past its Henry Bowen era, declared that "no man of his generation has left so strong an impress on the government and politics of this city as Thomas Kinsella." But, it added, "his influence" was neither "altogether for good" nor "altogether for evil."[125]

Somehow, despite his sins of divorce and remarriage, the local Catholic Church, which was a bit maverick compared to the Archdiocese of New York, stood by him. Father O'Reilly of St. Stephen's Parish offered him the last rites. Although no mass was said and the funeral took place in his home, the vicar general of the Brooklyn Diocese, William Keegan, officiated and orated. They also permitted his burial, late on a foggy afternoon, at Holy Cross Cemetery in Flatbush. His pallbearers, carrying him before a crowd stretching a block in both directions, included the city's most prominent Republicans, Henry Ward Beecher, Benjamin F. Tracy, Mayor Seth Low, and James Jourdan, joined by General Henry Slocum, ex-Mayor James Howell and others. Virtually every official of the City of Brooklyn and County of Kings attended the ceremonies,[126] but there was no sign of Henry C. Bowen.

The once poor Irishman had succeeded financially as well as professionally. His estate was estimated at $250,000.[127]

In 1896, nine years after Beecher had passed, never fully restored to glory, Bowen died in his famous Willow Street home at 82. He had transferred his devotion to the Pilgrim Congregational Church, where his eulogy was spoken by Dr. Richard Storrs. In the *Eagle* he was honored with a page-one obituary and a prolix editorial that stretched to a third long column.[128] The city in its final years had softened.

Nearly all the distinguished lawyers who had gathered about the Three Graces of Raymond Street lived to their ends in Brooklyn. Winchester Britton was the first to die, stricken suddenly in his home in 1886 before he had reached 60. The Brooklyn *Times* interestingly noted that his removal as district attorney was something that "a man of less learning and more of every day cunning could have avoided easily." His great adversary, Samuel Morris, addressed a memorial meeting of the Kings County Bar, and, referring to his and Britton's past differences, remarked that "the cloud soon passed away," and wished "peace to his ashes."[129] Morris himself, resident of Oxford Street, behind the new Academy of Music, made it to 1909, when, at 85, he was the second-oldest practicing attorney in the now Brooklyn Borough. He was remembered as a prosecutor who had been "a terror to evildoers," but "was charged with using the powers of his office to the extreme of propriety."[130]

Sarah Merrigan's persistent advocate, Patrick Keady, became a judge in the Court of General Sessions and lived to old age at 436 Clinton Street, three doors from the Kinsella household. He died there in 1908, and seventy carriages followed him to Holy Cross.[131] His opponent at the first Merrigan trial, D.A. John Winslow, thereafter practiced law on Montague Street and refreshed himself at local men's clubs until his death in Bay Ridge in 1898.[132] And Keady's, mentor, Benjamin F. Tracy, after moving on to national fame in Washington and enduring the loss of his wife and daughter in a house-fire there, returned to New York and ran for mayor in the first election of the consolidated city—and lost to Tammany Hall. He died in 1915 after being injured in an automobile that collided with a peddler's wagon—a clash between the centuries. His final return to Brooklyn was to be buried at Green-Wood Cemetery, attended by sailors from the Brooklyn Navy Yard.[133] His alter-ego, Isaac Catlin, passed less than six months later at the St. George Hotel on Brooklyn Heights. Like Tracy, he had been a failed mayoral candidate, and, at age 63, had stood on his one leg to volunteer for service in the Spanish-American War, but was denied.[134]

William W. Goodrich also outlived the City of Brooklyn. He lost a bitter campaign for the State Senate in 1879, then returned to private practice, and President Cleveland appointed him a delegate to the Maritime Conference of 1888.[135]

There was another devastating moment in his life, when his oldest son Frederick, manager of a quarry in Richmond, Virginia, died in a hotel room there in January 1890 after having apparently been severely beaten. It was conjectured that he had been attacked by an employee or employees whom he had dismissed,[136] but the case seems never to have been solved.

W. W. Goodrich was appointed presiding justice of the Appellate Division of the Kings County Supreme Court, and died in 1906, at

73, in his daughter's house on Park Slope's elegant Montgomery Place. All the courts of Brooklyn adjourned. His eulogy, like his brother's, was delivered by Rev. Theodore Cuyler, now pastor emeritus of the Lafayette Avenue Presbyterian Church. The famous old man could declare of him, unlike Charles, that "in all his career there was not the slightest stain of reproach."[137]

Henry Hyde remarried around 1883, and in 1900 lived with Isabel on Willoughby Avenue, a few blocks from where he previously had boarded. He appears to have remarried in 1912, and in 1920, at age 70, he was still working at his bookbinding trade. A Henry Hyde his exact age died in Brooklyn in 1926.[138]

Although Fanny may have fled the city of her ignominy, the other Windleys stayed on, moving to the substantial row-house section of Bedford-Stuyvesant in 1880. Alice, her sister, had married an English-born upholsterer in 1875 and would bear six children between that year and 1893, living not far from her parents at three locations in Fort Greene. Long after her husband had left her, she died in Brooklyn in 1935.[139]

Sam wed Annie, a New Yorker of English parentage, about 1881, and lived and labored in Brooklyn long enough to be proclaimed one of its venerable citizens. After his parents died in the 1890s, he and Annie occupied and eventually owned the house where they had rented at 407 Monroe Street in Bedford-Stuyvesant.[140] As he aged, the local press, while oblivious to his connection to the long-ago murder case, recognized him as a man with vivid reminiscences of old Brooklyn and New York. A 1929 *Eagle* profile tagged him America's "oldest weaver," still active in Williamsburg at 77. Five years later, he was listed as a long-lived Brooklynite in a piece about the centennial of the late city. His death-notice appeared in 1941. Adelbert, his son, died in Jamaica, Queens in 1975.[141]

It is doubtful that Sarah Dougherty ever got away from New York, for Cecilia, her child who had charmed the scene of her mother's murder trial, gave birth to a child of her own, Esther Noel, in New York, perhaps in Brooklyn, in 1897. Whatever became of Sarah—she may have been either of the Sarah Doughertys who died in New York City in 1895 and 1896—her daughter and granddaughter would have unstable lives. Esther at 13 was separated from her parents and living with her father's relatives in New Hampshire. She married at 15, lived in the South Bronx, and bore three children. The eldest was Cecilia, the enduring name of her Irish-born great-great grandmother. At 32 Esther was in Bay Ridge, Brooklyn, working at home as a seamstress and minding a fourth child by another man, who did not live with her. She survived to age 81. Descendants of hers, and of the Doughertys of Donegal and Williamsburg, and of the Merrigans whose name is lost to them, are still living.[142]

When Kate Stoddard's story was reprised, usually inaccurately, in the Brooklyn press during the next half-century and more, the accounts invariably mentioned Patrick Campbell's scheme for finding her dwelling-place as an exemplar of enterprising police-work. And, reviewing the case again in 1900, the *Eagle* it expressed nostalgia for "a time when there was much in the way of public scandal and crime of the first degree to keep reporters busy, the newspapers filled and the people properly thrilled." Most memorable was the year 1873, which heard "the first grumblings of the great ecclesiastical scandal" and saw "the arrest of William M. Tweed" and "the murder of [Margaret] Hamill," a year in which "the Fanny Hyde case was yet absorbing public interest, . . . the scandals in the City Treasurer's office became known" and "the police force of Brooklyn itself was turned topsy-turvy by the dismissal of Chief Campbell." And in that "year of serious accidents, mysterious deaths and of political sensations . . . the Goodrich mystery managed to keep the center of the stage."
"There are very few of these cases nowadays."[143]
It would be remembered in the *Eagle* well into the new century. In 1913, reminded of the case by the death of Mayor Gaynor and the role he'd played in it, columnist Julius Chambers, the well-known onetime investigative journalist and editor of *The World*, revealed that he, too, had covered her inquest and later hearings. Chambers had been, in effect, the male Nellie Bly, for, like her, he had had gotten himself admitted to an asylum to report on the treatment of the mentally ill. But his retrospective sympathies for Kate Stoddard and against other actors in her drama were misplaced. She was a "poor creature" who he "never thought . . . had fair treatment." "Cold-blooded" Mary Handley had "betrayed her to the police to obtain a reward."[51] The woman called "Kate Stoddard" was last remembered in 1931 in a laudatory piece about the old chief Patrick Campbell.[144]

Kate's parents, Isaac B. and Harriet Augusta Hoyt King—did either ever visit her again?—died in advanced age in Plymouth, where descendants of the family can be found today. Her sister Augusta, mother of three, lived on at Boston until at least 1910.[145]

By the time of Kate's arrival at Auburn it was becoming crowded, and a new residence was completed in 1892 in the village of Matteawan, in the Hudson Valley between New York City and Albany. Kate and her 260 neighbors, including Mary Ann Dwyer, were transferred there that year, and the Auburn Lunatic Asylum was closed. Its successor was named, more benignly, Matteawan State Hospital,[146] and more benign treatment of the mentally ill was its policy. Its authorities worked to limit stress, assigning its residents therapeutic jobs, encouraging social events, exercises, and games. But it too grew more and more populous, and, at least for male inmates, less benign.[147]

Census-takers visit even such places, and there in 1900 one found Lizzie L. King, "patient," 53, and alongside those entries is the oddly poignant initial "S" for "single." In 1910 another wrote down "Lizzie Lloyd King, inmate, 63," no occupation—nor any aliases.[56] That was her last full year; she died there on October 3rd, 1911.[148]

But the brownstone house on Degraw Street in which she shot and killed her lover Charles Goodrich still stands, with a different address, in a thriving Brooklyn neighborhood.

Notes

Newspaper Key

BDT: Brooklyn Daily Times
BSS: Brooklyn Sunday Sun
Eagle: Brooklyn Daily Eagle
Graphic: New York *Daily Graphic*
Herald: New York Herald
NYT: New York Times
SU: Brooklyn *Standard Union*
Sun: The Sun
Tribune: New York Tribune
Union: Brooklyn (Daily) Union

Chapter 1

1. Mild midwinter weather . . . in sparkling-new Prospect Park: *NYT, Eagle,* 1-21, 25-72.

2. a plain, slate-colored poplin dress . . . a brown ribbon that secured a black feather: *Union, Eagle,* 1-27-72.

3. into the bosom of her dress: *Official Report of the Trial of Fanny Hyde,* Fanny Hyde testimony. "Testimony" hereafter refers to this source; thick winter cloak . . . satchel: *Eagle, Union,* 1-27-72.

4. He had sold his machinery about ten days earlier . . . worked side by side with Fanny, now his only employee: *Union,* 1-27-72 (Ager Pixley interview); *Herald,* 1-28 (John Dexter interview).

5. the previous day she had quarreled with him: Fanny Hyde testimony.

6. They were seen talking, but were not heard over the machinery's hum: Ellen Curley, Mary Ann Kelley, Mary Gleason testimony.

7. At about eleven o'clock . . . "wild," she would call it, and "pale": Mary Dexter testimony; shawl: Kelley testimony.

8. There was a problem with third-floor toilet: Fanny Hyde testimony; also referenced by S. D. Morris in question to Mary Dexter (*Official Report of the Trial*, p. 53). At the inquest Margaret Manie (Mahony?) stated that the water-closet was "occupied": *Eagle*, 1-31-72.

9. knocked on the door of the velvet-weaving shop. . . . when she didn't come back as soon as he expected, he went back to work: Henry Potts testimony.

10. Fanny's stepmother . . . and that she looked "wild and very much excited": Mary Gleason testimony.

11. When she returned upstairs . . . on the third-floor landing, she saw George Watson: Fanny Hyde testimony.

12. It was Watson's habit to leave for lunch . . . three minutes after Fanny had stepped out: Mary Ann Kelley testimony; light overcoat: Ager Pixley testimony (recalled as witness, p. 22).

13. "I saw him there before I went up the stairs." . . . before he had grabbed her the second time: Fanny Hyde testimony.

14. what she said was the only bullet in the gun: Fanny Hyde testimony.

15. it struck him from several feet away . . . his splayed legs tilting upward onto the bottom stairs: *Tribune, Union*, 1-27-72; Dr. Joseph Creamer, Ager Pixley testimony.

16. A native of the little sheep-raising town of Plainfield . . . on Hicks Street on Brooklyn Heights: 1850 U.S. census; *Eagle Union*, 1-27-72.

17. Watson rented a room: *Eagle Union*, 1-27-72; in September 1853 he married Eliza Pixley: newspaper extracts (Barber Collection); <ancestry. com>.

18. Nottingham: *Columbia Gazetteer of the World;* "A History of Nottingham," <www.localhistories.org> (5-21-10); <wiki.answers.com>, *Official Report of the Trial of Fanny Hyde*, John Windley testimony.

19. Hattie Windley died . . . as soon as they were able.: John Windley testimony.

20. three-masted, iron-hulled British ships that were hybrids of steam and sail.: "ship "article, *Encyclopædia Britannica* Online Library Edition (5-14-2010).

21. John Windley, just turning 30 . . . a "boy" named "Francis": <ancestry.com>, birth, census, immigration (passenger list) records; John Windley testimony; about $30: *NYT*, 6-7-1865.

22. Something troubled Eliza Watson's health . . . she should move away from the sea.: *Union*, 1-27, 29-72; back to the bucolic Berkshires and

sold produce: 1860 U.S census; in the 1860s he picked up that trade again in Hartford, Connecticut: 1870 U.S. census.

23. The Windleys of Nottingham had New York connections . . . a dutiful student at night school and Sunday school": testimony of John Windley, John Marr, Sandra Marr, A. P. Bachman, Arthur M. Thomas.

24. five-feet-two . . . considered pretty: *Official Report of the Trial of Fanny Hyde*, Isaac Catlin's opening for the defense, Sarah Windley testimony; *Eagle*, 1-27-72.

25. the 1860s . . . Watson opened a shop that produced silk hair-nets: *Eagle, Union*, 1-27-72; *Union*, 1-29-72.

26. Ager Pixley . . . a "dutiful husband" who returned every other week to Hartford: *Union*, 1-27-72; the youngest of his and Eliza's children was a toddler, and the eldest was about the age of the teenage girls that her father employed: 1870 U.S. census.

27. A few years after landing . . . amid the factories and docks of Williamsburg: John Windley testimony.

28. Fanny transferred to the Bridge Street Primitive Methodist School . . . invited to speak at one of their evening presentations: testimony of John Windley, Sarah Marr, Howard Daisely, Jane Thatcher, Edwin Holloway.

29. John Windley conceded that he was more strict with his children . . . both her father and stepmother had been strict with her: testimony of John Windley, Fanny Hyde.

30. in February 1869, she reported to George Watson's third-floor hair-net shop: *Eagle*, 1-27, 31-72; William Newton testimony.

31. At 42, he was trim and handsome . . . prominent cheekbones and deep-set eyes: *Eagle*, 4-17-72; William Newton testimony; drawing of Watson at front of *Official Report of the Trial*.

32. Watson was sportive and indulgent with the girls. . . . She was not resisting him: Newton, Alexandre Amos, Ager Pixley testimony.

33. The same man . . . with him alone after everyone else had left: Newton, Mary Milford, Eliza Jackson testimony.

34. Fanny Windley's own recollection would be. . . . He also began to visit Fanny at her family's apartment: Fanny Hyde testimony; bedroom on the second floor: *Herald*, 1-28-72 (Henry Potts at inquest).

35. During these months, and into early 1870 . . . and increasingly irritable: John and Sarah Windley testimony.

36. "dysmenorrhea." . . . She refused to do either: Fanny Hyde testimony, Samuel D. Morris direct examination of John Byrne, M.D., *Official Report of the Trial*.

37. during that first part of 1870, John Windley heard a rumor. . . . He never mentioned it again": John Windley testimony.

38. in March, she left his home . . . who also began to work in Watson's shop. *Eagle*, 1-27, 2-2, 4-17-72; 1880 U.S. census; Kate Lown testimony.

39. On May 6th . . . she married him.: Margaret Hyde testimony.

40. John Windley did not know about it . . . "thought if she had married and made her bed, she had better lie in it": John Windley testimony.

41. Fanny did inform Watson of her coming marriage. . . . Within two months they had sex again: Fanny Hyde testimony; because the money . . . was better: Sgt. George W. Bunce, Thomas Langan testimony; $10 a week: Fanny Hyde testimony.

42. Fanny traveled to Washington in April. . . . "I feel that there is a curse hanging over me.": Margaret Hyde testimony.

43. dissolved his arrangement with Bachman . . . to operate a factory in New Britain, Connecticut: *Union*, 1-27-72 (interview with Ager Pixley).

44. Henry . . . sent Fanny in Washington a letter asking her to join him: Margaret Hyde testimony.

45. She traveled up about the first of May . . . "cried about it continually." Fanny Hyde testimony.

46. A friend of Henry Hyde remembered occasions . . . telling him that he was no longer welcome.: *Herald*, 1-28-73; *Eagle, Union*, 1-29-72 (inquest); Edward Weaving testimony.

47. she had sex with him again the next week: Fanny Hyde testimony.

48. One day around the middle of that month . . . purchased cartridges for it.: *Eagle*, 1-31-72 (inquest); Nelson J. Stowell and Fanny Hyde testimony.

49. Ellen Curley . . . then she bolted past him to tell the others: *Eagle, Herald, Union*, 1-27-72; Ellen Curley testimony, Ager Pixley testimony.

50. Pixley, then Henry Potts and Charles Merrill . . . was just pronouncing Watson dead: Pixley testimony; *Eagle*, 1-27-72 (Curley and Potts at inquest).

51. Ellen had run up to tell the news . . . "and I shot him": *Herald* 1-28-72 (Mary Dexter at inquest).

52. Sam grabbed the stair-post . . . swung himself over the victim and rushed up the stairs: Ager Pixley testimony; George Watson, obsessive in jealousy . . . she confronted him angrily before she left the shop: Fanny Hyde testimony, and testimony of Capt. Cornelius Woglom, recalled to the witness stand, *Official Report of the Trial*, p. 85.

53. Pixley took charge of the body . . . to take the body to his home on Hudson Avenue: Pixley testimony.

54. police surgeon Joseph Creamer conducted an autopsy . . . not to a struggle with his killer: Creamer testimony.

55. Between one and two o'clock . . . her idea to "give herself up,": Cornelius Woglom testimony, Fanny Hyde testimony; "the Chief of Williamsburg": Fales, *Brooklyn's Guardians*, p. 273.

56. She told her story and admitted the shooting to Woglom . . . and then to Chief Patrick Campbell: testimony of Woglom, Sgt. George W. Bunce and Det. Thomas Langan; *Union*, 1-27-72.

57. A man from *The Brooklyn Eagle* arrived . . . "very different from what would be expected in those of a malicious and ferocious murderer": *Eagle, Union,* 1-27-72; *Herald,* 1-28-72. Charles Reade: *Union,* 1-30-72.

58. The coroner's inquest began . . . before a jury of eight men who sat around them: *Union, Eagle,* 1-27-72, *Herald,* 1-28-72; blood that had been blanketed with ashes: *Herald*; Still wearing the plain gray dress . . . relieved in the morning by Sam: *Union,* 1-27-72.

59. The next night, Saturday, the venue switched . . . while the others pressed at the doors: *Herald,* 1-28-72.

60. Fanny was wearing her veil when she arrived . . . drew every eye in the courtroom: *Union,* 1-29-72.

61. Keady was now joined by Samuel D. Morris . . . that he had told his sister not to do it: *Herald,* 1-28-72; *Eagle, Union,* 1-29-72.

62. The curious masses thronged to the courthouse . . . "the trial of Mrs. Hyde will not be as fair and unsentimental as the trial of a man murderer would be.": *Eagle,* 1-31-72.

63. She was transferred the next day to the County Jail at Raymond Street . . . corridor of which she was free to walk in: *Eagle,* 2-2-72.

64. Watson "was perfectly innocent of any criminal relations to her" . . . that she shot him when he decided to end the deal: *Eagle,* 2-2-72.

65. "She is a small, thin undersized girl of eighteen . . . a sufficient reason for his death.": *Eagle,* 2-2-72.

66. "always find their apologists among decent people, who never saw the gashed, riddled or jellied corpse of the victim.": *Herald.* 1-28-72.

67. Laura Fair of San Francisco . . . acquitted on the insanity plea the second time around: <abncny.org> and Duke, pp. 65–67 (<google.com>, Google books. (7-1-10)).

68. the *Eagle* had ruminated. . . . Oh, for one year of Jersey justice in New York!": 1-26-72.

69. "Another Murder": *Union,* 1-26-72.

70. deadly attack near the Brooklyn Navy Yard on a quiet, slightly built, gentlemanly piano-instructor . . . in Mrs. Snow's parlor, he died the next morning.: *Eagle,* 1-25, 26, 27, 30, 2-2-72; *NYT* 1-25. 26. 27, 28-72, *Herald,* 1-26-72; *Union,* 1-27-72.

71. 24 officers of the Fourth Precinct . . . a race for a committee-seat.: *Eagle*, 1-29-72.

72. "Murder Mania" . . . and by the shooting of a young New York man by his father: *Eagle*, 1-27-72, *Herald*, 1-28-72.

73. 25-year-old Alfred East . . . Mrs. Snow's boarding-house.: *NYT*, *Union*, *Herald*, 1-29-72.

74. One account . . . "utmost intimacy.": *Herald*, 1-29-72.

75. The *National Police Gazette* . . . whispered over Fanny Hyde's shoulder: 2-10-72.

76. "a singular coincidence" . . . where Panormo and East had died: *Union*, 1-29-72.

77. rope, sugar and whisky: Syrett, p. 14, McCullough, p. 104.

78. growing faster than any comparably sized place in America . . . a tick under 400,000: <www.demographia.com/db-uscity1790.htm> (10-26-2011).

79. Thomas Kinsella, had left his editor's desk . . . return to the *Eagle* full-time at the start of '73: Stiles, v. II, pp. 1181–82, 1185–87; Biography Resource Center (*Dictionary of American Biography* Base Set), <www.galenet.com> (2-19-09); *Eagle, Union*, 2-11, 12-84. The "History of the Press" section of Stiles's history was authored primarily by W. E. Robinson, and "supplemented" by Stiles. Its biography of Kinsella was written by Laura C. Holloway. Henry McCloskey: Schroth, pp. 60–65; Stiles, v. II, p. 1181; Howard, p. 95; Hazelton, pp. 1412–13; *Eagle* 4-18-61, 4-29, 30-69.

clearing the many illicit whisky distilleries . . . a federal building in his bulging city: *Eagle*, 1-27, 2-2-72. Kinsella's *Eagle* supported the government and the war against the South, although it remained Democratic and critical of President Lincoln.: Schroth, p. 65. "chiefly responsible" for *New York Herald* publisher Horace Greeley's presidential run.:*Eagle*, 2-11-84.

80. radical Republicans, who one night at the start of the war . . . "hang out your flag," which he promptly did: Syrett, p. 21.

81. in September 1863, some party leaders established a paper. . . . Theodore Tilton, whom Bowen would also appoint editor of the *Union* in 1870: Stiles, v. II, pp. 1177–78, Syrett, p. 21, Shaplen, pp. 6–8, 27–31.

82. "The Trinity of Plymouth Church": Shaplen, p. 7.

83. Beecher was much more than the city's best-known citizen . . . in speaking-fees and from publications that included a collection of his sermons and a novel: Shaplen, pp. 18–25; McCullough, pp. 109–111; <plymouth-church.org> (7-23-10); "had humbly turned down": Applegate, p. 393; "the most famous man in America": Applegate.

84. 11 intercity ferries: *New York City Encyclopedia*, p. 199.

85. About half of its people were foreign-born, most of those Irish and Germans: *New York City Encyclopedia*, p. 151; Syrett, p. 13. Judd, p. 10.

86. from 1869 to the mid-1870s U.S. revenue officials enlisted federal forces, including Marines, in a series of invasions that became known as Brooklyn's "Whisky War," for they were stoutly resisted by the moonshiners and brick- and stone-flinging residents of the district. One raid, in 1870, deployed 1500 troops.: Miller, pp. 234–248; Brooklynology, <Brooklynpu-pliclibrary.org> (7-22-10).

87. "The Three Graces" . . . controlled all federal patronage in the city: Syrett, p. 57; *Eagle*, 2-10-1909, and multiple other newspaper references.

88. Tracy . . . Beecher: *American National Biography*, pp. 791–794; Stiles, v. II, pp. 1222–27; *Eagle*, *BDT*, 8-7-1915.

200 churches,: Syrett, p. 20.

89. Farther south on the Heights . . . "the Chrysostom of Brooklyn": Syrett, p. 20, *NYT*, 8-22-96.

90. DeWitt Talmage's . . . Free Tabernacle on Schermerhorn Street: Syrett, p. 20; 1911 *Encylopædia Britannica* Online (<1911encyclopedia.org> (7-23-10)).

91. Lafayette Presbyterian . . . most congregants of any Reformed church in America: *NYT*, 10-26-74; Abram N. Littlejohn: *NYT*, 8-4-1901.

92. Bishop John Loughlin . . . riots that required the deployment of the state militia: Sharp, vol. 1, pp. 271–276; Judd, pp. 15–16.

93. "It is admitted by strangers . . . the handsomest place of public outdoor resort of any city in the world": *Eagle*, 10-9-74.

94. "I am prouder of it than of anything I have had to do with." Roper, p. 403.

95. The towers of John and Washington Roebling's long-envisioned East River Bridge . . . the longest in the world: McCullough, pp. 29, 328, 564–565.

96. Government was messy, sharply contentious . . . , the particular properties of the municipal aldermen: Syrett, *passim*; "Hey, mister, your saloon's on fire!": Syrett, p. 31.

95. in the mayoral–election year of 1869 . . . butted him against party boss Hugh L. McLaughlin.: Syrett, pp. 56–57.

98. The 1871 election was no purer, and again Morris delivered indictments: Syrett, pp. 57–59; *Eagle*, 7-16, 17, 18, 19-73.

99. Frederick Schroeder . . . to relieve Brooklyn of another $200,000.: Syrett, pp. 67–68.

100. would be elected in 1875: Syrett, pp. 87–88.

101. Hugh McLaughlin . . . such as the proposed entrance-route to Prospect Park, for example: Syrett, pp. 70–86; *New York City Encyclopedia; Eagle*, 12-8-1904; sniped at Schroeder: Syrett, p. 6;."honest graft": Syrett, 83; "I seen my opportunities and I took 'em": William L. Riordan, *Plunkitt of Tammany Hall* (New York: Signet, 1995), p. 3.

102. Boss's McLaughlin's greatest nemesis would turn out to be Thomas Kinsella . . . it largely caused the election of Low.: Syrett, pp. 94–106.

Chapter 2

1. " 'Fanny, my child,' " . . . as had violated this trust.: reported in *Eagle*, 3-16-72.

2. She was arraigned on March 6th . . . to begin the trial on the 19th of the month.: *Eagle*, 3-6-72.

3. "a notable legal tourney": *Eagle*, 3-14-72.

4. the court granted Morris a postponement: *Eagle*, 3-19-72.

5. The Kings County Jail . . . each of the 448 new cells was equipped with a water-closet: <correctionhistory.org>, "Return to Raymond St. Jail," (8-26-10); Livingstone, p. 143; *Eagle*, 7-19-72, 6-23-73, 8-27-73, 5-16-74, 8-13-74, 10-5-74, 1-25-75, 5-21-75, 6-2-79, 8-2-79, 4-2-80; *Union*, 11-1-73; *BDT*, 1-7-75; He would call to her home on Wythe Avenue: Kate Lown testimony. "modeled after a West Point fortress": <correctionhistory.org>. "a relic of the age so fondly remembered": *Eagle*, 6-23-73. Fort Greene: <fortgreenepark.org> (8-26-10). "a mean" and "badly laid out prison": *Eagle*, 5-16-74. who ran it humanely . . . many improvements: *Union*, 11-1-73, *BDT*, 1-7-75. "that of the Black Hole of Calcutta . . . calculated to make criminals." *Eagle*,1-25-75. nine-by-six-foot cells; prisoners got drunk: *BDT* 1-7-75. "in admirable condition" . . . 80 in all: *Eagle*, 7-19-72. A later visitor . . . "just like home.": *Eagle*, 5-16-74. "polite and cheerful, as usual": *Eagle*, 8-27-74.

6. The end of Samuel D. Morris's nine-year span . . . had been involuntary: *Eagle*, 1-5-74.

7. Morris, 48, handsome. . . . He was district attorney at 38: Stiles, v. II, pp. 1236–37; *Eagle*, 5-23-72, 1-5-74.

8. In politics and prosecution . . . even after his life had been threatened: *Eagle*, 1-5-74, 11-1-1909.

9. Once, during a cholera epidemic . . . to be housed in tents: *SU*, *NYT*, 11-1-1909.

"few equals in this state," and to have once been complimented for his skill by Henry Clay: *Eagle*, 3-23-72.

10. In May 1870, Democratic Boss Hugh L. McLaughlin . . . obstruction of justice: Syrett, pp. 56–57.

11. charging that he had played with bail money . . . because the county had owed him the money.: *Eagle*, *NYT*, 5-31-70.: The matter made its way to the democratic governor . . . "but this was to be expected after

exposing their frauds.": *Eagle*, 5-14, 7-14, 8-31, 9-15, 16-70; Syrett, p. 57; Ackerman, pp. 54–55, 111; McCullough, pp. 125–26, 249.

12. in the fall of '71, . . . "heartily" endorsed the party's ticket: *Eagle*, 10-27-71. Morris had stated in a letter to Britton . . . then decided that it was not worthwhile to pursue any others.: *Eagle*, 3-4, 12, 20-73.

13. Winchester Britton, about two years younger than Morris . . . honesty, loyalty to friends, and exceedingly fine knowledge of the law: Stiles, v. II, pp. 1283–85; *Eagle*, 10-22-77; *Eagle*, 2-13-86; *NYT* 2-14-86; "his remarkably brilliant black eyes": Stiles, v. II, p. 1283. The contributor was L. B. Proctor.

"It is silvery white, but full of electricity . . . his fine eyes flash with the fire of combat": *Eagle*, 12-2-73.

"too bold, frank and outspoken" *Eagle*, 2-16-86.

14. two Greek Revival buildings designed by Gamaliel King about . . . equal in height:

Snyder-Grenier, p. 96; Conklin and Simpson, pp. 50, 55–56, 62; *Brooklyn Almanac*, p. 53; nyc.gov (10-18-10).

15. "an inordinate number of liquor establishments . . . almost anything at which money . . . [could] be made": Syrett, p. 17. He quotes *Union*, 4-27-70.

16. The courtroom was thick with prominent Brooklyn jurists . . . a pointed "imperial" beard descending from his chin, wore a black suit: *Union*, 4-15-72; *Eagle*, 4-16, 17-72. Morris would tell the jury . . . working for nothing.: *Official Report of the Trial*, p. 127. "No trial which has been before the courts in a great while . . . will be looked forward to with painful anxiety": *Union*, 4-16-72.

17. Although Morris felt that the district attorney's juror-challenges were excessive . . . by two o'clock.: *Official Report of the Trial*, p. 71, *Eagle*, 4-16-72.

18. "It would seem . . . to which she made no reply": *Official Report*, p. 15.

19. He then defined and explained the statute . . . the meaning of justifiable homicide: *Official Report*, pp. 15–16.

20. "[I]t will be your duty to rebuke this mawkish sensibility . . . shall be taken into the hands of private persons": *Official Report*, p. 17.

21. As testimony began, Morris conceded . . . bought at Stowell's shop: *Official Report*, p. 17.

22. Then Britton brought forth witnesses . . . the cross-examination of the first witness, Ellen Curley: *Official Report*, pp. 17–20.

23. After noontime recess . . . chatted briskly with her: *Union*, 4-16-72.

24. The following morning. . . . She wept nonetheless: *Eagle*, 4-17-72.

25. After the examination of Dr. Creamer . . . the prosecution rested: pp. 21–23.

26. "I submit to the Court that there is no proof" . . . after which General Catlin opened for the defense.: *Official Report*, pp. 23–25.

27. A powerfully built man of 36 . . . lost a leg at Petersburg: Stiles, v. II, p. 1254; *NYT*, 1-20-1916.

28. declared that the defense would present the case "in full" . . . as irresistible and uncontrollable as the decree of fate.: *Official Report*, p. 25.

29. Beginning in the year 1800 . . . could not distinguish right from wrong: Robinson, pp. 142–154; "wild beast": Robinson, p. 134; Carter, p. 1.

30. The McNaughtan (or "M'Naghten") case . . . "that he did not know that he was doing what was wrong": Robinson, pp. 163–182; Maeder, pp. 32–33; Carter, pp. 1–3; "The McNaughton Rule—not knowing right from wrong," Cornell Law School (<forensic-psych.com/articles/McNaughtonRule> (10-22-2010)); Williams, John M., Jr. "Insanity," *Encyclopedia Americana* (Grolier Online (10-22-2010)). The name of the defendant in this trial has been spelled various ways, and the "Rule" it spawned is usually written as "M'Naughten." Robinson (pp. 286–87) credits Richard Moran, in his book *Knowing Right from Wrong: The Insanity Defense of Daniel McNaughtan*, with having determined that this spelling is the correct one.

31. Scotsman James Prichard . . . "is in some instances irresistible": Robinson, pp. 160–61, 167–68, 176.

32. As early as 1844 . . . knowing that his or her criminal act was wrong: Williams, *Encyclopedia Americana*.

33. Although New York was not one of the states that had adopted "irresistible impulse" test by 1872: Carter, p. 3.

34. Daniel Sickles . . . had been driven temporarily mad by jealousy: <www.abcny/library>: "Crimes of Passion"; <wikipedia.org>, "Daniel Sickles."

35. "kindness which is usually shown to legitimate offspring": Robinson, pp. 168–69.

36. " 'Motherless!' . . . the wiles and treachery of the seducer": *Official Report*, p. 33.

37. God was "on Fanny's side" . . . "the poison and mildew of licentiousness are corrupting our society.": *Official Report*, p. 37.

38. the poor and weak against the wealthy and powerful . . . "to get some confession out of this defendant.": *Official Report*, pp. 26, 27.

39. The oration lasted two hours, during which many women in the courtroom wept: *Union*, 4-16-72.

40. Hardly had the defense testimony begun when the district attorney objected . . . "the person was a raving maniac, and had been all her life": : *Official Report*, pp. 38–40.

41. He then brought up Fanny's dysmenorrhea . . . perfectly irresponsible for any act they might commit while that was upon them": *Official Report*, pp. 38–41.

42. Britton responded that it was clear . . . was unconvincing to the prosecution.: *Official Report*, pp. 41–42.

43. At the end of the day . . . across the sidewalk on Joralemon Street: *Eagle*, 4-17-72.

44. "Very wild and very much excited" . . . "I cannot say for certain": *Official Report*, pp. 54–55.

45. Mary Dexter, Fanny's aunt . . . "because he was said to be out of his mind": *Official Report*, pp. 55–59.

46. After a brief examination of Sarah Windley . . . his life with his older daughter, and their falling-out: *Official Report*, pp. 62–64; "was not entirely in his right senses": p. 63.

47. The courtroom became silent for perhaps four minutes . . . "No, sir, I have not.": *Eagle, Union*, 4-18-72; *Official Report*, p. 64.

48. an account in *The Brooklyn Union* . . . who had been amorous with a friend of hers.: 1-29-72.

49. he asked if she had cried much about her situation: *Official Report*, pp. 64–65.

50. "the crowd surged forward" . . . wept into her handkerchief: *Eagle, Union*, 4-18-72.

51. The Hydes had boarded there at the home of a Mr. Woodhouse . . . "Did you go to his room while you were there, in the night, from your own?" . . . "No, sir": *Official Report*, pp. 66–67.

52. In re-direct examination, . . . have no recall of the act itself or the minutes immediately following it.: *Official Report*, pp. 67–69.

53. "How did you happen to have the pistol with you on that day?" . . . "It has cost me a good deal of money to try to find him": *Official Report*, pp. 68–70; "an accessory before the act": *Union*, 4-16-72.

54. Sam Morris arrived at court on Thursday morning . . . counted at "some forty": *Eagle*, 4-19-72; several "prominent New York lawyers" also attended: *Union*, 4-18-72.

55. Dr. John Byrne . . . "They are affected mentally to the extent of hysterical paroxysms": *Official Report*, pp. 72–74; solidly built, grey-haired: *Eagle*, 4-19-72.

56. Up then came Dr. Charles Corey . . . "I do not know that I am able to define the difference": *Official Report*, pp. 74–83; who had sat among the spectators on previous days; a tall, thin man with gray hair and a Lincolnesque beard, who wore gold-rimmed glasses: *Eagle*, 4-19-72.

57. "she said she did not mean to kill him," that "she could not help it. She was sorry for it.": *Official Report*, p. 87.

58. "she was worked up so in her mind that she shot him for satisfaction." : *Official Report*, p. 85.

59. Ellen Curley . . . stated that she had.: *Official Report*, p. 87.

60. he expected the case to go to the jury the next day: *Official Report*, p. 89.

61. two advocates for women's rights . . . "and are therefore the natural judges in all cases of woman. . . .": *Eagle*, 4-20-72.

62. The crowd that Friday, which began to form outside the courthouse . . . and her cadre of female supporters vocally greeted her: *Union*, 4-19-72.

63. He went right after the district attorney . . . "sent to an awful or ignominious death upon the scaffold. . . .": *Official Report*, p. 92.

64. She and her stepmother wept. . . . smiled derisively: *Eagle*, 4-20-72.; "This is not a case of blood-hunting . . . we are supposed to elicit the facts and the evidence": *Official Report*, p. 95.

65. "oh what can be said when a person is executed . . . Better that ninety-nine guilty go free": *Official Report*, p. 105.

66. On and on then he went with citations . . . intellectual and moral insanity: *Official Report*, pp. 114–15; "no man can conceive of the misery that exists in the world today, following on the track of the libertine": p. 119.

67. "Look at her now, a wreck . . . reduced to a skeleton": *Official Report*, p. 125.

68. He addressed some points of law. . . . the charge was that "or nothing": *Official Report*, p. 119.

69. that Samuel Windley had remarked, "Fanny, I told you not to do it!": *Official Report*, p. 120.

70. "a gross outrage upon all propriety": *Official Report*, p. 122.

71. "a miserable sneak, worse than a spy . . . some of the gold that had been paid to Charley Spencer": *Official Report*, p. 121.

72. "Oh, gentlemen, I beg of you. . . . God bless you, Fanny Hyde!": *Official Report*, p. 129.

73. Many in the crowd applauded . . . 5 hours and 20 minutes: *Eagle*, 4-20-72.

74. They began an hour early on Saturday . . . "his voice partakes of the same characteristics": *Eagle*, 4-22-72.

75. "must have caused a smile upon the countenances of some of the gentlemen in this courtroom. . . .": *Official Report*, p. 130.

76. "Here is a woman who, early in life . . . she then prepares herself with a pistol and shoots him": *Official Report*, p. 134.

77. "Some women would have quailed at this contemplation. . . . some of the worst crimes are committed by women": *Official Report*, p. 149.

78. "a growing feeling in the community against capital punishment . . . a particular reluctance to inflicting this penalty upon women": *Official Report*, p. 145; "there is more deference to women among the educated American people than any other on the face of the earth": p. 146.

79. "petty, contemptible . . . overturn the results of the experience of ages": *Official Report*, p. 135.

80. He mocked Morris's elaborate efforts . . . "the question here is; is this such a case? That is all.": *Official Report*, p. 136.

81. "a mode of proof that has crept into jurisprudence" . . . "it is left to the jury alone and exclusively to apply those general principles and opinionate the facts of the case.": *Official Report*, p. 136.

82. "Men in pursuit of a single idea . . . are unsafe judges of such questions when you come to apply them to specific acts": *Official Report*, p. 137.

83. "a score of witnesses on each side": *Official Report*, p. 139.

84. "Did it occur to you . . . a sham and a farce": *Official Report*, p. 138.

85. Britton excused himself for this . . . it was not clear and convincing enough to properly introduce.: *Official Report*, p. 132.

86. "there is no getting away from the conclusion that her husband connived in this matter; . . . that he gave his assent to this relation": *Official Report*, p. 148.

87. "some ways below," at least three feet: *Official Report*, p. 150.

88. they were free to convict her of third-degree manslaughter: *Official Report*, p. 153.

89. 3 hours and 40 minutes: *Eagle*, 4-22-72.

90. "if sympathy is to determine the case . . . not to the wicked and vicious alone": *Official Report*, p. 154.

91. applause was again stifled by the bench, and the court recessed: *Eagle*, 4-22-72.

92. "a contest between the two men. . . . Mr. Britton surpasses Mr. Morris in subtlety": *Eagle*, 4-22-72.

93. "present[ed] issues not ordinarily found even in cases of great celebrity": *Official Report*, p. 155; the gentlemen not be swayed by sympathy or passion: p. 157. He defined first-degree murder and manslaughter . . . or that she was insane at the time: pp. 156–7; He reviewed the meaning of insanity, which must be established beyond reasonable doubt: *Official Report*, p. 160.

94. The jurors began deliberating about a quarter to two, as the room remained crowded with expectant, speculating and contending spectators: *Herald*, 4-21-72; *Eagle*, 4-22-72. (There is inconsistency regarding the time

of these events between newspaper reports and the "official" trial report. The author has found the newspaper accounts to be more probable.)

95. At about six they sent a note to Tappen . . . and they brought the printed matter back to their room: *Official Report*, p. 161; *NYT* 4-21-72; *Union*, 4-22-72.

96. All evening Fanny, now doubly veiled, and her family sat in their places. . . . He had to ask them to go back and deliberate further: *Official Report*, p. 161; *Eagle*, 4-23-72.

97. "Your honor, it will be impossible for us to agree if we stay together until next January." But back they went, many of them smiling wryly: *Herald*, 4-21-72; *Eagle*, 4-23-72.

98. Much of the crowd . . . not back to Raymond Street but to a local restaurant: *Eagle*, 4-23-72.

99. the jurors came in again at 12:30. . . . Then he cleared the courtroom: *Union*, 4-22-72; *Eagle*, 4-23-72.

100. The Hydes and Windleys retired to a private room . . . Voorhees and Johnson while they slept: *Eagle*, 4-23-72.

101. The twelve weary men took their seats again at exactly seven . . . every eye focused anxiously on the foreman as Tappen spoke: *Union*, 4-22-72.

102. "Gentlemen of the jury". . . . She groaned and sobbed, and her stepmother wept once more: *Eagle*, 4-23-72.

103. Judge Tappen remarked that if it were any day but Sunday . . . ten for acquittal and two for manslaughter in the third degree: *Union*, 4-22-72; *Eagle*, 4-23-72.

104. The *Eagle* got the attention of several jurors. . . . " 'I would convict her! She is a [whore], always has been a [whore].' ": 4-23-72.

105. A reporter found the dissenters at their lower Manhattan offices on Monday. . . . "If ever a man had a vacant look, he has it": *Eagle*, 4-24-72.

106. It became known . . . "the public would have been entirely willing to permit them to gratify themselves": *NYT*, 4-23-72.

107. "growing disinclination to hanging people" . . . "as revolting as anything in the records of our courts": *Eagle*, 4-23-72.

108. "every native-born citizen . . . here long enough to really understand our institutions": *Union*, 4-24-72.

109. On the morning of Tuesday, April 24th, two bondsmen posted $2,500 bail . . . predicted that she would never be tried again: *Eagle*, 4-23-72.

110. on Friday, the 27th . . . captured the previous night in Philadelphia.: *Eagle*, *Union*, 4-27-72; "defiant-looking": *Union*, 4-27-72.

111. Britton moved to retry her in October . . . won a postponement.: *Eagle*: 10-8, 16-73

112. When the case came to court again on January 21st, 1873 . . . who demanded payment on the bond.: *Eagle*, 1-21-73.

113. on March 23rd. . . . She "only wish[ed] that it was all over": *Eagle*, 3-24, 25-73.

114. He and others submitted an elaborate list of 11 charges . . . "Go to hell!": *Eagle*, 2-28-73.

115. Van Buskirk . . . eventually died in Brooklyn City Hospital.: *Eagle*, 8-30, 31; 9-1, 2, 5, 6, 20, 21, 25; 10-4, 5; 12-28-71; *NYT*, 10-4-71.

116. "a monstrous outrage against society": *Eagle*, 1-18-73.

117. In April '73 Morris defended Dr. Lucius Irish . . . a witness whom he wanted to cross-examine: *Eagle*, 6-7, 24-72; 7-16, 19-72; 12-10-72 through 1-3-73.

118. ". . . permit me to volunteer a little advice." . . . "there was evidence of suffering on his part from aberration of intellect.": *Eagle*: 1-16-73.

119. Victoria Woodhull . . . was a regular visitor to the Tilton home on Livingston Street.: Shaplen, pp. 130–161, passim; Applegate, pp. 412–414; *Columbia Encyclopedia*, articles on Henry Ward Beecher and on Victoria Woodhull and Tennessee Claflin.

120. "I conceive that Mrs. Tilton's love for Mr. Beecher was her true marriage . . . and that her marriage to Mr. Tilton is prostitution": Shaplen, p. 160.

121. deposited the sisters in New York's Ludlow Street Jail for a month on the charge of circulating obscene literature.: *Eagle*. 11-5-72; Shaplen, pp. 163–166.

122. "almost every man in Brooklyn has an ax to grind." James Morgan to *Eagle*, 1-21-73.

123. how many mistresses the pastor preached before: Applegate, pp. 391, 398, 412, 421.

124. Edna Dean Proctor . . . believed to have fathered a daughter: Applegate, pp. 267, 293, 302–05, 365–66, 375–77.

125. And Tilton, tall, curly-haired . . . a young woman who lived in his house as an unofficial daughter. : Shaplen, pp. 45–51, 81. Also on Tilton: <mrlincolnandnewyork.org>, (1-3-11).

126. Bowen was accused of different sins, such as vindictiveness and unscrupulous business practices: Shaplen, pp. 77–84.

127. his wife and mother of ten, Lucy Maria . . . her own intimacy with the minister: Shaplen, pp. 8–9; "amative": Shaplen, p. 160

128. They disputed over money . . . to shake the Christian world.: Applegate, *passim*, Shaplen, p. 9.

129. He betrayed Tilton . . . made up with the great clergyman.: Applegate, pp. 400–407; Shaplen, pp. 77–88, 101–03. 400–407; Waller, pp. 190–193.

130. In her dissertation on the scandal . . . for Plymouth was the church that Bowen had largely built: Waller, pp. 177–205; Applegate, pp. 202–05.

131. "Machiavellian," one author has described Bowen. Shaplen, p. 77.

132. to prevent the election of the presumably disloyal papist Francis Kernan: *Union*, 11-3-72.

133. the nativism that had infected Brooklyn . . . 20,000 people Sharp, v. 1, pp. 271–76; Murphy, *Catholic Charities*, p. 7; Judd, pp. 12–14.; *Eagle*, *NYT*, 6-5-1854; *Eagle*, 11-8, 9, 10, 11-1854.

134. "hauteur" . . . "if we wanted a friend to swear by we would choose Kinsella": the *Brooklyn Sunday Sun (BSS)*, 11-30-73.

135. a member of the Board of Education for five years: Biography Resource Center (<www.galenet.com> (2-18-09)); chairman of the committee for the local school. . . . Kinsella got him fired.: *Eagle*, 4-2, 10-73.

136. he had failed to remove his hat or the cigar from his mouth . . . and asked a teacher to fix him a brandy-and-water: *Union*, 4-9-73.

137. "boor," half-drunken, profane loafer": *Union*, 4-10-73; "a man of low, even brutal instincts," "an Irish importation of questioned naturalization": *Union*, 4-9-73.

138. "well known," . . . a member of his own household": *Eagle*, 4-12-73.

139. That spring a corps of 100 laborers . . . essentially complete: *Eagle*, 4-5-73.

140. In the fall . . . end their historic partnership.: Rybczynski, pp. 312–13, Lancaster, p. 66.

141. she had lately received anonymous letters . . . at a certain time that afternoon at Olmstead's Hotel: *Union*, 4-16-73.

142. It was said that Field had discovered . . . barred the editor from their home: The *National Police Gazette*, 6-5-80.

143. Accounts of the rides through Prospect Park and the incident at Olmstead's Tavern were published in the *Union* on 4-16 and 4-17-73, and on 4-17 the *Union* included excerpts of accounts from the *New York Herald*, New York *World*, New York *Evening Telegram* and *Brooklyn Daily Times (BDT)*.

144. Emeline, aged 23 or 24 . . . Kinsella was 40, and Elizabeth about the same age: 1870, 1880 U.S. censuses <ancestry.com>; New York Port arrival record, 9-12-83 <ancestry.com>; *Eagle*, 12-29-75.

145. "a neat, frame dwelling of the better class of country inns". . . . "He won't, but I will. I mean to see this thing out": *Union*, 4-16-73.

146. "the scene furnished another of those peculiar evidences . . . Mr. Thomas Kinsella": *Union*, 4-16-73.

"Oh, this thing was bound to come out sooner or later". . . . "I tell you his position is terrible": *Union*, 4-17-73.

147. "coarse and commonplace lust": *Eagle*, 4-2-73. The exact phrase, quoted earlier, is "coarse and commonplace life of economical lust."

148. "——— master" who managed "the Ring Organ": *Union*, 4-16-73.

149. The educational meeting at the Academy of Music: both the *Eagle* and the *Union* reported the speeches on 4-19-73.

150. In May and June, Reid got his hearing . . . "I think I can show that he is." *Eagle*, 4-24, 6-3-73.

151. at a Republican Association meeting . . . a past "presiding officer" of one of its engines, the Order of the American Union, in the city's sixth ward. *Eagle*, 6-10-73.

152. the Teachers' Committee delivered its finding . . . he hadn't doused his cigar or doffed his hat.: *Eagle*, 6-23-73.

153. He had admitted as much about the cigar . . . not left it in his mouth: *Eagle*, 6-3-73.

Chapter 3

1. They had been born in 1831 and '33 in the Finger Lakes region. . . . To family and friends he was "Billy": *NYT*, 3-23-73; *Eagle*, 4-2-72; *Eagle*, *SU*, 11-21-1906.

2. And Charles was "Charlie". . . . a widower for six years: *Eagle*, 3-24, 4-2, 4-5-73; *NYT*, 3-23, 4-5-73.

3. After Charles moved into 731 Degraw Street there in March 1873, William often stopped to see him in the morning.: *Eagle*, 3-29-73; 59 Wall Street: *Eagle*, 3-26-73.

4. There was one newspaper report . . . revolver under his pillow: *NYT*, 3-23-73.

5. On Thursday, March 20th . . . left the pail at the entrance and went to work: *Eagle*, *NYT*, 3-29, 4-2-72.

6. A messenger named Bunker Hill . . . talking to another man that afternoon.: *Eagle*, 3-28-73.

7. three persons would state that he had been on the Fifth Avenue car . . . Alderman William Richardson, who exchanged bows with him.: *Eagle*, *NYT*, *Herald*, 3-29-73.

8. W. W. Goodrich stopped again . . . "as if he was glad somebody had come": *Eagle*, 3-29-73.

9. He opened the shutters . . . "colored coachman": *Eagle*, 3-21, 29-73; *Union*, 3-21-73; *NYT*, 4-2, 5-73; dressed in a brown "business coat" and vest, dark-blue check "pantaloons, dress-shirt, collar and tie."

10. "Oh, Joseph". . . . "He was crying when he told me this": *Eagle*, 3-24-73.

11. In a front-page newspaper list . . . the city's eight millionaires.: *Eagle*, 7-27-71. a bundle of real-estate investments he had begun to transact the previous year . . . four contiguous lots on the north side of Degraw Street, between Fifth and Sixth Avenues: property conveyance records, Kings County Register's Office.

12. "bleak and desolate," and "dotted over with little shanties": *NYT*, 3-23-73, *Eagle*, 3-21-73.

13. At the end of 1871 . . . "peaceably and quietly have, hold, occupy, possess and enjoy the above-granted premises.": property conveyance records, Kings County Register's Office.

14. FOR SALE . . . C. GOODRICH: *Eagle*, 4-18, 19-72

During that period . . . move his parents into another.: *BDT*, 3-22-73; *Union*, 3-24-73; *Eagle*, 4-2, 7-73.

15. A local stove-dealer . . . "temperate and quiet." *Union*, 3-24-73.

16. some more substantial houses, both brick and frame . . . "What scuffle?", seeming quite annoyed: *Eagle*, 3-21-73 (including quotes), 4-2-73.

17. It was the only time . . . known him to be a gentleman: *NYT*, *Eagle*, *Herald*, 4-2-73.

18. His brother would describe him . . . rustle of her dress in an adjoining room: *Eagle*, *NYT*, 3-29, 4-2-73.

19. letter from a unknown woman who had been Charles Goodrich's lover: *Eagle*, *NYT*, *Herald*, 4-2-73.

20. The eastern end of Degraw Street . . . Superintendent John S. Folk: *Eagle*, 4-5-73; Fales, p. 345.

21. Thousands feel" . . . "preventive of crime": *Graphic*, 3-21-73; "All honor to the Governor's firmness": *The Diary of George Templeton Strong*, v. 4, pp. 472–473 (3-14-73).

22. The pistol immediately suggested suicide . . . watch, pocketbook and seal ring were missing: *Eagle*. 3-29-73.

23. Folk and Videto did not agree . . . the window had been broken for some time.: *Eagle*, 3-21, 22, 4-5-73.

24. Coroner Whitehill, who was not a physician: *Eagle*, 10-16-68; began his own examination . . . caused by a blunt instrument: *Eagle*, 3-21-73.

25. In the evening . . . "he couldn't have committed suicide": *Eagle*, 3-22, 4-2, 5-73; *NYT*, 3-24-73.

26. Still the Brooklyn police . . . forgotten that he had done so: *Eagle*, 3-21-73.

27. "If you had a brother that committed suicide. . . .": *Eagle*, 3-22-73.

28. "people who deny that he has committed suicide. . . .": *Eagle*, 3-26-73.

29. The *Eagle's* reporter made fun of "the old veteran" . . . "exquisitely ridiculous": 3-22-73.

30. "absurd to everybody" . . . other valuable items upstairs: *NYT*, 3-23-73.

31. "The chimerical idea of suicide . . . upon which some of the detectives have departed": Eagle, 3-22-73.

32. "We no more believe . . . from all labor or care in working up the case": *Eagle* 3-26-73.

33. "occasioned more excitement in the city. . . .": *Eagle*, 3-22-73.

34. *Graphic* illustrations: 3-24-73.

35. It was noon on Saturday, the 22nd. . . . "He was murdered for his money. I'm quite sure of it": *Eagle*, 3-22-73.

36. he had died intestate . . . $3,000: *NYT*, 3-27-73; would later state that Charles had owed him $15,000: *Eagle*, 8-27-74; offered $2,500: *Eagle*, 3-25-73.

37. began to sob . . . "scowled at the reporter, who laughed in return": *Eagle*, 3-23-73; a dressmaker who lived on E. 59th Street: 1870 U.S. Census.

38. "of considerable beauty": New York *Sun*, 3-24-73; "profusely curled" . . . "honorable": *NYT*, 3-24-73.

39. "that she was engaged to be married to Mr. Goodrich": *NYT*, 3-25-73; this was also mentioned in *Graphic*: 3-25-73.

40. Adeline Palm: *Eagle*, 7-14-73.

41. in the kitchen icebox: *Eagle*, 3-22-73.

42. removed on Saturday, the 22nd, and laid out . . . would be laid in the family vault: *Eagle*, *NYT*, 3-24-73; "a man of fretful and even misanthropic disposition"; "it was impossible to view the coffin.": *NYT*; "His daily walk was that of a quiet, unostentatious Christian. . . .": *Eagle*.

43. On Monday, the 24th, the *Eagle's* reporter . . . "or whom he had refused to marry": *Eagle*, 3-24-73.

44. "bold and scheming adventuress" . . . washed his head and "laid him out": *Eagle*, 3-24, 25-73.

45. There was no speculation . . . "one of the highest officials in the county.": *Eagle*, 3-25-73.

46. "I have never, from the first," he said, "entertained the least shadow of belief that it was other than a murder.": *Eagle*, 3-25-73.

47. some members of the force . . . attempt to muzzle it or its sources: *Eagle*, 3-26-73.

48. "The name of the woman . . . recognized as true by the authorities today": *Eagle*, 3-26-73.

49. "The system is the creature of politics . . . brain fever": *Eagle*, 3-25-73.

50. Father Briggs and General Jourdan . . . all seven of Brooklyn's gas concerns: Fales, pp. 47–8, 75–80; Murphy, *Brooklyn Union*, pp. 7–9 and passim; Syrett, p. 57.

51. "smartest man in Brooklyn": *NYT*, 12-14-1890.

52. replaced its longtime publisher, Isaac Van Anden, on the police board: Fales, p. 47.

53. the police had found a dozen letters . . . but with another name, which was not yet revealed: *Eagle*, 3-27-73.

54. Exactly a month after that letter had been written. . . . "What," she asked, "have you had me brought here for?": *Eagle*, 3-28, 10-27, 11-21-73.

55. Campbell, 46. . . . His customary manner was genial: Fales, pp. 118–22; "one of the most skilful detectives in the country": Walling, p. 543.

56. "Do you know Mr. Goodrich?" . . . "and if I have got to stay here I will stay": *Eagle*, *Sun*, 3-28-73.

57. The latter they learned from the coachman . . . "mighty unwilling" to come: *Eagle*, 3-28-73.

58. ""If I go . . . a parrot that never talks": *Sun*, 4-5-73.

59. Campbell and others . . . in the janitor's room: *Eagle*, 3-28-73.

60. 27 press representatives . . . buzzed with news about the capture of Charles Goodrich's "mistress.": *Eagle*, 3-28-73.

61. A newsman who had interviewed Professor Boyle . . . "a female who had dissipated in one way or another to some degree": *Eagle*, 3-28-73; missing teeth: *Eagle*, 4-2-73. about 30: *Herald*, 3-28-73.

62. Campbell soon realized that this woman was not the killer: *Eagle*, 3-29, 8-23-73.

63. "She's a Yankee woman" . . . "they will be thunderstruck!": *Eagle*, 3-28-73.

64. the *Eagle*, determined to identify Campbell's captive, put a man on the ferry . . . nudged her daughter to be silent: 3-28-73.

65. The *Eagle*'s man in Manhattan moved on to 13 Stanton Street . . . "an' no one knows the misery of the poor": 3-28, 29-73.

66. "The Song of the Shirt,": *Herald*, 3-30-73.

67. Coroner Whitehill was given use of a regular courtroom . . . the story of finding his brother's body: *Eagle*, 3-28-73; *NYT*, *Herald*, 3-29-73.

68. continued his testimony on April 1st . . . signed "Amy G": *Eagle*, *NYT*, *Herald*, 4-2-73.

69. William Goodrich had learned. . . . "I was greatly shocked.": *NYT*, 4-2-73; *Eagle*, 8-23-73.

70. Lucette took the stand for more than three hours on April 1ˢᵗ . . . but was "not he": *NYT*, 4-2-73.

71. the coroner called "Samuel Roscoe" to the stand. . . . "it is on the Camden and Amboy Railroad": *NYT*, *Herald*, 4-2-73.

72. In successive days non-Roscoes (and non-Spaniards) were picked up . . . "a totally different person from that described in the telegram from New York": *Eagle*, 3-31, 4-1, 2-73; *NYT*, 4-3-73.

73. The *New York Times* declared its certainty. . . . "in a few days he will be arrested": 4-3-73.

74. Whitehill did not release her . . . Raymond Street: *NYT*, 3-29-73.

75. A lawyer . . . petitioned for her release: *NYT*, 3-29-73; a drunk . . . offered to post her $1,000 bail.: *NYT*, *Eagle*, 4-2-73.

76. But for many days, . . . everything would her done for her comfort: *NYT*, *Eagle*, 4-2-73.

77. Her residence was described by a New York reporter . . . dismal-looking cells on either side": *Graphic*, 10-4-73.

78. When the Goodrich murder inquest resumed on the evening of April 4ᵗʰ, 1873 . . . "was keeping bachelor's hall" on Degraw Street: *Herald*, *NYT*, *Eagle*, 4-5-73.

79. He was followed by Dr. Reuben Smith . . . he had lent Charles, his friend "up to the day of his death," a total of $3,000": *Herald*, 4-5-73.

80. The papers reacted to the evening's accounts . . . "loathing and abhorrence" *Eagle*, *NYT*, 4-5-73; *Herald*, 4-6-73; *Graphic*, 4-7-73.

81. The following day's featured informer was 22-year-old Charles Green . . . after Tuesday morning he never more saw either one of them: *NYT*, *Herald*, 4-6-73; *Eagle*, *Sun*, 4-7-73.

82. "offensiveness": *Eagle*, 4-7-73.

83. "a coarse and commonplace life of economical lust": *Eagle*, 4-2-73.

84. "By degrees there will be a better understanding . . . so much that is good and evil in humanity." *Herald*, 7-13-73.

85. George Templeton Strong . . . "seek to become second-rate men, or bad imitations of men": Strong, v. 4, p. 474 (3-28-73).

86. If she is meant to work like a man . . . why is she so frail and gentle?: *Union*, 10-18-73.

87. One stratagem they conceived . . . no new intelligence.: *Herald*, *NYT*, 4-12-73; Lucette was released . . . on April 14ᵗʰ: *NYT*, 4-15-73.

88. On that same day . . . "butchery in Degraw Street": *Eagle*, 4-15-73; "so far as the police force is concerned the Goodrich case is practically at an end": *Eagle*, 4-28-73.

89. the department issued an order . . . for which an arrest had not yet been made: *Eagle*, 4-29-73.

90. living in rural Connecticut: *Eagle*, 4-26-73.

91. on the evening of the 29th . . . "some other person": *NYT*, 4-30-73.

92. an Irish gangster from West 16th Street, New York . . . claimed to know nothing of Goodrich, and apparently didn't: *NYT*, 5-11,12-73; *Eagle*, 5-12-73.

93. W. W. Goodrich and District Attorney Winchester Britton were vacationing in Europe.: *Eagle*, 6-11, 24-73.

94. As the Brooklyn Common Council was approving a $1,000 reward: *NYT*, 6-3-73.

95. In the early morning of June 3rd, 1873 . . . abused and threatened his former wife, Frank's mother, and would not let up: *NYT*, 6-4, 7-1, 2, 3-73; O'Brien, pp. 172, 181, 201ff.

96. "A most uncommonly shocking murder . . . concealed weapons a felony." Strong, v. 4, p. 483 (6-3-73).

97. But at the same moment Coroner Whitehill was canceling a resumption of his inquest: *NYT*, 6-3-73.

98. They had interviewed. . . . Myers, who had known her well: *Eagle*, 7-11-73.

99. Miss Mary Handley . . . became Campbell's hired agent, at a salary of two dollars a day: *Eagle*, 7-11, 12; 8-23, 25-73; 11-25-74; *NYT*, 7-13-73.

100. "a handsome brunette": *NYT*, 7-13-73; "of medium height, firmly built" . . . "a captivating mode of address": *Eagle*, 7-12-73.

101. Jourdan, in fact, had wanted to dump the chief months earlier. . . . But Briggs wouldn't consent.: *Eagle*, 8-22-73.

102. And Campbell, when the time was right. . . . This picture, added Campbell, had been given to Jourdan by Lucette.: *Eagle*, 8-23-73.

103. Mary Handley had lived with the woman she had known as Kate Stoddard during the first half of 1872 at 45 Elizabeth Street . . . and moved to the "Working Woman's Home.": *Herald*, 7-11-73; *Eagle*, 7-12-73; 11-25-74; *NYT*, 7-13-73.

104. Agent Handley pursued Kate mainly in New York City. . . . Kate's correspondence was again showing up at 12th Street: *NYT*, 7-11-73; *Eagle*, 7-12; 8-23-73; 11-25-74; *Herald*, 7-13-73.

105. Jourdan now appointed his own detective. . . . "This was after the Commissioner had told the Chief to discharge Mary Handley.": *Eagle*, 8-22-73.

106. He had sent her back to 12th Street and handed her a five-dollar bill for expenses: *Eagle*, 7-12; 8-23-73.

107. she kept the money in her hand . . . "the woman was no other than Kate Stoddard": *Eagle*, 7-12-73.

108. She bid the driver to stop the car. . . . It was close to noon: *Eagle*, 7-12; 8-23-73; 11-25-74.

109. Before them the Brooklyn tower of the East River Bridge . . . lifted by three huge derricks: McCullough, pp. 223, 564–65.

110. Near the ferry-house . . . he complied: *Eagle, Sun*, 7-10-73; *Eagle*, 7-12-73, 11-25-74.

111. "looked as if she was goin' to faint first. . . . I'll go along with you": *Eagle*, 7-10-73.

112. On the way to the Second Precinct house . . . "did not know until he got to the station house who he had arrested": *Eagle*, 7-12-73.

113. Although Kate said nothing, she did something . . . "rather an advantage than otherwise to its possessor": *Graphic*, 7-12-73; *NYT, Herald*, 7-13-73.

114. The commander of the Second Precinct was Captain John McConnell. . . . Mullins, who operated a dry-goods store: *Eagle*, 7-12, 17-73.

115. "It did not take me long . . . skirt, shawl and hat were all she possessed": *Sun*, 7-10-73.

116. "No. . . . She was a bony lookin' woman"; McConnell telegraphed Chief Campbell at headquarters, and he rushed down to York Street: *Sun*, 7-10-73.

117. General Jourdan, once more examining his supposed photograph of Kate . . . who was sure he had her: *Eagle*, 8-23-73.

118. But she would not give her name . . . overnight in McConnell's office: *Eagle*, 7-14; 8-23-73.

119. "At last" . . . just to stop his questioning: *SU*, 12-9-1906.

120. Forty years later . . . also provided by that 25-year-old man: *Eagle*, 9-12-1913.

121. They liked a story that she had shot him, not on the Friday, March 21st. . . . She told the chief that she had indeed called to Charles . . . returned to Brooklyn on Sunday and appeared at Charles's funeral: *Tribune, Eagle*, 7-12-73; 3-12-74; *BSS*, 7-19-74; *SU* 12-9-1906.

122. Then there was the episode of the gold locket . . . "That is Charles Goodrich's blood.": *Eagle*, 7-12-73; Two sketches of her drawn at the inquest would clearly depict it: *Graphic*, 7-14-73; *Frank Leslie's Illustrated Newspaper*, 7-26-73.

123. "A queer thing is crime. A queerer thing is woman.": *Eagle*, 7-11-73.

124. Twenty-two years after Kate's arrest. . . . "I have tested your loyalty and I say to you that I will never forget you as long as I live.": *Eagle*, 3-4-95.

125. When he was interviewed again . . . "in a cool, sneering way": *SU*, 12-9-1906.

126. In one of the two trunks in Kate's High Street room . . . by one account, $40, by another, just 16: *Eagle*, *NYT*, 7-12-73.

127. Also here was what she was reported to have stated was the murder weapon . . . his father could not identify this one as his son's: *Eagle*, 7-11, 12, 14-73.

128. Every account seemed to add . . . that his father remembered an older one: *NYT*, 7-13-73; *Eagle*, 7-14-73.

129. In any case, there were also lots of letters . . . "it is better for both that we should separate": *Eagle*, *NYT*, 7-15-73, *Sun*, 7-16-73.

130. a bunch of letters, too, from her 54-year-old mother. . . . Lizzie Lloyd King: *NYT*, 7-12, 13-73; born in Plymouth on May 27th, 1847: *Eagle*, 7-14-74.

131. No. 127 High Street was a building much like thousands. . . . On my mother wishing to hear it, and my brother to read it, she got up and left the room": *Eagle*, 7-11-73; they rented her a room for $2.50 a week: *NYT*, 7-13-73.

132. "as many names as lovers": *NYT*, 7-14-73; "Gilmore": *NYT*, 7-13-73; "Amy Marlowe": *Herald*, 7-13-73; *Sun*, 7-14-73; a sad and wild stay in Attleboro Falls . . . "Emma Chase": *Eagle*, 8-4-73 (per *Attleboro Chronicle*); In Attleboro Falls. . . . She had claimed that she carried a pistol.: *Eagle*, 8-4-73.

133. She learned to make straw bonnets. . . . Providence, Hartford, perhaps? *Eagle*, 7-14, 15-74, *Herald*, 7-16-73.

134. Isaac and Harriet King . . . "all efforts to administer comfort were in vain": *Herald*, 7-16-73; Mr. King, said to employed as a mason: *Herald*, 7-15-73.

135. W. W. Goodrich was a member of the Society of Mayflower Descendants: *Eagle*, 12-22-1906.

136. When the long-interrupted Goodrich murder inquest resumed. . . . Kate's never subsided while the witness remained on the stand: *Eagle*, 7-12, 14-73; *NYT*, *Herald*, 7-13-73.

137. The newspapers . . . continued to speculate about his involvement in the murder and his current whereabouts: e.g., *Eagle*, 7-14-73.

138. When Alderman Richardson, the jury chairman, asked Lucette to lift her veil . . . their common lover had told her that Kate was his sister from Brooklyn: *Eagle*, 7-12-73; *Herald*, 7-13-73.

139. Since Counselor DeWitt had prevailed upon his client . . . "pistol-shot wounds in the head, inflicted by Lizzie Lloyd King, alias Kate Stoddard, with intent to cause death": *NYT, Herald*, 7-13-73; *Eagle*, 7-14-73.

140. Keeper Howard Conrady. . . . One of them was Fanny Hyde: *Eagle*, 7-11-73; *NYT*, 7-13-73; *Sun*, 7-16, 18. "Howard": *Herald*, 7-14-73.

141. Fanny, "looking better than ever" . . . sat and sung side-by-side at Sunday services: *Eagle*, 7-14-73; "a fellow feeling" . . . "fairly loves Fanny": *Herald*, 7-18-73; who told the press that Kate would not speak about her case, but had been writing a full account of it for her lawyers: *Eagle*, 7-14-73.

142. Within a week . . . removed to the witness room: *Eagle*, 7-24-73.

143. the new inmate was remarkably well-treated . . . "the spotted cow in the yard": *Eagle*, 7-15-73; *Sun*, 7-16-73.

144. the baneful influence of tawdry romantic fiction: *Herald*, 7-16-73; *Graphic*, 7-17-73; Shakespeare and Ossian . . . *Othello*: *Herald*, 7-18-73; read and prayed: *Eagle*, 7-15-73.

145. "A dozen newspapers . . . justifying murder as a means of redressing personal injuries": *NYT*, 7-15-73; "Most women know the difference between right and wrong . . . a few of the responsibilities of the wrong": *NYT*, 7-18-73.

146. *Herald* was attacked by other papers. . . .": *Eagle*, 7-14-73; *NYT*, 7-15-73.

147. Sympathizers, mostly female . . . "hardly probable.": *Herald, Sun, Graphic*, 7-18-73.

148. On July 22nd her father, Isaac King, came to her . . . gathering witnesses from Massachusetts: *Eagle*, 7-23-73; taking responsibility for expenses: *Eagle*, 7-21-73.

149. A Democratic governor of Maryland in the early 1850s. . . . "The Historical Destiny of Women.": Caleb Clarke Magruder, "Enoch Louis Lowe, Governor of Maryland, 1851–54," (extracted from the Year-Book of the American Clan Gregor Society, 1909 and 1910; accessed at <www. archive. org>, 3-18-11).

150. On August 21st . . . "let this matter stand over until tomorrow, when Gen. Jourdan will be here": *Eagle*, 8-21-73.

151. And on that morrow a slightly longer letter was delivered . . . , Campbell had allowed gambling and prostitution to flourish in the city.: *Eagle*, 8-22-73.

152. The next day Commissioner Briggs was asked his opinion of Patrick Campbell. . . . "The force," Campbell lamented, "had been set against me.": *Eagle*, 8-23-73.

153. Even the *Union* conceded . . . "bungled" the case of Professor Panormo: *Union*, 8-22-73.

153. In September 1873 Charles Videto was also gone. . . . The flags at Court and Livingston Streets were lowered to half-mast: *Union*, 9-8-73.

Chapter 4

1. The women had met when the adolescent Sarah Dougherty . . . the only "confidential friend . . . I ever had in my life.": *Eagle*, 10-31-74.

2. Margaret, who lived at 236 West 48th Street, New York, had inherited money from her father, and drew an income from rents on residential property that he had left to her and her brothers.: *Eagle*, 10-28, 29-74; *NYT*, 7-23-75.

3. She was named godmother of Sarah's boy. . . . They browsed together at New York's Broadway picture-galleries: *Eagle*, 10-29, 31-74.

4. they became disciples of fortune-telling, and their fervor for it intensified as the year 1873 wore on.: *Eagle*, 10-28, 29, 31-74.

5. One day that summer a gypsy named Bertha came to her door . . . "I felt that she had told me more of the truth than the others had done": *Eagle*, 10-31-74.

6. Bertha told her that she was very intelligent . . . not one who concerned herself with the things of this world: *Eagle*, 10-29-74.

7. The gypsy also told her that she was pregnant, which Sarah did not think she was: *Eagle*, 10-31-74.

8. Bertha came a second time. . . . "Don't let anyone see how foolish we are": *Eagle*, 10-31-74.

9. "excused herself for not admitting me". . . . the visitor asked Sarah to come look at them: *Eagle*, 10-28-74.

10. Sarah agreed . . . told Mrs. Knowles, that she had left her friend for too long: *Eagle*, 10-28, 29, 31-74.

11. Mrs. Knowles next saw Sarah that night about ten. . . . That night the Merrigans stayed at Sarah's parents' house. *Eagle*, 10-28, 29-74; *Herald*, 10-28-74.

12. David Coe. . . . She paid the boys 75 cents: *Eagle*, 10-28-74.

13. Coe came home that night about nine o'clock. . . . The rope had been newly cut with a sharp instrument, and "was drawn tight": *Eagle*, *NYT*, 9-9-73; *Eagle*, 10-28-74.

14. born Sarah Cecilia Dougherty in 1850: *Eagle*, 10-31-74; in what was still the Village of Williamsburgh: J. M. Stearns, History of the Town of Williamsburgh, (Stiles, Kings Co. v.1, p. 298).

15. Eighteen-fifty is also the year at which the historian Emmet Larkin . . . more than doubled during the 1860s and 1870s: Larkin, p. 644.

16. By 1870, nearly 300,000 residents of New York and Brooklyn were Irish-born: *New York City Encyclopedia*, "Immigration," p. 584.

17. Sarah Dougherty attended one of those schools . . . in the same neighborhood until she was 17: *Eagle*, 10-29, 31-74; illiterate parents: <ancestry.com> 1880 U.S. census.

18. Neighbors would remember her as a mild-mannered, well-behaved girl . . . "she took the shoes off her feet one day and gave them to a poor woman": *Eagle*, 10-31-74.

29. The convent . . . "who wish to do penance for their iniquities and lead a truly Christian life": Le Brun, Charles. "Our Lady of Charity of the Good Shepherd." *The Catholic Encyclopedia*, vol. 6. (1909) <http://oce. catholic.com> (4-19-2011).

20. Although she had taken the vows. . . . It was January 1870.: *Eagle*, 10-28, 29-74.

21. The period that followed was the first of several in which Sarah was known to have been sick. . . . She also suffered severe headaches: *Eagle*, 10-29, 30-74; She was 20; he was 21: <ancestry.com>, 1870 census; a girl, named Cecilia: <ancestry.com>, 1880 census.

22. nine dollars-a-month: *BDT*, 9-5-73.

23. Matilda Knowles . . . "seemed to be her ideal.": *Eagle*, 10-28-74.

24. "consulted for this purpose "Madame La Rosa" on Canal Street, New York . . . "expressed a strong desire to be in better circumstances, to go in good society." *Eagle*. 10-29-74.

25. "greatly frightened": *Eagle*, 10-31-74.

26. "After she went to live in the rear of No. 199 . . . my daughter remarked it and the neighbors spoke of it": *Eagle*, 10-28-74.

27. A drawing of Sarah Merrigan at this period: *Graphic*, 9-12-73.

28. "She is a well built woman, perhaps weighing 140 pounds . . . she shows them very pleasantly": *Eagle*, 6-20-74.

29. "Prepossessing" . . . "indicate the owner to have been a woman of character." *Union*, 9-10-73.

30. David Coe's little pail of water. . . . She gave Mary Jane her baby boy to hold, and picked him up later at the Knowles's apartment: *Eagle*, 9-11-73, 10-28-74; "The fire is all out now" . . . "there was nobody up in his rooms": *NYT*, 9-9-73.

31. Police Officer Edmund Brown arrived . . . "she supposed Miss Hamill had upset the kerosene lamp": *Eagle*, 10-29-74.

32. a local doctor, the same Samuel Brady . . . "not think it at all possible that deceased had committed suicide": *Eagle*, 9-11-73.

33. Captain Woglom also heard Sarah's story . . . talk that she had stolen things from Maggie, and perhaps others, in the past: *Eagle*, 9-8-73.

34. he wanted to know if she had taken jewelry from her friend's body. . . . There was jewelry there: *BDT*, 9-6-73; *NYT*, 9-8-73; *Eagle* 9-8-73, 10-29-74; "very feeble and sick": *Eagle*, 10-29-74; "would give a beggar a quarter rather than arrest him": *Eagle*, 7-26-1904.

35. On that Saturday the scorched remains of Margaret Hamill were laid to rest . . . she had died at age 33: *Herald*, 9-7-73; *Union*, 9-8-73.

36. Patrick Keady . . . Democratic assemblyman and a lawyer only since 1869.: *Eagle*, 5-23-72, 9-9-73; *NYT*, 10-8-1908.

37. He believed that Sarah was innocent . . . "hundreds of dollars" of his own into the cause: *Eagle*, 10-29-74; *NYT*, 7-23-75.

38. "whom an errant spider throws into convulsions," . . . perpetrated by Sarah alone: *Eagle*, 9-9-73.

39. the inquest that began in the district courtroom on the evening of Monday, September 8th. . . . "It's mine—mine": *Eagle*, 9-9-73; *NYT*, 9-11-73.

40. "We must have" or "will have a separation:" *Eagle*, 9-12-73.

41. A parade of workingmen with Irish names. . . . "Mr. Merrigan was very much vexed about it, saying he was so tired, he had a good mind to lie down in the lots": *Eagle*, 9-11, 12-73; *NYT*, 9-11-73; St. Patrick's Mutual Alliance: *Herald*, 9-7-73.

42. Mrs. Cecilia Dougherty testified . . . "that a dead body was in the room": *Eagle*, 9-12-73.

34. a foul smell was plainly detected shortly afterward . . . had come home and discovered that smell after being away for some days: *Eagle*, 9-9-73.

44. At the inquest's end . . . was returned to the Kings County Jail: *Eagle*, *Union*, 9-12-73.

45 "It is a matter not altogether unworthy of a little consideration three of the meagrest and meekest looking women in the country. . . .": *Eagle*, 9-15-73

46. Fanny Hyde was released from the jail . . . had shuffled off to Washington on Sam Morris's advice: *Eagle*, 9-3-73.

47. "not far distant". . . . "before the time of her full compensation will come": *Eagle*. 9-4-73.

48. During her first month or so in prison, Kate, that able wordsmith, had completed her "pamphlet" . . . "knew he had killed himself": *Eagle*, 3-11-74.

49. Kate did not receive Sarah at all well at Raymond Street. . . . "I have nothing to complain about and neither has she, only she wants to put on airs and give the keepers trouble": *Eagle*, 10-27-73, 11-19-73.

50. demanding to be sent to another floor to be away from her . . . upsetting the whole jail with her early-morning shrieks: *Eagle*, 10-27-73.

51. One of the other inmates was Lucette Myers . . . while the nemesis expressed resentment: *Eagle*, 10-2, 6-73; *Union*, 10-20-73.

52. A visitor stated . . . no one but the person who brought her meals. *Graphic*, 10-4-73.

53. She had been detained again . . . threatened to perforate her if she squealed: *Eagle*, 10-2-73; *Graphic*, 10-4-73; *Union*, 10-28-73.

54. The *Union* scored a long interview with Dr. Park . . . got a fellow collared who was no more Beach than the soap-salesman at the inquest had been the wicked Roscoe: *Union*, 10-30-73.

55. It was said that Park even provided her with new teeth: *Eagle*, 10-28-73.

"Lucette's story of the murder" . . . "I must confess that she is a mystery to me": *Union*, 10-30-73.

56. "expected when arrested to make some money . . . though she has cost us something": *Eagle*, 10-27-73.

57. "the biggest liar I ever met" *Eagle*, 11-3-73; "Dogberry": *Eagle*, 11-8-73.

"Laughing and smoothing her dress". . . . " 'I never saw him, that I know of' ": *Eagle*, 11-10-73.

58. She wrote a letter to D. A. Britton . . . "she was laughing immoderately": *Eagle*, 11-20-73.

59. On October 5th James Merrigan had been re-arrested: *NYT*, 10-6-73.

60. He, Sarah and Kate were all arraigned on October 7th . . . he and his partner, D. B. Thompson, were not ready for trial: *Eagle*, 10-7-73.

61. A crowd followed Sarah and Kate back to Raymond Street . . . "whose face everybody desired to look at": *Union, Eagle*, 10-7-73.

62. Kate's lawyers had received a commission from the court to search for witnesses . . . possibly would establish that no crime had been committed at the Merrigan apartment: *Eagle*, 10-23-73.

63. Britton was patient with these appeals. . . . The price was $2500, the same as for Fanny Hyde: *Eagle*, 11-3-73.

64. Kate granted an interview to the *Union* in November . . . "was the last to leave the sidewalk when his coffin was placed in the hearse": *Union*, 11-13-73.

65. Tall, slim and trimly bearded, Tracy at 43 . . . "father of the fighting navy": *American National Biography*, v. 21, pp. 791–94; Stiles, v. II, pp. 1222–27; *Eagle, BDT*, 8-7-1915; Syrett, pp. 102–04.

66. "he was seldom defeated in a case which he fully and maturely prepared": Stiles, v. II, p. 122; "a worker, a man of great ability, and a lawyer of learning": *Eagle*, 6-19-74.

67. In March 1873 Governor Dix asked him to respond to the list of charges against him, and he denied them all.: *Eagle*, 3-12-73.

68. who held hearings on December . . . when Morris himself stood up to interrogate Britton.: *Eagle*, 12-1, 2, 3, 4, 5, 8, 10, 11, 12, 13, 15, 16-73.

69. "the men from Albany . . . laugh at our folly in thus exposing our domestic differences and internal disagreements.": *Eagle*, 12-5-73.

70. two boys visited Morris at his home . . . because it had been manufactured in Morris's own camp.: *Eagle*, 2-2, 3, 4, 5-74; Syrett, pp. 62–3.

71. The ruling was issued on February 20th . . . charges against the city collector.: *Eagle*, 2-20-74.

72. Most lawyers in the city . . . "too thin": *Eagle*, 2-23-74.

73. "probably fear[ed] that a civil war was about to break out": Syrett, p. 63.

74. Morris's ally, A. C. Davis, approached Sam Morris in a county courtroom. . . . the strong implication that they were headed to a saloon.: *Eagle*, 2-21-74.

75. The man whom Dix appointed to succeed Britton . . . replaced in May by Republican John Winslow: *Eagle*, 5-8, 11-74, 10-17-98; *NYT*, 5-8-74.

76. Britton was re-elected by a wider margin than . . . 1871: *Eagle*, 11-8-71, 11-4-74.

77. She had fired all her lawyers . . . "is not that she is insane at the present time, but that she was at the time of the offense, if any was committed by her": *Eagle*, 3-3-74.

78. Her 16-month-old boy. . . . "Oh, if I could have been there to see its little body laid in the grave!": *Eagle*, 5-16-74.

79. "There were convulsions" . . . "and she was weak." *Eagle*, *NYT*, 10-30-74.

80. A few days after this attack, Dr. Charles Corey . . . would wait to compare his observations with those of others: *Eagle*, 5-20-74.

81. "Why, the idea! I'm not insane at all . . . that's what I ought to have done": *Eagle*, 5-21-74.

82. but the impression among employees . . . a "dodge": *Eagle*, 5-20, 21-74.

83. General Tracy was in Albany . . . the judge agreed to postpone the trial until October: *Eagle*, 6-20-74; yet another Civil War general, wounded during the Seven Days: Sifakis, p. 321; Stiles, v. II, pp. 1277–80; no close relation to Charles Pratt: interview with Paul Schlotthauer, Pratt Institute archivist, 7-13, 15-2011.

84. sold the paper in October 1873 to a group of fellow Republicans, including Benjamin Tracy and Controller Frederick Schroeder: *Eagle*, 10-11-73; *BSS*, 11-30-73.

85. "regret that a former proprietor of the paper . . . should never have been printed": *Union*, 1-7-75.

86. "Brooklyn's Lesser Scandal": *Sun*, 12-23-74.

87. Kinsella agreed to pay $15,000 to Field. . . . his nomination as co-respondent in the divorce case.: *BDT*, 12-22-74; *Union*, 12-22, 28-74; *Eagle*, 1-8-75.

88. Field stipulated . . . "an enduring monument to the man's infamy," *Sun*, 12-23-74;

"the reclamation of fallen women": *BDT*, 12-30-74.

89. Emeline didn't want the money. . . . "the best years of my girlhood and youth with a man lost to all sense of manhood." *BSS*, 1-10-75.

90. some tasty details of its history were produced at a December 29th hearing . . . "a number of letters from Kinsella, making appointments and containing many expressions of love and devotion.": *Sun*, 12-30-74.

91. Field hired a detective. . . . ordered refreshments such as milk punches, brandy, and pints of Piper-Heidsieck champagne.: *Sun*, 12-30-74.

But it actually was she. . . . the Stileses had a home in Lake George for years.: *Sun*, 1-7-75; *Eagle*, 10-25-1902; Stiles, *The Stiles Family in America*, p. 331 (<google.com> (9-9-2011)).

92. The *Sun* later published excerpts from the Kinsella letters . . . blamed the spilling of events there on the Republican politician William Booth, who had been present in the hotel parlor.: 1-7-75.

93. "I . . . find that the defendant debauched and carnally knew". . . . entitled to receive $15,000 from the defendant: *Union*, *BDT*, 1-6-75; *Sun*, 1-7-75.

94. Kinsella's revealed that he intended to appeal the case and gain a public trial: *Eagle*, 1-8-75.

95. a nasty quarrel erupted between the parties regarding the custody of their child. . . . "Then, sir, I will kill you!": *Sun*, 1-7-75.

Chapter 5

1. "A Crazy Mother": *Eagle*, 6-3-74

2. "been insane for some time" . . . "not legally responsible": *Eagle*, 6-4-74.

3. Born in Ireland probably in 1846. . . . were alive at the start of June, 1874: *Graphic*, 6-2-74; *Eagle*, *NYT*, 6-3, 4, 5-74; 7-9-74.

4. Michael was a member of the United Association of Coopers . . . a union meeting in Williamsburg: *NYT*, 5-5, 9, 23, 24-74; 6-2, 3-74.

5. either stayed out and got drunk and returned home the next morning, or went home and got up early . . . but now he said no, not yet—maybe in a few days: *Eagle*, 6-3, 5-74; *NYT*, 6-3-74.

6. Mary Ann was also up; Murphy . . . could hear her moving about.: *Eagle*, 6-5-74.

7. "She was very kind to her children," . . . They never cried or anything like that." *Eagle*, 6-5-74.

8. "better woman never lived": *NYT*, 6-3-74.

9. "Do you think my children and me could all starve to death . . . that is all there is about it, now I tell you": *Eagle*, 6-3-74.

10. The Slavins, an older couple. . . . "She said that it said, 'Oh, mamma.'" *Eagle*, 6-5-74.

11. In her precinct cell she recounted to a reporter that she had struck the baby first. . . . And my brain is not quite right sometimes, and that's the way it happened": *NYT*, 6-3-74.

12. Outside the police station a crowd of hundreds . . . "that it seemed as if Brooklyn had given birth to a race of female murderers": *Graphic*, 6-2-74; drawing: 6-3-74.

13. Dr. William DeLong found that her first deranged episode had occurred "after the birth of her second child" . . . "caused a sudden and violent reaction": *Eagle*, 6-4-74.

14. The inquest began in the presence of the children's bodies. . . . Charles Pratt, the oilman for whom Michael Dwyer would not work without his union's blessing: *NYT*, 6-4-74; *Eagle*, 6-5-74.

15. Michael had been admitted to the Fourth Street Hospital. . . . Brady spoke optimistically of his recovery: *Eagle*, 6-4-75.

16. "the commission on lunacy": *Eagle*, 6-5-75.

17. Since 1872 the New York State Legislature. . . . introduced the bill that would finally become law: *Eagle*, 1-22-74, 6-22-74; *NYT* : 1-22, 4-4, 5-8-74; <politicalgraveyard.com/bio/prince>.

18. The primary intent of the bill . . . to sign certificates of commitment: *Eagle*, *NYT*, 2-18-74.

19. With the endorsement of two state-licensed physicians . . . who could then conduct his own inquiry: *Eagle*, 6-22-74, and reference to article in *American Journal of Insanity*, 1874, vol. 31, pp. 80–89": "Code of Laws Relating to the Insane in the State of New York, Passed May, 1874" at <psychiatryonline.org>.

20. These guidelines then extended to the criminal courts in cases of persons accused of arson, murder or attempted murder . . . "where such person shall remain until restored to his right mind": *Eagle*, 7-14-74.

21. The law did not take effect until weeks after its passage . . . Kings County clerk received his official copy on June 21st: *Eagle*, 6-22-74.

22. When the Fourth Grace took her place in Kate's corridor . . . that a doctor was called to her., *Eagle*, *NYT*, 6-9-74.

23. Whitehill reopened the inquest on July 8th . . . "we are of the opinion that she was insane at the time of the commission of the act.": *NYT*, 7-9-74.

24. "Do you think I'm insane?" . . . "almost unruly temper": *Eagle*, 6-24-74.

25. The morning was warm . . . but the prisoner had not been allowed to go with her: *Eagle*, *NYT*, 7-14-74.

26. one reporter detected traces of the blacking in her hair the next day: *Eagle*, 7-15-74.

27. It was stated later that Sarah Merrigan had brought the stuff to her: *Eagle*, 7-18-74.

28. District Attorney Winslow explained how the new law applied to Lizzie Lloyd King. . . . "Now sit down," Moore concluded, and she was quietly led back to her chair: *Eagle*, *Herald*, *NYT*, 7-14-74 (the dialogue is put together from these three sources.)

29. "She was with me all the time up to the age of thirteen. . . . She has not been home since, except for a single night in the Fall of 1867": *Eagle*, 7-14-74, primarily, and also, *Herald*, *NYT*, 7-14-74.

30. She was not yet 19 when she took off from Plymouth to Boston. The following year word got back that she was in a hospital there. Her father, Isaac King, went up to look for her and found that she had been admitted to a "lunatic asylum" in Taunton.: *Herald*, 7-16-73; *Eagle*, 7-14-74.

31. it was from there that she had arrived at nearby Attleboro Falls . . . had used the name of "Alice Howard.": *Eagle*, 7-14, 15-74.

32. At Attleboro she told the story that she had run away from the hospital . . . before arriving in that town: *Eagle*, 8-4-73, 7-14, 15, 24-74; "ragged, dirty and haggard.": *Eagle*, 8-4-73 (reprinted from the Attleboro *Chronicle*.)

33. Kate would repeat the story . . . at least the third time she had tried to escape.: *Eagle*, 7-14, 24-74.

34. one of her Brooklyn attorneys, D. B. Thompson. . . . "They are a disgrace to Brooklyn!": *Herald*, *NYT*, 7-14-74.

35. A man who had rented a room to her in Providence . . . she had been medically treated in Boston in the spring of 1867: *Eagle*, *Herald*, *NYT*, 7-14-74.

36. Dr. Charles Corey took the stand . . . of what she would do if she were permitted to go at large": *Eagle*, 7-14-74.

37. Dr. Brown agreed that her mind had long been and continued to be "unsound": *Eagle*, *NYT*, 7-14-74.

38. Dr. MacDonald appeared first . . . which "lunatic asylum" he would send her to: *Eagle*, *NYT*, 7-14-74.

39. Many in the crowd followed her onto the sidewalk . . . trailed by 500 people: *Eagle*, 7-15-74.

40. deposition of Taunton's Dr. Folsom's . . . he believed that she was still insane when she "ran away." *Eagle*, 7-15, 16-74; *NYT*, 7-15-74.

41. Moore stated that he would write an order committing Lizzie King. . . . "Kate Stoddard and her famous case disappeared from public view": *Eagle*, *NYT*, 7-14-74.

42. Judge Moore's formal commitment . . . "the State Lunatic Asylum for insane criminals at Auburn": *Eagle*, 7-17-74.

43. Opened in 1859 . . . first institution in America designated for that purpose: <www.prisontalk.com> (7-5-2011).

44. At Raymond Street Kate protested . . . "I have been to one once, and I know what it is": *Eagle*, 7-17-74; "rather be hanged": *Eagle*, 7-14-74, quoting *The Rochester Democrat*.

45. The *Eagle* tried to interview her, but found her to be protected. . . . Kate, remembering that she would be tried if she would later be found to be sane, at last determined to do so: *Eagle*, 7-17-74.

46. "Your Honor's attention I wish to call to the wording of your commitment of me. . . . Raymond Street Jail, Brooklyn, L. I.: *Eagle*, *NYT*, 7-18-74.

47. "It is thought that having to talk so much with such hopeless lunatics as the Brooklyn detectives unsettled her mind": quoted in *Eagle*, 7-18-74.

48. Moving day for Kate and Mary Ann was July 21st . . . and nearly all the articles were Goodrich's: *Eagle*, *NYT*, 7-22-74.

49. A special correspondent for the *Eagle* . . . "and as we walked away we heard her sobbing like a child": *Eagle*, 7-24-74.

50. Benjamin F. Tracy . . . "has only just begun": Shaplen, pp. 185–200; *Eagle*, 8-29, 9-1-74; *American National Biography*, v. 21, p. 792.

51. Mrs. Merrigan, dressed in black . . . and that the murder was committed on the second day of September: *Eagle*, *Union*, 10-27-74; *Herald* 10-28-74.

52. A witness would testify that she had paid Hamill $66 in rent. . . . James was in the habit of keeping money in the chest: *Union*, 10-28-74; *Eagle*, 10-29-74.

53. But also in the chest was a "hair anchor" or "anchor charm" . . . she thought she also heard two women's voices: *Union*, 10-27-74; *Eagle*, *Herald* 10-28-74.

54. "a sort of scuffle"—"like two or three persons having a scuffle": *Eagle*, 10-28-74. "somebody was thrown down heavy on the floor" . . . she thought Maggie had been burned in the fire: *Eagle*, *Herald*, 10-28-74.

55. The Merrigans' former landlady testified . . . would include Sarah in her will: *Eagle*, 10-28-74.

56. Patrick Keady opened for the defense . . . "deed of blood of which she stands accused": *Eagle*, 10-29-74.

57. she was lucid when they interviewed her: *Eagle*, 5-20, 21-74.

58. Keady offered exactly ten evidences of his client's lunacy: *Eagle*, *Herald*, 10-29-74.

59. They called on four physicians . . . to be consistent with a certain form of epilepsy: *Eagle*, 10-30-74.

60. Epilepsy as a basis for defense was unusual . . . considering the dead person to be a possible victim of an epileptic attack: *NYT*, 7-2-73; O'Brien, p. 210; <http://www.google.com/search?sourceid=navclient&aq=0& oq=epilepsy+defense> (5-19-2011).

61. Testimony followed from Williamsburg policemen and Daniel Dougherty. . . . One of the women was said to be "inclined to be violent.": *Eagle*, *Union*, 10-30-74.

62. On morning of October 30th, 1874 . . . the whole thing seems to me like a dream, or like something that happened in very early child-hood. . . ." *Union*, 10-30-74; *Eagle*, 10-31-74. The words are verbatim from these sources, but the sequence has been altered; "in a low, quiet voice, occasionally a little tremulous": *Union*, 10-30-74.

63. "I don't know whether I remained at my sister-in-law's that night". . . . Or going to jail, or of having a fit and fainting spells there: *Union*, 10-30-74; *Eagle*, 10-31-74.

64. Commenting on this "extraordinary case". . . . as to baffle the police as to the murderer's mode of entrance": *Eagle* editorial, 10-29-74.

65. The testimony wound down on October 30th. . . . Sarah Merrigan "received the announcement of the result without the movement of a muscle." *Eagle*, *NYT*, 10-31-74.

66. a neurologist and pioneer in the field of criminology . . . epilepsy would be defined as one of the principal causes of moral insanity.: Lombroso-Ferrero, p. 53 and passim.

67. The disease has a dizzying number of forms and variations: cf. *Churchill's Medical Dictionary*, pp. 629–635.

68. for well over a century it has been understood that epileptic epi-sodes in the temporal lobes of the brain may have particular psychic char-acteristics: <epilepsy.com, medsscape.com>, "temporal lobe epilepsy."

69. "temporal lobe epilepsy of the dominant hemisphere predisposes to psychotic manifestations": Flor-Henry, p. 363.

70. further investigations distinguished between psychotic violent epi-sodes that occurred during, after and between epileptic attacks: Mendes, <psychiatryonline.org>.

71. two murders known to be committed by epileptic children; "Many episodes of violent behavior . . . strange feelings of unreality. . . .": Pincus.

72. A more recent study determined that psychosis occurs up to seven days after a seizure . . . "irritable and aggressive behavior, and hallucinatory experiences." Arnedo, Devinsky, Nadkarni.

73. a chart of criminal offenses "related to epileptic automisms" . . . stabbing a wife and locking a daughter in a cupboard: "Epileptic Automisms in the Criminal Courts: 13 Cases Tried in England and Wales between 1875 and 2001," *Epilepsia*, Jan. 2008.

74. "Aggression . . . religious preoccupation. . . .": Appelbaum and Borum.

75. Other researchers compared this to what William James . . . called "patients with epilepsy and religiosity conform to those who William James referred to as having, with respect to religion, 'an acute fever.'": Freeman and Trimble, p. 407.

76. James declared that St. Paul "certainly had an epileptoid, if not an epileptic seizure": *The Varieties of Religious Experience* (New York: New American Library (Mentor), 1958), p. 29.

77. "gravidarium" . . . "catamenial" . . . "arise in relation to menstrual periods": *Churchill's Medical Dictionary*, pp. 630–631.

78. ambulatory epilepsy . . . " 'sleepwalking' and postictal wandering and confusion": Appelbaum and Borum, pp. 762–63, *Churchill's Medical Dictionary*, p. 630.

79. Tappen would not admit her to bail . . . in a case where eight jurors had voted for conviction.: *Eagle*, 10-31-74.

80. "kindest of treatment" . . . there, and indeed, that she owed "the preservation of her life": *Eagle*, 5-29-75; At another time frequently visited and comforted her.: *BDT*, 1-7-75.

81. "She says she will never live with him again": *Eagle*, 11-5-74.

82. Benjamin Tracy was detained at The Trial of the Century . . . another split vote, nine to three in Beecher's favor. Shaplen, pp. 215 ff.; Stiles, (L. B. Proctor), v. II, pp. 1225–26; *Eagle*, 1-19-75.

83. he managed to slip away for its opening on the 16th . . . he assigned the prosecution to his first assistant, Thomas S. Moore. *Eagle, NYT*, 6-16-75.

84. Once again the two Cecilias . . . and to have been through further illness: *Eagle*, 6-16-75.

85. The witnesses repeated their previous testimony . . . had been heard from the Merrigan's apartment.: *Eagle*, 6-17, 18-75.

86. he motioned the bench for an acquittal. . . . The judge needed to think some more.: *Eagle*, 6-18-75.

87. the next morning . . . very unlikely that he could have got away long enough to go home and kill somebody: *Eagle, Union*, 6-19-75; *Herald*, 6-20-75.

88. "Is the case now closed?" . . . and a ripple of laughs went through the crowd.: *Union*, 6-19-75.

89. Tracy boldly brought forth no witnesses. . . . "The secret of the death will never be known until the secrets of all hearts are revealed": *Eagle, Union*, 6-21-75.

90. Moore, granted a second closing speech, argued that the circumstantial case against Sarah was strong enough to convict her.: *Union, Herald*, 6-22-75.

91. The jurors retired at half-past three on June 21st . . . a narrow escape for Sarah Merrigan: *Union, Herald*, 6-22-75.

92. "in a muddle". . . . "It is not likely that Mrs. Merrigan will ever be tried again": *Eagle*, 6-22-75.

93. "By what curious psychological jugglery does assassination lose its hideous colors when practiced by a woman?": *Eagle*, 5-12-74.

94. "The amount of compassion lavished . . . sweetened all the cannibals in Carriba": *Eagle*, 9-4-73.

95. "for money.": *Eagle*, 1-5-79.

96. "The history of American criminal law has nothing more interesting in it than the case of *The People vs. Fanny Hyde*": Stiles, v. II, p. 1260.

97. "the most sensational and mysterious [tragedy] in the criminal history of Brooklyn." *Eagle*, 1-5-90.

98. she was next seen making a social visit to her old quarters . . . "appeared to be pleased": *Eagle*, 12-9-73.

99. in May 1874, the *Eagle* referred cryptically . . . "she had relied on virtue and frugality for advancement": *Eagle*, 5-12-74.

100. a man who claimed to be named Watson asked if a *nolle prosequi* . . . if their relations have only been guilty enough": *Eagle*, 9-2-77.

101. In August 1878. . . . She was dismissed with a warning: *New York Post*, 8-24-78.

102. a different judge sent her back to Raymond Street . . . when she either would not or could not pay a five-dollar fine.: *NYT*, 2-28-80.

103. In the 1880 U.S. census 31-year-old Henry Hyde is listed as an unmarried bookbinder boarding at 193 Franklin Avenue, Brooklyn: <ancestry.com>.

104. She was last heard of as Mary F. Windley, "alias Fanny Hyde,". . . . Her only injury was "a slight scalp wound.": *Brooklyn Union-Argus*, 12-10-81.

105. At the end of her second trial, in June 1875, she remained at Raymond Street . . . released on July 22nd after he had reduced it by a third: *NYT*, 7-23-75; *Eagle*, 2-6-78.

106. "inflammation of the lungs" . . . said to be doubted: *NYT*, 3-18-76.

107. In November of that year "ad infinitum": *Eagle*, 2-6-78.

108. a much improved Sarah, "whom few would recognize" . . . with a *nolle prosequi*?: *Eagle*, 1-24, 2-6-78; *NYT*, 2-6-78.

109. Pratt denied her: *Eagle*, 2-14-78.

110. Their marriage was doomed: *Eagle*, 8-7-81.

111. in 1877, when a lawyer suing him . . . "his right to prove his innocence of such a horrible crime": *Eagle*, 1-31, 2-1-77.

112. became Sarah Dougherty again . . . had become a schoolteacher.: <ancestry.com>, 1880 U.S. census.

113. she wrote to D.A. Winslow . . . "death to incarceration in a madhouse": 8-25-74.

114. Kate was next heard from in October . . . she was doing as well as could be expected: *NYT*, 10-10-74.

115. The City's $1000 reward . . . finally got her full payment: *Eagle*, 8-26, 27, 28, 11-20, 21, 12-1, 2-74.

116. W. W. Goodrich would not produce the $2500 he had offered . . . that she had killed his brother.: *Eagle*, 8-27-74, 1-2-75.

117. In 1880, not being allowed to handle a pen. . . . Such a law, she charged was "*ex post facto*": *NYT*, 5-14-80; *New York Evangelist*, 6-24-80 (American Periodical Series Online); Syracuse reporter . . . "most of her time reading.: Syracuse *Sunday Courier*, 7-24-81.

118. Thomas Kinsella continued to lead the *Eagle* . . . the Liberal Republican candidacy of Horace Greeley: Biography Resource Center (*Dictionary of American Biography* Base Set), (<www.galenet.com> (2-19-2009); *Graphic*, 5-26-80, *Eagle*, *Union*, *BDT*, 2-11, 12-84.

119. After winning his divorce from his straying wife Emeline . . . a 30-year-old former public-school principal: *Eagle*, *BDT*, 12-29-75.

120. who would live in the Bushwick neighborhood . . . until his death at 61 in 1881: <ancestry.com>, 1880 U.S. census; *Eagle*, 11-26-81.

121. Kinsella . . . did not marry Emeline Van Siclen until May 19th, 1880.: New York Newspaper Extracts (Barber Collection), 1880 <ancestry. com>; "obtained in some other state than New York.": The *National Police Gazette*, 6-5-80.

122. Elizabeth removed for a time to the "quiet little town" of Stamford. . . . "I have been annoyed in this town more than I ever was in Brooklyn": *NYT*, 6-17-80.

123. Kinsella sailed with Emeline to England and . . . Ireland: <ancestry.com>, passport application, 5-19-83, "Pavonia" ship-passenger list, 9-12-83; *Eagle*, 2-11-84.

124. It was a trip intended to improve his health . . . died at his Clinton Street home on the afternoon of February 11th, 1884, aged 51: *Eagle*, 2-11-84; *Union*, 2-12-84.

125. 200 employees gathered to honor him: *NYT*, 2-13-84; "poor Irish printer" . . . "almost unthinkable" in London: *NYT*, 2-12-84; "no man of his generation has left so strong an impress" . . . neither "altogether for good" nor "altogether for evil." *Union*, 2-12-84.

126. Father O'Reilly of St. Stephen's Parish . . . every official of the City of Brooklyn and County of Kings attended the ceremonies: *Eagle*, 2-11, 13, 14-84; *NYT*, 2-14-84.

127. His estate was estimated at $250,000: *Union*, 2-14-84; *NYT*, 2-15-84.

128. Bowen died in his famous Willow Street 1896 at age 82: *NYT*, 2-27-96; He had transferred his devotion to the Pilgrim Congregational Church . . . a prolix editorial that stretched to a third long column *Eagle*, 5-25-96.

129. Winchester Britton was the first to die . . . "a man of less learning and more of every day cunning could have avoided easily": *Eagle*, *BDT*, 2-13-86; "the cloud soon passed away," and wished "peace to his ashes": *Eagle*, 2-16-86.

130. Morris himself . . . the second-oldest practicing attorney in the now Brooklyn Borough: *Eagle*, *SU*, 11-1-1909; "a terror to evildoers . . . the extreme of propriety.": *Eagle*, 11-1-09.

131. Patrick Keady. . . . seventy carriages followed him to Holy Cross: *Eagle*, 10-7, 8, 9-1908.

132. D.A. John Winslow death in Bay Ridge in 1898: *Eagle*, 10-17, 18-98.

133. Benjamin F. Tracy. . . . attended by sailors from the Brooklyn Navy Yard: *NYT*, 6-1, 8-7, 10-1915.

134. Isaac Catlin . . . service in the Spanish-American War, but was denied: *NYT*, 1-16, 20-1902; *Eagle* 1-20-1902.

135. William W. Goodrich . . . the Maritime Conference of 1888: *SU*, *BDT*, 11-21-1906; *BDT*, *Eagle*, 11-22, 23-1906.

136. There was another devastating moment in his life . . . had been attacked by an employee or employees whom he had dismissed: *NYT*, 1-2, 3-90; *Eagle*, 1-2-90.

137. W.W. Goodrich was appointed presiding justice of the Appellate Division . . . "in all his career there was not the slightest stain of reproach." *SU*, *BDT*, 11-21-1906; *BDT*, *Eagle*, 11-22, 23-1906.

138. Henry Hyde remarried around 1883. . . . A Henry Hyde his exact age died in Brooklyn in 1926: <ancestry.com>, 1900 and 1920 U.S. censuses; <italiangen.org/nycdeaths> (Italian Genealogical Group) (6-27-2011).

139. Windleys stayed on. . . . 407 Monroe Street in Bedford-Stuyvesant: <ancestry.com>, U.S. censuses, 1880–1930; <itiliangen.org/nycdeaths> (6-2011); *Eagle*, 8-16-97.

140. A 1929 *Eagle* profile tagged him America's "oldest weaver," still active in Williamsburg at 77.: 4-21. Five years later, he was listed as a long-lived Brooklynite in a piece about the centennial of the late city. *Eagle*, 4-8-1934; His death-notice appeared in 1941. *Eagle*, 6-27; Adelbert . . . 1975: <ancestry.com>, Social Security Death Index.

141. Cecilia, that child who had charmed the scene of her mother's murder trial . . . the Doughertys of Donegal and Williamsburg, and of the Merrigans of whose name is lost to them, are still living: <ancestry.com>, 1880, 1910, 1920, 1930 censuses; <italiangen.org/nycdeaths>.

142. in 1900 it expressed a certain nostalgia for. . . . "There are very few of these cases nowadays": *Eagle*, 3-25-1900.

143. In 1913. . . . "Cold-blooded" Mary Handley had "betrayed her to the police to obtain a reward.": *Eagle*, 9-13-1913.

144. The woman called "Kate Stoddard" was last remembered in 1931 in a laudatory piece about the old chief Patrick Campbell.: *Eagle*, 6-3-1931.

145. Kate's parents . . . until at least 1910: <ancestry.com>, 1900 and 1910 U.S. censuses.

146. a new residence was completed in 1892 . . . Its successor was named, more benignly, Matteawan State Hospital: Hurd, pp. 241–43; "Fishkill Correctional Facility," <correctionhistory.org> (7-5-2011).

146. more benign treatment of the mentally ill was its policy . . . at least for male inmates, less benign.: "Fishkill Correctional Facility," <correctionhistory.org> (7-5-2011); Gilfoyle, pp. 291–299.

147. in 1900 one found Lizzie L. King, "patient," 53 . . . no occupation—nor any aliases: <ancestry.com>, 1900 and 1910 U.S. censuses.

148. she died there on October 3rd, 1911.: New York State Department of Health records at the National Archives at New York City.

Bibliography

Books Consulted

Ackerman, Kenneth D., *Boss Tweed: The Rise and Fall of the Corrupt Politician Who Conceived the Soul of Modern New York*. New York: Carroll and Graf, 2005.

American National Biography. New York: Oxford University Press, 1999.

Annual Reports of the Brooklyn Police Department (no. 2, Apr. 1871–Apr. 1872; no. 4, Jan. 1873–Jan. 1874). New York: Collins and Sesnon.

Applegate, Debby, *The Most Famous Man in America: The Biography of Henry Ward Beecher*. New York, et al.: Doubleday, 2006.

Benardo, Leonard, and Jennifer Weiss, *Brooklyn By Name: How the Neighborhoods, Streets, Parks, Bridges, and More Got Their Names*. New York: New York University Press, 2006.

Biographical Dictionary of American Journalism (Joseph P. McKerns, ed.). New York et al.: Greenwood Press, 1989.

Brooklyn Almanac (Margaret Latimer, ed.). Brooklyn: The Brooklyn Educational and Cultural Alliance, 1984.

The Catholic Encyclopedia, vol. 6. New York: Robert Appleton Company, 1909. (http://www.newadvent.org/cathen/06647c.htm).

Chillemi, Stacy, and BlancaVazquez, *Epilepsy and Pregnancy*. New York: Demos Medical Publishing, ca. 2006.

Churchill's Illustrated Medical Dictionary (Ruth Koenigsberg, managing editor), New York, et al.: Churchill Livingstone, 1989.

The Columbia Encyclopedia, Sixth Edition (Paul Lagassé, ed.). New York: Columbia University Press, 2000.

The Columbia Gazetteer of the World, vol. 2 (Saul B. Cohen, ed.). New York: Columbia University Press, 1998.

Conklin, William J., and Jeffrey Simpson, *Brooklyn's City Hall*. New York: The City of New York Department of General Services, 1983.

Crimes of Passion (author unknown). London: Verdict Press, 1975.

Douglas, George H., *The Golden Age of the Newspaper*. Westport, CT, and London, UK: Greenwood Press, 1999.

Duke, Thomas S., *Celebrated Criminal Cases of America*. San Francisco: The James H. Barry Company, 1910 (google.com, Google books. (7-1-10)).

Emery, Edwin; Michael C. Emery, Nancy L. Roberts, *The Press in America: An Interpretive History of the Mass Media*, 9th ed. Boston et al.: Allyn and Bacon, 2000.

Encyclopedia Americana. (Grolier Online, http://go.grolier.com (2010, 2011)).

Encylopædia Britannica Online. (1911 encyclopedia.org).

Encyclopædia Britannica Online Library Edition, 2010. (http://library.eb.com/eb/article-259199) (5-14-10).

The Encyclopedia of New York City (Jackson, Kenneth T., ed.). New Haven and London: Yale University Press; and New York: The New York Historical Society, 1995.

Fales, William E. S., *Brooklyn's Guardians; a Record of the Faithful and Heroic Men Who Preserve the Peace in the City of Homes*: Brooklyn, self-published, 1887.

Fialka, John J., *Sisters: Catholic Nuns and the Making of America*. New York: St. Martin's Press, 2003.

Fox, Richard Wightman, *Trials of Intimacy: Love and Loss in the Beecher-Tilton Scandal*. Chicago and London: University of Chicago Press, 1999.

Gilfoyle, Timothy J., *A Pickpocket's Tale: the Underworld of Nineteenth-Century New York*. New York and London: W. W. Norton & Company, 2006.

Haag, Pamela, *Consent: Sexual Rights and the Transformation of American Liberalism*. Ithaca, NY: Cornell University Press, 1999.

Hazelton, Henry Isham, *The Boroughs of Brooklyn and Queens, Counties of Nassau and Suffolk, Long Island, New York, 1609–1924*, vol. II. New York and Chicago: Lewis Historical Publishing Company, 1925.

Howard, Henry W. B., assisted by Arthur N. Jervis, *The Eagle and Brooklyn: the Record of the Progress of the Brooklyn Daily Eagle, Issued in Commemoration of its Semi-centennial and Occupancy of its New Building; Together with The History of the City of Brooklyn*. Brooklyn: Brooklyn Daily Eagle, 1892.

Hudson, Frederic, *Journalism in the United States, from 1690 to 1872*. (1873) rpt. New York: Haskell House, 1968.

Hurd, Henry H., et al., *The Institutional Care of the Insane in the United States and Canada*, v. 3. Baltimore: The Johns Hopkins Press, 1916 (google.com/books).

Jones, Ann, *Women Who Kill*. New York: Holt, Rinehart and Winston, 1980.

Lancaster, Clay, *Prospect Park Handbook*. New York: The Greensward Foundation and Long Island University Press, 1972.

Lee, Alfred McClung: *The Daily Newspaper in America: The Evolution of a Social Instrument.* New York: Macmillan, 1947.

Leonard, Thomas C., *News for All: America's Coming-of-Age with the Press.* New York: Oxford University Press, 1995.

Lewis, Dorothy Otnow, *Guilty By Reason Of Insanity: A Psychiatrist Explores the Minds of Killers.* New York: Fawcett Columbine, 1998.

Livingstone, Colin H., *The Citizen Guide to Brooklyn and Long Island.* Brooklyn: R. Wayne Wilson and Company, 1893 (archive.org/stream/citizenguidetobr).

Lombroso, Cesar[e] and Ferrero, William [Guglielmo] Ferrero, *The Female Offender.* New York and London: D. Appleton and Company, 1920.

Lombroso-Ferrero, Gina, *Criminal Man According to the Classification of Cesare Lombroso.* New York and London: G. P. Putnam's Sons (The Knickerbocker Press), 1911.

Maeder, Thomas, *Crime and Madness: The Origins and Evolution of the Insanity Defense.* New York: Harper & Row, 1985.

McCullough, David, *The Great Bridge.* New York: Simon and Schuster (Touchstone), 1982.

Mott, Frank Luther, *American Journalism, a History: 1690–1960.* New York: Macmillan, 1962.

Murphy, Robert E., *Brooklyn Union: A Centennial History.* Brooklyn: The Brooklyn Union Gas Company, 1995.

———, *History of Catholic Charities, Diocese of Brooklyn, 1899–1999.* Brooklyn: Catholic Charities, Diocese of Brooklyn, 2002.

Nash, Jay Robert, *Almanac of World Crime.* New York: Bonanza Books, 1986.

O'Brien, Geoffrey, *The Fall of the House of Walworth: A Tale of Madness and Murder in Gilded-Age America.* New York: Henry Holt and Co., 2010.

Official Report of the Trial of Fanny Hyde for the Murder of Geo. W. Watson, from the Short-hand Notes of William Hemstreet, Official Reporter of the Court. New York: J. R. McDivitt, 1872 (pds.lib.harvard.edu/pds/view/5777948 (retrieved 2-23-2010)).

Osrtander, Stephen M., *A History of the City of Brooklyn* (Alexander Black, ed.). Brooklyn: 1894, published by prescription.

Paneth, Donald, *The Encyclopedia of American Journalism.* New York: Facts on File, 1983.

Payne, George Henry, *History of Journalism in the United States.* New York and London: Appleton-Century Co., 1940.

Robinson, Daniel N., *Wild Beasts & Idle Humours: The Insanity Defense from Antiquity to the Present.* Cambridge, MA: Harvard University Press, 1996.

Roper, Laura Wood, *FLO: A Biography of Frederick Law Olmsted*. Baltimore: Johns Hopkins University Press, 1973.

Schroth, Raymond A., *The Eagle and Brooklyn: A Community Newspaper, 1841–1955*. Westport, CT, and London, UK: Greenwood Press, 1974.

Schwarzlose, Richard Allen, *Newspapers: A Reference Guide*. New York et al.: Greenwood Press, 1987.

Shaplen, Robert, *Free Love and Heavenly Sinners: The Story of the Great Henry Ward Beecher Scandal*. London: Andre Deutsch, 1956.

Sharp, John K., *History of the Diocese of Brooklyn, 1853–1953: the Catholic Church on Long Island*, vol. 1. New York : Fordham University Press, 1954.

Showalter, Elaine, *The Female Malady: Women, Madness and English Culture, 1830–1980*. London: Virago Press, 1987.

Sifakis, Stewart, *Who Was Who in the Civil War*, vol. 2. New York: Facts on File, 1988.

Snyder-Grenier, Ellen, *Brooklyn! An Illustrated History*. Philadelphia: Temple University Press, 1996.

Stansell, Christine, *City of Women: Sex and Class in New York, 1789–1860*. Urbana and Chicago: University of Illinois Press, 1987.

Stiles, Henry R., editor in chief, *The Civil. Political, Professional and Ecclesiastical History and Commercial and Industrial Record of the County of Kings and the City of Brooklyn, from 1683 to 1884*, vols. I and II. New York: W. W. Munsell and Co., 1884.

———, *The Stiles Family in America: Genealogies of the Connecticut Family*. Jersey City, NJ, 1895 (Google Books).

Strong, George Templeton, *Diary of George Templeton Strong*, vol. 4: *Post-War Years, 1865–1875*, ed. Allan Nevins and Milton Halsey Thomas. New York: Macmillan, 1952.

Syrett, Harold Coffin, *The City of Brooklyn, 1865–1898*. New York: Columbia University Press, 1944.

Rybczynski, Witold, *A Clearing in the Distance: Frederick Law Olmsted and America in the Nineteenth Century*. New York: Scribner, 1999.

Twain, Mark and Charles Dudley Warner, *The Gilded Age: A Tale of Today*. New York: Trident Press, 1964.

Waller, Altina Laura, *The Beecher-Tilton Adultery Scandal: Family, Religion and Politics in Brooklyn, 1865–1875* (rpt. of doctoral dissertation, University of Massachusetts, 1980). Ann Arbor. MI: University Microfilms International, 1986.

Walling, George W., *Recollections of a New York Chief of Police*. New York: Caxton Book Concern, Limited, 1888.

Walter, John, *Handgun: From Matchlock to Laser-Sited Weapon*, illustrated by John Batchelor. New York: Sterling Publishing, 1988.

Wyllie, Elaine, *The Cleveland Clinic Guide to Epilepsy.* New York: Kaplan Publishing, ca. 2010.

Villard, Oswald Garrison, *Some Newspapers and Newspaper-Men.* New York: Alfred A. Knopf, 1923.

Articles

Appelbaum, Kenneth L.; Randy Borum, "Epilepsy, Aggression and Criminal Responsibility," *Psychiatric Services,* vol. 47, no. 7. (July 1996) pp. 762–763.

Arnedo, Vanessa; Orrin Devinsky; Siddhartha Nadkarni, "Psychosis in Epilepsy Patients," *Epilepsia,* vol. 48 (Dec. 2007) supplements, pp. 17–19 (Wiley Online Library (5-17-11)).

Bradshaw, Wesley, "The Goodrich Horror. Being the Full Confession of Kate Stoddart, or Lizzie King. Why She Killed Charles Goodrich. Showing a Deserted Woman's Vengeance" (booklet). Philadelphia: Old Franklin Publishing House, 1873 (rpt., Gale Making of Modern Law Print editions (print on demand, 2011).

Carter, Robert Allan, "History of the Insanity Defense in New York State" (Albany, NY: Legislative and Governmental Services, New York State Library, 1982 (nysed.gov).

Chaudry, Neera; Geeta Khwaja; Gurubax Singh, "Epilepsy and Religion," *Annals of Indian Academy of Neurology,* vol. 10, no. 3 (July–Sept., 2007) pp. 165 ff. (galegroup.com, document no. A169443874 (5-16-11).

Cornell Law School, "The McNaughton Rule—not knowing right from wrong," (forensic-psych.com/articles/McNaugtonRule).

"Epileptic Automisms in the Criminal Courts: 13 Cases Tried in England and Wales between 1875 and 2001," *Epilepsia* (Series 4), vol. 49 (Jan. 2008), issue 1, p. 141 (web.ebscohost.com (5-18-11)).

Flor-Henry, Pierre, "Psychosis and Temporal Lobe Epilepsy; a Controlled Investigation, *Epilepsia,* vol. 10, issue 3, Sept. 1969, p. 363: abstract: Wiley Online Library (http://onlinelibrary.wiley.com/doi/10.1111/j.1528-1157.1969.tb03853.x/abstract (5-24-11)).

Fornazzari, Luis, et al., "Violent Visual Hallucinations and Aggression in Frontal Lobe Dysfunction: Clinical Manifestations of Deep Orbitofrontal Foci, *The Journal of Neuropsychiatry and Clinical Neurosciences,* vol. 4, no. 1 (Winter 1992) pp. 42–44.

Freeman, Anthony; Trimble, Michael; "An investigation of religiosity and the Gastaut-Geschwind syndrome in patients with temporal lobe epilepsy," abstract, *Epilepsy and Behavior,* vol. 9, no. 3 (Nov. 2006), p. 407 (www.ncbi.nlm.nih.gov/ pubmed, of (5-24-2011)).

Gladwell, Malcolm, "Damaged," *The New Yorker*, 2-27-97 (www.gladwell.com/1997 (7-12-2010)

"Insanity Experts," *Christian Advocate*, Dec. 1, 1881 (American Periodical Series Online).

Ireland, Robert M., "Frenzied and Fallen Females: Women and Sexual Dishonor in the Nineteenth-Century United States," *Journal of Women's History*, vol. 3, no. 3 (Winter 1992), pp. 95–117 (Project MUSE online (12-5-2010)).

Judd, Jacob, "Brooklyn's Changing Population in the Pre-Civil War Era," *Journal of Long Island History*, vol. IV, no. 3 (Spring 1964), pp. 9–18.

Larkin, Emmet, "The Devotional Revolution in Ireland, 1850–75," *The American Historical Review*, vol. 77, no, 3 (June, 1972), pp. 625–652 (The University of Chicago Press, http://www.jstor.org/stable/1870344 (3-26-2011)).

Mendes, Mario F., "Postictal Violence and Epilepsy," *Psychosomatics*, vol. 39, pp. 478–480 (October 1998) (http://psy.psychiatryonline.org/cgi/content/full/39/5/478psychiatryonline.org (5-16-2011)).

Miller, Wilbur R. "Moonshiners in Brooklyn: Federal Authority Confronts Urban Culture, 1869–1880," *Long Island Historical Journal* (Stony Brook University, State University of New York), vol. 2, no. 2 (Spring 1990), pp. 234–250.

Miyakawa, Taihei, Akira Ogata, "Religious experiences in epileptic patients with a focus on ictus-related episodes," *Psychiatry and Clinical Neurosciences*, vol. 52, issue 2 (May 1998), pp. 321–325 (Wiley Online Library (5-18-11)).

"Newspapers and Editors," *Harper's New Monthly Magazine*, vol. XLVI, no. 274 (Mar. 1873), pp. 585–593.

New York City Bar, "Crimes of Passion," (www.abcny/library).

Pickover, Clifford, "Transcendent Experience and Temporal Lobe Epilepsy," (www.science-spirit.org), Sept./Oct. 1999, and meta-religion.org (5-18-2011).

Pincus, Jonathan H., "Can Violence Be a Manifestation of Epilepsy?" *Neurology*, vol. 30 (1980), pp. 304 ff. (neurology.org (5-16-2011)).

"Pleas of Insanity by Persons Under Indictment," *The Albany Law Journal: A Weekly Record of the Law and the Lawyers*, Sept. 4, 1975 (American Periodical Series Online).

Williams, John M., Jr., "Insanity," *Encyclopedia Americana* (Grolier Online).

Additional Websites

ancestry.com: Biography and Genealogy Master Index

bbc/co.uk/science

fultonhistory.com/Fulton.html: an archive of "Old New York State Historical
Newspaper pages"
Mrlincolnandnewyork.org
wikipedia.org

Index